JUN 2 5 2013

A Letter from Legendary Newsman Stan Chambers

Dr. George's place in television news broadcasting is unprecedented. When Dr. George's reports came along, it was out with the old and in with the new. He established the vital link for the viewer that weather was a science. And he engaged us with his professorial instincts. Dr. George has laid much of the groundwork of what our best TV meteorologists exemplify today.

Nothing could have prepared Dr. George better for his television news career than the years he spent teaching his science classes in New Mexico. The time he spent encouraging the questions and interest of his students had suddenly blossomed into a television career where he's reaching audiences "from the desert to the sea, to all of Southern California."

Since his arrival in the early 1970s, Dr. George had such a huge impact on all of us. His exhaustive research and innovative approach have left his friends not just glad to know him, but always intrigued by whatever he has to share.

Dr. George, looking at all the great days spent at KABC Channel 7 News with Jerry Dunphy, Christine Lund, and all the rest—where would our Los Angeles television news be without you? Congratulations on your brilliant career and your fascinating new book.

Stan Chambers

KTLA News
1947–2010

Dr. George

Dr. George

My Life in Weather

George Fischbeck

with Randy Roach

UNIVERSITY OF NEW MEXICO PRESS 🌿 ALBUQUERQUE

Library of Congress Cataloging-in-Publication Data

Fischbeck, George, 1922–
   Dr. George : my life in weather / George Fischbeck with Randy Roach.
     pages cm
   ISBN 978-0-8263-5332-0 (cloth : alk. paper) — ISBN 978-0-8263-5333-7 (electronic)
1. Fischbeck, George, 1922–
2. Meteorologists—California—Los Angeles—Biography.
3. Television weathercasters—California—Los Angeles—Biography.
4. Science teachers—United States—Biography.
I. Roach, Randy, 1948–
II. Title.
   QC858.F45A3 2013
   551.5092—dc23
   [B]
                        2012046034

Designed and typeset by Lila Sanchez
Text composed in Warnock Pro 10.75/14.25
Display type is Warnock Pro

Dedicated to my beloved family,
Sue, Nancy, and Spring. I am so
proud of them and love them dearly.

Contents

Foreword

There are very few journalists who will ever have as much to be thankful for as I do. For thirty-five years, I was a part of what may be the most successful local news operation in the history of television—Channel 7 Eyewitness News at KABC-TV in Los Angeles. Along the way, I have worked with some of the real giants of L.A. news: Marc Brown, Jerry Dunphy, Paul Moyer, Dallas Raines, Christine Lund, Harold Greene, Laura Diaz, Ann Martin, and Regis Philbin. I have also served alongside the finest reporters, producers, writers, camera crews, and technical people in broadcast journalism.

But during my more than three decades on the job, no one has even come close to reaching out through the television screen and touching viewers like the man I call the best teammate anyone could have wished for. He's so beloved, you only have to say his first name to know who I'm talking about—Dr. George.

L.A.'s love affair with George Fischbeck began in 1972 when he was first introduced as a member of the Channel 7 Eyewitness News team. At first glance, he looked more like your uncle. But Dr. George was the quintessential professor, turning the news set into a classroom as he taught viewers why weather was so important and how it could affect their daily lives. Then again, teaching was nothing new to this innovative instructor.

For twenty-three years, Dr. George taught science courses in classrooms ranging from elementary and junior high school through college and graduate levels across New Mexico. His invaluable school lessons were also featured on public education television in Albuquerque and syndicated nationwide. For his work in teaching science, Dr. George earned three Ohio State University Awards for Excellence, the coveted Seal of Approval of the American Meteorological Society, and the Education Television Award for the "best systematic television school instruction in the United States."

When Los Angeles television came calling, this prolific teacher was an instant hit and grew into a legend with a marvelous broadcast news career that spanned more than a quarter of a century. Dr. George became the cornerstone of Channel 7 Eyewitness News, giving it a face and an unforgettable personality. On-the-air TV news careers can flourish or die based on the results of the all-important Q Ratings, which measure a person's popularity and familiarity with the viewing audience. Dr. George scored the highest Q Ratings in the history of Los Angeles television news—more than 90 percent.

This visionary guided Southern California through decades of weather phenomena, with storms, floods, searing heat waves, snow—even tornadoes. We all learned his lessons very well. Dr. George was a welcome visitor to your living room each night. He became part of your family. Who else would refer to his loyal viewers as "my friends"? Dr. George could take an ordinary newscast and turn it into magic.

To borrow a line from the legendary sports columnist Jim Murray—to describe Dr. George as "just a weatherman" would be like calling the Taj Mahal just another building or Mount Everest as just another hill. There are only a handful of people who you could say shaped local television news in the City of Angels, and Dr. George is clearly one of them. His impact on Los Angeles was, and always will remain, indelible. He charmed us all. He made us think. He made us better. And anyone who missed an opportunity to work with Dr. George has been cheated out of a most wonderful experience that you could cherish for life.

Along with Dodgers Hall of Fame announcer Vin Scully and legendary TV reporter Stan Chambers, Dr. George is a member of a most exclusive club, having won both the prestigious Governors Award from the Academy of Television Arts & Sciences, and the Lifetime Achievement Award at the Golden Mike Awards from the Radio and Television News Association of Southern California. To his colleagues, Dr. George wrote the book. We were merely the footnotes.

Dr. George Fischbeck is also the greatest humanitarian I have ever seen in TV news. For years, he was the driving force behind Channel 7's

Toys for Porterville campaign as he raised public awareness of the disadvantaged and mentally impaired. Dr. George has helped raise millions of dollars and at the age of ninety is still raising for two fire-fighters' burn survivors charities.

I can't imagine there is a hospital in the Southland that hasn't been graced by a visit from Dr. George. A handshake and a hug from this gentle angel is the best medicine a grateful patient could ask for. And for more than a decade, Dr. George paid weekly visits to the Los Angeles Zoo as a volunteer tour guide to spread his warmth among visitors, staff—and yes, even the animals. If you have a cause, Dr. George has the time and a most gracious generosity of spirit. He has never accepted a dime for doing what he loves to do, and what you get in return is priceless.

In my thirty-five years as a journalist, I have never seen Los Angeles ever embrace a news figure like Dr. George. And I can tell you this—what you saw on the air is really who he is. Dr. George doesn't have an off and on switch like many television personalities. He's no three-act play. Dr. George is as genuine as they come. We have all been so enriched by the pleasure of his company. That's why it is my distinct pleasure to invite you on a most remarkable journey . . . "Dr. George: My Life in Weather" . . . from one friend to another.

RANDY ROACH
Journalist
KABC-TV Eyewitness News
1974–2009

PREFACE

There is no way that I could ever begin a book or a journal on the wonderful career that I have been blessed with without referring to you, the people who made it all possible, as "my friends." It was "my friends" who invited the Channel 7 Eyewitness News team into their living room each day. And there wasn't a day that I was not thankful to have been a member of the team I still cherish.

The most powerful people in the television industry aren't the top network executives you find in Los Angeles or New York City making crucial decisions that could affect what America watches (and how many commercials they think the audience will endure). It's not the general managers and news directors who decide which broadcasters will deliver the news on the air. And it's not the managers, assignment editors, and producers who select which stories their reporters will cover that day. No, the most powerful people in television are the viewers themselves. The power rests with you. Nobody who has ever succeeded in television news could have done it without a sizeable amount of viewers choosing to watch their product.

Whenever you turn on a TV set, you have a choice to make. Those choices by the viewers can make or break the careers of television anchors, reporters, sportscasters—and yes, even the folks in the weather department. It's not hard to forecast what will happen at a station when those storm clouds roll in produced by bad ratings. Television management spends a fortune of money on consultants, volumes of research, and endless viewer groups to try to figure out what you, the audience, want to watch.

Because I needed to earn a paycheck to feed my family on a regular basis, I will always be grateful that I found a place in the television family at KABC-TV Channel 7 in Los Angeles. Eyewitness News was billed as "The Southland's Number One News Team." Thanks to our loyal viewers who allowed us to make that claim with top ratings, I was able to keep Mrs. Fischbeck and our little ones happy (and well-fed) on payday.

The success we enjoyed at Channel 7 is extremely gratifying when you consider just how tough the competition was. The rosters at both KNBC (Channel 4) and KNXT (now KCBS Channel 2) were packed with extremely talented journalists both on- and off-camera. Covering news, sports, and weather in Los Angeles is one pressure cooker of a job. You have to give your best each and every day. But in the end, it's the viewers who will fill out your report card with the choices they make that will ultimately decide whether or not your newscast made the grade.

Los Angeles may be the second largest city in the nation in terms of population. But you'd be hard-pressed to find another place that has a richer heritage when it comes to local television news than the City of Angels. When I first arrived in 1972, I was in awe when I looked back at this broadcast history and wondered how a humble small town school-teacher like me would ever fit in.

The dawning of an era began one afternoon on April 8, 1949, when a little girl was playing in a field in San Marino with her sister and cousin. But in the flickering of a moment, three-year-old Kathy Fiscus vanished. She had fallen into an abandoned water well that had been forgotten. The hole was only fourteen inches wide. And the attempted rescue of Kathryn Anne Fiscus became what has been called a landmark event in the annals of American television. KTLA-TV Channel 5 canceled all programming and commercials as reporters Stan Chambers and Bill Welsh provided twenty-seven and a half hours of live uninterrupted coverage from the scene as rescuers desperately tried to dig their way to save little Kathy. When their worst fears were realized and her tiny body was brought to the surface, rescue workers wept openly. And Southern California television viewers mourned the loss of a little girl they didn't know—but had grown to love. The Kathy Fiscus tragedy is one of the finest television reporting achievements ever seen in Los Angeles. It was journalism at its finest. The marker at Kathy's gravesite reads: "One little girl who united the world for a moment."

The behind-the-scenes mastermind of this unprecedented live coverage by KTLA was a genius named Klaus Landsberg. There isn't a person who has ever worked in television that doesn't owe a deep debt of gratitude to this pioneer for what he dreamed about and accomplished. He was remarkable. He was revolutionary. If Klaus Landsberg thought an event was important enough to be broadcast live, there was no mountain he wouldn't move to allow Channel 5 viewers to be an eyewitness. His résumé reads like a life achievement award, including the historic remote telecasts of a live atomic bomb test from the Nevada desert in both 1951 and 1952. Landsberg's dream of turning a helicopter into a flying television station would later revolutionize the landscape of television news. However, he never lived to see KTLA's Telecopter, which would provide live dramatic coverage of the Baldwin Hills Dam disaster and the Watts Riots in the 1960s. On September 16, 1956, Klaus Landsberg lost his battle with cancer. He was just forty years old. Those of us who have had the honor and the privilege of working in the L.A. market owe so much to this visionary for whom doing the impossible was just another day on the job.

When an unknown junior high science teacher named "Dr. George" agreed to accept the challenge of doing the news in a major metropolitan city called Los Angeles, I knew (oh-so-dauntingly) that I would be trying to follow in the footsteps of some real broadcast giants. In the dictionary, the word *anchor* is defined as a source of stability, a reliable support, a mainstay. And no anchor in the history of Southern California has ever been more influential and had more clout than George Putnam in the 1950s on KTTV Channel 11. He dominated the ratings with his bold, deep-voiced delivery and his pull-no-punches commentaries called "One Reporter's Opinion." Quite simply, George Putnam put television news on the map in the City of Angels. He enjoyed a career in TV and radio that spanned nearly six decades. And at one point, Putnam even earned a bigger paycheck than Walter Cronkite.

In 1960, the CBS-owned station in Los Angeles, Channel 2 KNXT (now KCBS-TV) decided to launch the first one-hour newscast in the country. It was given a simple name—*The Big News*. But it made a huge impact. Jerry Dunphy, who had worked as an anchor in Milwaukee and a sports reporter in Chicago, was hired to be the anchorman of *The Big News*. And he became a Southland institution. As John Severino, my former boss at Channel 7 who later hired Dunphy to anchor Eyewitness News, said, "He owned the market." Perhaps my former colleague, anchor Laura Diaz, said it best when she told the *Los Angeles Times*, "When I was a kid, I would watch Jerry on *The Big News*. To me, Jerry was the news."

Success breeds competition. And when it comes to local television news, Los Angeles is perhaps the most competitive marketplace on the airwaves. Look at the anchor lineup that KNBC-TV Channel 4 fielded to head up its news team in the late 1960s and early '70s: Tom Brokaw, Jess Marlow, and Tom Snyder. Bryant Gumbel was the station's number two sports anchor. And oh yes, Channel 4 News also had a weatherman you may remember—Pat Sajak, who has found his own "Wheel of Fortune" hosting one of the most popular game shows in the history of television.

With this rich heritage of news spanning twenty-five years, can you possibly imagine how I felt when Channel 7 plucked me out of Albuquerque, New Mexico, in 1972 to bring me to Los Angeles to forecast the weather on Eyewitness News? I didn't have the vision of a Klaus Landsberg. I didn't have the talent and the versatility of Stan Chambers. And I certainly didn't have the journalistic résumé of George Putnam, Jerry Dunphy, or Tom Brokaw. Boy, going in, I realized that I was going to have to be a quick learner. Then again, that was the one thing I had going for me in L.A. You see, before coming to Southern California, I had spent twenty-three years in the classroom preparing for what would become the biggest challenge of my life. And I invite you to join me as we begin that journey in chapter 1.

Acknowledgments

A Thank-You Note

Appreciation can make a day, even change a life.
Your willingness to put it into words is all that is necessary.
~ Margaret Cousins ~

First and foremost, I want to thank the leadership of my longtime television home in Los Angeles—KABC-TV. President and General Manager Arnold J. Kleiner and Vice President and News Director Cheryl Fair have been so gracious in sharing the many pictures that made this walk down memory lane so special. Winning is a habit at ABC7, that even to this day is rightfully called "Number One in News—Number One in Southern California". They specialize in teamwork at Eyewitness News. As a wise man once said, "No one can whistle a symphony. It takes a whole orchestra to play it."

I want to express my deepest thanks to the greatest reporter of them all, Stan Chambers, and his talented son, Dave Chambers, for their unwavering support and guidance in helping me put this book together. Quite simply, this couldn't have been done without them. Stan's book on his extraordinary career, *KTLA's News at 10: 60 Years with Stan Chambers*, was the inspiration for this project. On behalf of each and every person who has ever worked in Los Angeles television news: "We all look up to Stan Chambers!"

I am so indebted to Heidi Brown, the daughter of my mentor Dr. Wayne Bundy, who has helped keep her father's dream on air as it broadcasts only the finest in public education television at KNME-TV in Albuquerque. I want to thank my former teammate in the KABC-TV Eyewitness News weather department, Rick De Reyes, for all of his invaluable help. Talk about a success story—Rick is now the Public Information Officer for ABQ Ride, the transit agency in my beloved Albuquerque.

I have so many people to thank who served with me at Channel 7 Eyewitness News in Los Angeles. They include Dianne Barone, who was so unselfish with her pictures and memories from our time in weather; Martin Orozco, who shared a number of photos from his continuing three decades–plus career at ABC7 as an award-winning cameraman; professor, author, and political commentator Bruce Herschensohn; sportscaster, newsman, and friend-extraordinaire Ed Arnold; the incomparable anchor and reporter Gene Gleeson; a most talented camerawoman and videotape editor who dedicated thirty-two years to serving the viewers of Channel 7, Heather MacKenzie; and a journalist who has logged nearly forty memorable years as a newswriter on the roster of Eyewitness News, my dear friend Joe Ashby.

There aren't enough words to express my thankfulness to one of my former students who has gone on to become a giant in the world of entertainment. Most importantly, he is my friend—Ron Miziker. Thanks to Bob Morris for helping me tell his father's story of inspiration, the late anchor and reporter Barney Morris and to psychotherapist Nickie Shoemaker Haggart, who has dedicated her life to helping those in need, for graciously allowing me to use the poem written by her beloved father (Rev. Sam Shoemaker), "I Stand By The Door."

I have been so blessed to know some real-life heroes who are so dedicated to reaching out to care for others in a world that is starving for love and encouragement. They include executive director Tom Propst of Firefighters Quest for Burn Survivors; two former presidents of the Alisa Ann Ruch Burn Foundation, retired fire captain Rick Pfeiffer and Barbara Horn, and Scott Vandrick, who as executive director, was the guiding light of this foundation from 2006 to 2012;

former Porterville Developmental Center program director Gary Johnson, who gave thirty-nine years of his life to serving the center's residents with severely challenging disabilities; and Ruth Butler, a most valuable human being who has served the Porterville Center for forty-five years.

While we're on the subject of people who are godsends, my thanks to executive assistant Tobi Jabson of the Lincoln Training Center; to award-winning television meteorologist Kyle Hunter; to the Radio and Television News Association of Southern California and its impeccable executive director Rick Terrell; to the Academy of Television Arts & Sciences and three members of that wonderful team: Adam Philbin, Laurel Whitcomb, and Liz Korda; and my gratitude to two most talented photographers, Craig T. Mathew of Mathew Imaging and Henk Friezer of Friezer Photography.

My deep appreciation to Dave Stolte, who has created and operated a Dr. George letters page on the Pup 'n' Taco website and to a member of my own family, Rich Fischbeck (and his camera), for capturing those unforgettable moments when I was presented the Governors Award at the Emmys and the Lifetime Achievement Award at the Golden Mike Awards dinner. Rich has also been instrumental in helping put together a Facebook page on which our friends, former colleagues, and even some ex-students of mine are able to reminisce by sharing memories and photos.

A special thank-you note from Dr. George to Jason Jacobs, Ann Noble, Leinani Bernabe, and Kirin Daugharty of the Los Angeles Zoo; to Mark Chamberlain and his invaluable roster of teammates at Chamberlain Restoration; to the generosity of Don Wanlass, the managing editor of the WAVE Newspaper Group in Los Angeles; and to the dedicated team of young women and men at the ImPress Center at OfficeMax in Oak Harbor, Washington (especially Dawn Robison, Eana Randall, and David Parker), for their help, guidance, and encouragement along the journey of putting this project together.

I must make a confession at this point. This book was originally written on an old computer that wasn't hooked up to the Internet using the ancient Windows 98 operating system. It wasn't until we were in the middle of chapter 16 that we discovered we really had no way to retrieve the book from Windows 98 and send it to the publisher. A high-tech guru named John Hellmann of The Computer Clinic in Oak Harbor came to our rescue and saved the day (not to mention, the book) by utilizing his genius and a simple giant paper clip.

And finally, I want to thank all of you, who have graced this wonderful life that God has blessed me with, for watching our newscasts all these years, for taking the time to write those many letters that you sent, for stopping me on the street so that we could share a hug and a smile, and for always making me feel so special. The Lord would have to give me another ninety years of life to even begin repaying all of that happiness you have given me. You are the reason I was able to wiggle my nose and mustache with joy all those times that we spent together.

My friends, please enjoy this book. And may all your days be sunny and bright!

— Dr George !! —

You Want Heroes?

A caring teacher hands children their passport to the future.
~ JENLANE GREE ~

In all my years in television in Los Angeles, I saw how news coverage helped put a number of people up on a pedestal for public worship. They included movie and TV stars, singers, sports celebrities, politicians, the rich and the famous. Yes, at times, even criminals and those accused of a crime have attracted adoration from the public because of all the media attention. Andy Warhol once said: "In the future, everyone will be world famous for fifteen minutes." And hasn't that become seemingly true . . . so help me Kato Kaelin.

Human beings seem to have a need for hero worship—as in looking up to others with esteem. The dictionary defines a hero as one admired for his exploits. But have you ever noticed that many of our true real-life heroes never receive any of the attention they really deserve? You want heroes? How about the dedicated men and women who walk into a classroom every day to provide invaluable guidance to our students? You won't read about them in newspapers or see their accomplishments on television news. They are ordinary people who do extraordinary things as teachers. They have been described as beacons of light who, like a potter is to clay, mold us in our formative years and shape our future in a most influential way. And the lessons we learn from them will remain with us for the rest of our lives.

I know firsthand just how special teachers are in our society because I worked alongside them for much of my professional life. You see, before I became a TV weatherman for Channel 7 Eyewitness News in Los Angeles, I was a schoolteacher in New Mexico for twenty-three years. Please don't think that I'm trying to put myself on any kind of pedestal. My friends, you know me better than that. But each day during my weather segments, I tried to turn our news set into a virtual classroom so that I could teach our viewers why weather is so important, and how the local forecast might influence their daily activities. First and foremost, I am a teacher. I always have been—I always will be. The teachers I have worked with over the years are proud of the vital role they have had in trying to transform students into becoming successful citizens through education.

It's a lifelong mission they are devoted to. Teachers deserve our deep appreciation, encouragement, and support for laying the foundation of knowledge for students in classrooms across America. Educators see it as their duty to instill in their students a desire to learn and to make it as rewarding as possible. Teachers have a responsibility that is crucial. They don't seek fame, fortune, or public attention. But on graduation day, when one of their students is handed a diploma, teachers can look on with pride at a job well done.

But as I have learned, you can't teach unless you have been taught. And I grew up in a family that was brimming with teachers. This is a story that begins in the small community of Wallington, New Jersey, population 1,000. That became 1,001 on July 1, 1922, when I was born at home, the first of four children in a family blessed with loving parents, farmer George Stelling Fischbeck and his wife, Johanna. Mom was a farmer's daughter who became a farmer's wife. But before my mother was married, she was a schoolteacher for years. Mom had three sisters, and they all became schoolteachers. My mother's father, Henry Mohlenhoff, had this thing about education, and he taught his children the importance of going to school. It was indeed a lesson learned, as all of his daughters went on to become elementary schoolteachers.

As my mother explained, there weren't many jobs for women back in those days. Because Mom and her sisters loved young children, it led them to seek careers in teaching.

It's a trait that runs in my family. Not only did I grow up to become a teacher, so did one of my sisters, Honor, who retired after a long career in the classroom. Honor's daughter, Carol, continues to teach school to this very day. My brother, two sisters, and I were raised on a farm. At the tender age of five, I began attending kindergarten at our small public school in Wallington. I took an immediate liking to my teacher, Miss Kachinski, who had the exceptional unique ability to make her class interesting to students. And that was the key. As a small child, I found myself looking forward to going to school each day. And it all started because of my very first teacher, Miss Kachinski.

But in 1927, tragedy struck our family. Our farm burned down. We didn't own it. We couldn't afford to. We were renting the farm, but it was everything we had in life. One day around noon, my father received a phone call that the barn was on fire—apparently started accidentally by some of the hired hands who had been smoking inside. It wasn't long before the fast-moving flames had spread to the house. I can vividly remember the family throwing our belongings out the window from the second floor in a desperate attempt to save anything. In the end, the house and barn burned to the ground, along with everything left inside. For months, my father, mother, younger brother Kenneth, and I lived in a small shed on the property. Our family had no income. We had no farm. If life indeed teaches us lessons, this is one that I will never forget, because this tragic loss taught me the true meaning of family, strength, and love.

I have always believed that when one door closes, God will open another. After all, if we had all the answers, it wouldn't be called faith. My mother's father, Henry Mohlenhoff, bought a farm sixty-five miles to the south in the small community of Farmingdale, New Jersey. Grandfather wanted our family to run it. It consisted of forty acres of land that had been farmed since the Civil War years in an area called West Farms. The property was bordered on the north by the Manasquan River, which my brother and I turned into our personal swimming hole. But as Kenneth and I soon found out, there wouldn't be much time for swimming on this farm.

Farming was a full-time job, even for small kids like me. We planted radishes, parsley, peppers, leeks, celery, and all kinds of vegetables. At the time, it was called truck farming because we would work the fields by day and drive our crops by truck to market at night. A farmers' market was located about twenty miles from our farm. That's where we put up a little food stand and sold the fruits of our labors to both families and merchants from grocery stores. Each member of our family was always busy. If you worked the fields one day, you'd trade off the next day and help run the food stand. One of us always had to spend the night sleeping at the food stand to protect what little we had.

Talk about getting an education in life. That's where little children like Kenneth and I learned to work with adults—and how to handle any number of situations in a workplace. We were also taught invaluable lessons about people themselves. You see, our farm was a melting pot for the human race because we hired a number of immigrants to work with us. I'll never forget one field worker we called Old Joe, who spent hours entertaining us with stories about his native Italy that he loved. It was an environment in which our family learned to respect and appreciate other races and ethnic cultures as they blended together on our farm. What a wonderful experience. Prejudice and discrimination should never ever be a part of anyone's vocabulary.

Of course, moving to a new community meant going to a new school. I began attending first-grade classes at the West Farms Elementary School. It was a very interesting school by today's standards. Instead of students in each grade having their own classroom, the first, second, and third graders were all placed in the same classroom and taught by the same teacher. West Farms Elementary School was just that small. In the class, the students in each grade were assigned to sit together, two rows per grade. While the teacher would be giving lessons to the first-grade students, the second and third graders would be doing their assignments until it was time for the teacher to begin working with them. There was no magic formula to this. That's just the way it was, the way it had to be. And it worked. In all, there were about thirty students in our classroom. The teacher had to keep the window closed because there was a huge pig farm located next to the school. And because the pigs liked to exercise their First Amendment rights to speak out, it was best we kept that window shut.

After completing the first three grades, I was moved to another classroom where the fourth-, fifth-, and sixth-grade students were assigned together. Mrs. Stewart was my teacher for those three years. I can remember her lessons in math (especially fractions), poetry, and history. Mrs. Stewart lived near the ocean, and she would bring shellfish and horseshoe crabs to class to help encourage our love of nature. By this time, my mother had resumed her career as a teacher, working at a different school than the one I was attending. Along the way, there was another population explosion within the Fischbeck clan as Mom gave birth to two daughters, Dorothy (1928) and Honor (1932). With my schoolwork, my farm chores, and helping to take care of my little sisters, responsibility was becoming a very important lesson for me to learn in my young life.

For the seventh and eighth grades, I attended Adelphia Middle School. Since it was eight miles from our family farm, I took the school bus. I never missed a day because our next-door neighbor drove the bus. In the morning, I was the first student to be picked up on the way to school. And in the afternoon, I was the last to get off on the way home. Adelphia was also a small school; seventh and eighth graders were assigned together in the same classroom. Mrs. Griblin was our teacher. She opened our educational doors to history, geography, and music appreciation—especially symphonies and classical music, which I still love to listen to.

But it was in high school where I was first introduced to the world of science, which changed my life in ways I could have never imagined back then. Freehold High was the biggest school I had ever attended. Students were required to attend basic high school classes like English and math, as well as chemistry, physics, and biology. Unlike my elementary and middle schools, each grade at Freehold High had its own classroom and teacher. One instructor stood head and shoulders above all the others. His name was Mr. Stout, and he was my science teacher. Mr. Stout went the extra mile in helping students learn his lessons. He always had us thinking.

One time in class, Mr. Stout asked me to explain what causes thunder. I replied, "When two clouds bump each other." All the other students laughed at me. Everyone but Mr. Stout, who gave me the assignment of finding the right answer. He knew that's how you learn. The next day,

I gave our class this oral report on my homework: "Thunder occurs when negative energy in the air is attracted to positive energy on the ground. And when a lightning bolt is discharged, the air rushes in to fill the void and produces thunder." I received an A for content and an A for effort. Lesson learned. There were times when Mr. Stout would even come out to our farm for a visit. He just wanted to see how I was doing, and he would teach me a thing or two about science while we took nature walks. That was so special to me. Mr. Stout was a dedicated educator who went out of his way to reach out to students. He was my hero—a science teacher who cared.

It was while I was attending Freehold High that I met another student who became a lifelong friend. George Voorhis was enrolled at Red Bank High School in neighboring Little Silver, New Jersey. We got to know each other at football games involving our two schools. George was a real clown. He even had a clown outfit and was later hired to help promote a local fast food restaurant called McDonald's. George became the original Ronald McDonald. Years later, my friend was still on the job helping to teach positive values to children as McDonald's "chief happiness officer."

Back on the home front, my father learned he had to be innovative if he was to support his family from the farm year-round. After the summer crops had been harvested, Dad planted winter crops such as chives and wild mint, as well as small flowers, which I sold to motorists along the highway. My father also built a makeshift tennis court on our farm property. It was a great meeting place for all the kids in the neighborhood.

One day we looked up and saw the German passenger airship *Hindenburg* flying overhead on its way for a landing at the Lakehurst Naval Air Station, fifteen miles away. We were eyewitnesses to history. The date was May 6, 1937. A short time later that day, at 7:25 p.m., while our family was sitting at the dinner table, we felt a huge vibration that rattled the kitchen dishes. We had no idea at the time what had happened, but the news spread fast. The *Hindenburg* had exploded and burst into flames during its attempt to dock at Lakehurst. Of the ninety-seven people on board the *Hindenburg*, thirty-five died in the inferno. One person was killed on the ground. It's a tragedy that has been called the "*Titanic* of the Sky." The next day, our school bus had to take a long detour because of all the traffic heading to the crash site. As a reporter for Pathé Media described it, the *Hindenburg* was "a conquering giant of the skies that perished in the mighty grip of fate."

I graduated from high school at the age of sixteen. My family insisted that I go to college. They drove me to New Brunswick, New Jersey, where I enrolled at Rutgers University. New Brunswick was a pretty big town to this farm boy, with a population of 34,555. I lived in a dormitory on campus. I didn't particularly want to go to college at this point in my life. But I always did what my family wanted me to do. My parents also told me to major in agriculture at Rutgers. I did as instructed; however, it was only a few months before I dropped out of school. I came home and told Mom and Dad that I didn't want to train to be a farmer. My father accepted that and said I could go to any school I wanted. But there was one condition. I was going to have to get a job to pay for my education.

So my parents drove me to an even bigger challenge in the largest city in the entire state of New Jersey. Newark, with a population of more than four hundred thousand people, was unlike anything I had ever seen in my young life. I enrolled in the Newark School of Fine and Industrial Arts. I got a room across the street from school. At night, I worked as a coil winder at a local plant to pay for my room and tuition. I was even able to send some money home to my family. I'll tell you this: working as a coil winder is about as far removed from being a weatherman at Channel 7 Eyewitness News in Los Angeles as you can get. But it was a job. Soon, my bosses talked me into leaving the Newark School of Fine and Industrial Arts and enrolling at Newark Vocational School to study electrical engineering. The plant I worked for paid all my education expenses. But it wasn't long before I had to answer a calling from the biggest boss of all—Uncle Sam.

On December 7, 1941, the Japanese attacked Pearl Harbor, and the United States was plunged into war. I didn't wait for my country to come for me. I volunteered. I was inducted into the military at Fort Dix, New Jersey. In a matter of days, I was transferred to Southern California and to a famed horse racing track in Arcadia that had been turned into a huge U.S. Army training base called Camp Santa Anita. As the song goes, "You're in the army now." Camp Santa Anita is where I underwent basic training—boot camp—as I was transformed from college student to soldier. I wasn't alone. In fact, there were so many newly inducted trainees that we had to be housed in the grandstands at the Santa Anita Race Track. I may not have been as fast as Seabiscuit, but I learned quickly that it was best to stay at least one step ahead of my ever-demanding drill sergeant.

If there was one basic lesson in boot camp, it was to survive. It was a grueling eight-week challenge that tested trainees to the max both physically and mentally. The army had a slogan: "Be all that you can be." But that never seemed to be enough for my drill sergeant.

After I learned to become a soldier during basic training (which to this day remains debatable), it was time for the army to train me for a job. That meant crisscrossing the country to the Aberdeen Proving Ground in Maryland, where I underwent several months of training to become a tank mechanic. Now you may look at me and wonder what in the world was I going to do under the hood of a military tank? That's a question that crossed my mind as well—but the army never bothered to tell me. And I figured that if we wanted to win the war, I best go to where they ordered me. That journey led me all the way to Hawaii, where I spent World War II fixing tanks that had been brought in by ship after breaking down at the war front. Being a tank mechanic did have its benefits; at one point, I was promoted to corporal. But in Hawaii, there weren't all that many tanks for a mechanic like me to fix. So I spent much of my time washing dishes on KP (kitchen patrol), or even worse, on latrine duty. And my friends, excuse me for repeating myself, but I'll tell you this—washing dishes and performing latrine duty is about as far removed from being a weatherman at Channel 7 Eyewitness News in Los Angeles as you can get. Trust me, I know.

After several years of making sure the dishes were clean and the bathrooms were spotless, I had had enough. And after the war had ended, I decided to do something about it. On Christmas Day in 1945, I was on duty in the day room when I saw our officers drinking beer and having a party in the mess hall. I couldn't have been more infuriated. I figured it was time for Corporal George Fischbeck to go to war and play a holiday practical joke on his commanding officer. I called over to the motor pool, told them my plans, and asked if they could loan me a staff car. The guys at the motor pool hated our commanding officer so much, they even threw in a major's uniform for me to wear. Two of my friends, Ken and Bob, accompanied me as I drove to the mess hall and held an immediate inspection of all the beer-drinking officers on hand. Being a "major," I outranked the officers (or so they thought).

Never having done this before, I ordered all the officers to line up for a fingernail inspection. And things seemed to be going pretty well until I got down to the end of the line and started inspecting the fingernails of my commanding officer, who suddenly recognized me. That's when the captain screamed at the top of his lungs, "It's Fischbeck!!" along with some highly profane words that I don't think are well suited for this book. To make a long story short, the captain ordered my military career be terminated—effective immediately. But because I was already eligible for discharge, having served thirty-three months, my exit from the military was still declared "honorable." And because we had won the war, I figured the army and I were even. It's a truce that remains in place to this day.

As for the two friends that had been my co-conspirators—Ken (Kenneth Randall) went on to become a church pastor, while Bob (Robert Hoffman) became a schoolteacher and principal in Philadelphia. At one point, Bob taught a high school geometry class. You may have heard of one of his students—Bill Cosby. I never did find out what happened to our captain after all these years. But he did have nice fingernails.

Back in the states, Newark, New Jersey, hadn't changed much by the time I returned after the war. There weren't any military tanks roaming the streets that needed a mechanic, but the old plant where I had worked as a coil winder wanted me back. And since I had gone to school and studied electrical engineering, they actually promoted me to electrician. I even joined the union. Life for me was going pretty well at that point. My parents had moved to the community of Bloomfield, just outside Newark, and it was nice to have them nearby again. But little did I know what door was about to open.

When Cupid shoots his arrow of romance, he's usually on target. And with me, Cupid only had to aim once in my life. I was a bit more than smitten, shall we say, when I was first introduced to the secretary of one of our plant's general managers. Her name was Susanne June Reif. Mere words cannot possibly describe the courage it took me to finally ask Susanne out for a date a while after we had met. The way I looked at it, there were only two things she could say. Being dumb and not knowing any better, I figured that I had a fifty-fifty chance of it not being *no*. And Susanne and I went out on a first date.

If fate was indeed smiling on me that night, Mother Nature certainly wasn't. It snowed in Newark during our date. And it snowed. And it continued to snow. And then it got heavier. Real heavy. Viewers always seem to blame the TV weatherman for causing bad weather. On this evening, I might have been fired for even thinking of putting this blizzard in my forecast. It got so bad that Susanne and I had to seek refuge at my parents' home in Bloomfield. There was no way to "weather" the weather. And so Susanne spent the night with my mom, dad, and two younger sisters—who absolutely loved her. But as for George Fischbeck—well, that's another story. In all honesty, Susanne didn't really like me at first. And that likability factor rapidly declined when she learned how much I had gushingly told my parents about her even before our first date. But you know, God has a plan for each one of us. And the Bible teaches that His plan includes putting two people together. Our Heavenly Father knows best. And on April 17, 1949, George and Sue became Mr. and Mrs. Fischbeck forever.

But, if I may, let me backtrack a bit in this story. While Sue and I were still dating, I decided to expand my horizons. The lessons I had learned as a child working on our family farm with immigrants from around the world had created a curiosity within me to learn more about other ethnic groups and their heritage. And I had developed a particular interest in Native Americans. One summer, I had a chance to take some classes in sociology—the study of human social activity—at the University of Maine, some 462 miles northeast of my home in New Jersey. For living expenses, I worked part time at a local canoe factory. A number of my co-workers at the factory were members of the Penobscot Indian Nation, who lived in the small town of Orono along the Stillwater River. The Penobscot Indians were one of four tribes who were the original inhabitants of the area now known as Maine. I was fascinated by the culture and language of my new friends. It was another lesson in life that taught me to have a deep appreciation for others. Wouldn't this world be a wonderful place if we could all just learn to have respect for each other?

After returning to New Jersey, there was nothing I wanted to do more than to build on the invaluable lessons I had learned in Maine, both inside and outside the classroom. And with the GI Bill now "footing the bill" for my education, I was free to choose whatever I wanted to study and wherever I wanted to study it. Anthropology had become my favorite subject. It's the study of humans past and present and the complexity of cultures across all of history. I chose to attend the University of New Mexico because I felt it offered the best anthropology program in the nation. New Mexico is also home to twenty-two American Indian tribes. And I looked forward to the chance of being able to continue my study of the unique and rich history of Native Americans. My goodness, this was an opportunity that I couldn't pass up.

By this time, I was going steady with Sue. Even though I would be going to school more than two thousand miles away, she knew I'd still be coming home for the holidays to see her. I knew I'd miss her. But I didn't realize how much. At one point, I joined the Air National Guard as a reservist, where I was assigned to work in the weather department. But if there was one thing I learned in the Air National Guard, it was that I certainly didn't want to fly solo for the rest of my life. So I went back to Newark and married Sue. And boy was the new Mrs. Fischbeck about to undergo a geographic extreme makeover. You see, Sue was born and raised in a big city. She had always lived in a fast-paced town with bright lights and lots of people. Moving to the much-smaller (and quieter) community of Albuquerque, New Mexico, was going to be quite a change for my wife—a radical change. At first glance, I think she thought of the word *desolate*. But at least we were together.

At the University of New Mexico, I focused on earning a college degree. Even though I still didn't know what I wanted to do for a career, I graduated with a bachelor's degree. In addition to anthropology, my studies also included geology and archaeology. I must have walked all over northern New Mexico studying the ancient settlements of the Pueblo Indians. I had an insatiable quest for knowledge, and I decided to continue my education by seeking a master's degree. But my country had some other ideas—that's when Uncle Sam came calling again. The United States was at war in Korea, and it wasn't long before my Air National Guard unit in New Mexico was activated. Here I was, back in the military full time. But what I learned this time would have an everlasting impact.

I was assigned to the 188th Fighter Squadron at Kirtland Air Force Base in Albuquerque. My unit never made it to the war front in Korea during my time on active duty, but we had a motto: Be prepared. Our mission was to have our jet fighter squadron completely ready for combat at all times—no matter what. My work in our unit's weather department was an essential tool in this mission. My job was to make sure our pilots knew the latest weather conditions and how those conditions could change at a moment's notice while they were in flight. I had the best training in using the latest technology in meteorology. It was also my responsibility to supply all weather information from New Mexico to the National Weather Service headquarters in North Carolina. Like a gunfighter in the Old West, I had to be fast, but I needed to be accurate. There were times when my emotions on the job changed faster than the weather, but it was exciting.

It was also an education that would lay the foundation for a life-changing career in meteorology. But let's not put the cart in front of the horse just yet. Unbeknownst to me, there were other challenges that lay ahead. As I was about to learn, the experience of life itself is the greatest teacher of all. There will never be a time when you will have mastered all that life has to teach you. I've come to believe that the smarter you get, the more you will realize how much more there is to learn.

When our Air National Guard unit was finally deactivated and placed on reserve status, I still had to attend monthly National Guard meetings. But I was free to go back to school with the GI Bill paying my way. I needed to study a subject that would lead to a job and hopefully a career. My résumé included part-time work as a stevedore at a harbor terminal and grape, tomato, and peach harvesting at a cannery. I had worked for a fire department in a national forest. I had made automobile batteries, raised flowers commercially, and even managed a drive-in restaurant.

I had taken a number of classes either on campus or through correspondence courses that included genetics (University of Maryland), engineering (University of California), fine arts and advertising (University of Hawaii), history (Army University Center), and industrial management (Rutgers University, Newark campus). I loved anthropology. But I knew if I went into that field, I would be traveling all over the country pursuing the study of humankind through time.

While anthropologist isn't exactly a well-known career, it can be one of the most rewarding academically.

But I wanted to live and work in New Mexico. After all, that's where my wife was. And at this point in life, I really wanted to reach out and share with others all of the invaluable lessons that I have been blessed to learn. The word *teach* is defined in the dictionary as to impart knowledge, to instruct, to cause to learn by example or experience. You know, that sounded like a nice job. So I went back and hit the books again at the University of New Mexico. And once I had my master's degree in education in hand, I set out as a teacher, with a goal of helping to mold the minds of our nation's most precious resource—its children.

The Challenge of a Classroom

A good teacher is like a candle.
It consumes itself to light the way for others.
~ AUTHOR UNKNOWN ~

When you put together a television newscast each day, you have to decide what stories your team of journalists is going to cover. And that includes deciding how much importance you are going to assign each issue. These are tough decisions made daily in newsrooms across America. But when you really think about it, the issue of education may be the most important of all. It's like making an investment. Today's students are the future of tomorrow. If you can invest a sound, well-rounded, and thorough education in our students, it will pay positive dividends for society in the years ahead. But it all begins with the teachers, who need to present their material in a way that is both interesting and relevant so that students will be able to apply these lessons long after class is dismissed, and the challenges of the real world have begun. To both teacher and student alike, the learning process is crucial. And the responsibility that teachers face each and every day couldn't be of more importance. And as a young man still in his twenties, that is the responsibility a college graduate named

George Fischbeck decided to take on as a new chapter in my life was about to be written.

Going from being a student to teacher overnight didn't really scare me. I felt that after years and years of schooling, I was qualified. And thanks to my education teacher at the University of New Mexico, Mr. Ivans, I had confidence. Mr. Ivans gave me this piece of invaluable advice: "George, you're only going to be passing on what you already know." But it's a good thing that I didn't know what lay ahead of me on my first day on the job. I was hired to be the ninth-grade science teacher at what was considered to be the roughest and toughest school in all of Albuquerque at the time—Lincoln Junior High School. And being the brand new teacher on campus, I was assigned the worst class of all, comprised of the "baddest" students who were ready to chew up a rookie teacher and spit him out.

As the school bell rang to begin the day, I walked into my classroom and addressed the students: "I'm going to be your science teacher, and you're going to learn biology, chemistry, and physics." The students all laughed at me, and I wasn't even thirty seconds into my first day. I had to think fast. So I reached into a jar I had brought to class and pulled out a large, living tarantula, which I then placed on the sleeve of my shirt. I had intentionally worn a white shirt so that the tarantula would stand out even more in case I needed him. As the tarantula began walking up my arm, the class gasped in astonishment. When he got up to my neck, the students screamed out in horror. I think I had their attention. Being a brave soul, I let my eight-legged teaching aid walk up to the top of my head, at which time I scooped the tarantula up with my hand and placed him back in the jar. The class let out a loud and collective sigh of relief. By then, I knew what moments before had been the roughest and toughest students were now in the palm of my hand. And I said to myself, "Now I can teach them anything." Yes—it was another lesson learned.

It didn't take me long to realize that when you're the new teacher on the block, with the least seniority, you'd better keep your bags packed. Wherever there is a need, the teacher at the low end of the totem pole will be the first one transferred to fill that need. After eight months of teaching at Lincoln, I was reassigned to Ernie Pyle Junior High in Albuquerque. That's where I not only taught ninth-grade science, but

U.S. history and civics classes as well. By this time, I was becoming quite comfortable in my new career. After all, how many people in the world actually get to make a living doing what they really want to do in life? And at a salary of $2,600 a year, who could ask for anything more?

My students at Ernie Pyle Junior High were extremely receptive, which made a big difference for me in the classroom. Teaching had become an even more enjoyable canvas on which to paint, and I worked for a principal who appreciated his teachers. Principal Adolfo Chavez liked me from the very beginning. Under his tutelage, I would show up early for school daily, go to the furnace room on campus, write out my lessons for the day, and then submit them to Mr. Chavez before heading to the classroom. Mr. Chavez never made any changes to my lesson plans, but his guidance and the discipline he taught me made George Fischbeck an even better teacher. It was a lesson I never forgot.

About this time, there was a population explosion in the House of Fischbeck. My wife, Sue, and I became the proud parents of newborn twins, Nancy and George Junior (we called him "Fritz"). Albuquerque was going through some growing pains as well. With more and more people moving to the "Duke City," school officials had to figure out a way to accommodate all of the new students. One of the solutions was to build a new school from scratch out in the middle of "nowhere" in the open lands of Albuquerque's high plains area. In the beginning, the new Monroe Junior High School was nothing more than a couple of army barracks. But it had a great principal. Mr. Borland was my original principal at Lincoln Junior High. When he told me I was on his "most wanted" list for teachers at Monroe, I came running. It's so nice to be wanted. One of the most gratifying experiences of my entire life is to have had a hand in building the foundation of what became a very special institution of learning.

As a teacher, I was finding new ways of reaching out to my students to develop a positive connection that would ignite their desire for knowledge. A teacher needs to get his or her students involved. I guess you might call this Dr. George's "No Child Left Behind" program. I would begin a new class by learning to call each of my students by their first name. A simple gesture like this helped personalize our classroom. Students learned to be alert and ready to answer questions if I happened to call their name.

Teaching at a new school like Monroe with a small faculty also meant instructors needed to expand the academic subjects we taught. In addition to science, U.S. history, and civics, I was also teaching classes in chemistry, physics, and biology. Along the way, I learned to take advantage of a variety of resources at my disposal. Some of my students had parents working at the Sandia Base in Albuquerque, which for twenty-five years was the principal nuclear weapons installation of the U.S. Defense Department. The base played a key role in our country's research, development, assembly, and storage of nuclear weapons during the Cold War. But even though Sandia's multi-faceted assignments were classified as top secret . . . my students' fathers and mothers who worked at the base were allowed to visit our class to speak on a potpourri of fascinating topics. What science teacher wouldn't take advantage of that?

Then there is the concept of teamwork, which Andrew Carnegie once described as "the fuel that allows common people to attain uncommon results." Dennis Kinlaw has been quoted as saying a team player is "one who unites others toward a shared destiny through sharing information and ideas." That's why I reached out to my colleagues across the Albuquerque Public Schools (APS) to form the Science Teachers Association. A bunch of us science teachers got together, and we decided that we could enhance our own individual science classes by sharing our lessons, ideas, and resources with each other. Someone once spelled out the word "team" as "together everyone achieves more."

In the words of one well-known philosopher named Magic Johnson, "Ask not what your teammates can do for you. Ask what you can do for your teammates." Working together, the members of the Science Teachers Association parlayed individual participation to achieve collective results in our classrooms. It was a formula that succeeded far beyond our expectations. And our students were the big winners. One project we were particularly proud of involved milk and rats. Our association talked some local milk companies into funding an extensive study into what effect milk had on rats and why some rats received nutrients from the milk, while others did not. This study was carried out by students in school science classes across Albuquerque. The comprehensive results of our study, which detailed how milk and milk products affected the growth and activity of rats, were applauded by the scientific community. It was indeed a profile in excellence by our students, who made their teachers extremely proud.

While we're on the subject of animals in the classroom, let me share with you some experiences that got me anything but an A for effort from my family. Earlier in this chapter, I told you about a tarantula I pulled out of a jar for my students to see on my very first day as a teacher. That night, I brought my eight-legged friend home, where my little son's curiosity got the best of him. While I wasn't looking, George Junior took the tarantula out of its box to see what it was. The fearsome-looking spider frightened him so badly, George screamed and tossed it into the air. The tarantula went flying—landed on little Nancy, our daughter—and bit her on the knee. Nancy wasn't seriously hurt. But my wife, Sue, spent some nervous moments talking on the phone with an emergency room doctor, while the tarantula and I stood facing the wall in a corner as punishment.

At school, you never knew who might show up at our classroom, especially since we were located in old army barracks in the middle of a remote area eight to ten miles away from anything that resembled a city. One day, a student asked me to come to the doorway of the classroom to see who was there. Lo and behold, it was a live rattlesnake. He was only about a foot to a foot-and-a-half long. So I picked the snake up, put him in a glass jar, took him to the front of the class, and taught my students an hour-long class on rattlesnakes. As a teacher, I didn't want to look a gift horse in the mouth, so to speak. That night, I decided to take the snake home so I could study him further. My unassuming wife drove over and picked me up at school. I got into the car on the passenger side. And my beloved Sue will regret for the rest of her life asking, "George, what have you got in the jar?" I thought I'd never talk my screaming wife into getting back in the car.

Then there was the time I brought home a harmless little old gopher snake from class. Sue wasn't home at the time. I thought this would be an excellent opportunity to teach our infant twins, Nancy and George Junior, all about nature. So I placed the gopher snake in their crib to play with. Then my wife came home. By this time, our little twins were passing the snake back and forth in amazement. Sue didn't scream . . . she was speechless. However, my wife did turn a color that not even a science teacher like me can describe. Let me put it this way—from that point on, I was forbidden from ever bringing work home again.

That didn't mean I couldn't take things from home to my work. My wife, Sue, understood that I was anything but a "textbook" teacher. As a science teacher, I never did anything by the book. It's been said that science is about understanding the world around us. It's also about discovery. Whatever I could do to enhance that experience of discovery and understanding in the classroom, I would do. It was anything goes. I wanted to bring the world to my students in every way possible. Whenever I found something I thought would expand my students' knowledge and appreciation of the world we live in, I kept it at home until that particular lesson was ready to be shared in the classroom.

For example, did you know that there are animals whose body temperature drops significantly when they go into hibernation for the winter? When that happens, they can sleep under any conditions. It was a school lesson that actually began in my kitchen at home. I decided to experiment with a ground squirrel in hibernation by placing him in the refrigerator for an entire weekend. The squirrel was asleep. I kept a record on his body temperature. And my animal friend spent the weekend sleeping in the fridge. I took the squirrel to class Monday morning. After I woke the squirrel up in front of my students, we all watched the squirrel's body temperature rise rapidly as he emerged from hibernation. The class was able to compare this information with the data I had collected during the weekend at home. It was a lesson that couldn't have been taught by merely reading a textbook. In the weeks that followed, I continued my experiment by placing hibernating animals such as horned toads and lizards in my refrigerator at home so that I could share this information with my students as well. The class loved it. But my wife, Sue, never got used to being surprised when she would open the refrigerator door to make dinner and discover my "homework."

There were times when the House of Fischbeck actually resembled a scene right out of television's *Wild Kingdom* show. Animals made for some absolutely wonderful lessons at school. At home, I had to house many of the animals, like scorpions and a hognose snake, in cages or large glass containers to keep peace in my family. But there were other little critters that had the run of the place at times. They included two ground squirrels named Chipper and Nipper, a pair of skunks (descented, of course) that we named Blue Max and Flower, a kangaroo rat, Honey Bunny the rabbit, and Pedro the parakeet. A local religious group called Sisters of Santa Cruz donated another animal to my class called Sally the salamander. And our family pet, Dutchess the schnauzer, got along with everyone. Dutchess especially liked chasing the skunks and the rabbit in the backyard. I gave my family a break at times by rewarding good students and allowing them to take home one of the animals for the weekend.

On campus, the teachers and students of Monroe Junior High School were also rewarded after spending our first year in army barracks. I'll never forget that wonderful day when we were allowed to move into Monroe's brand new main school building after it was first built. That meant my science classes would be held in a modern classroom, the best that public education had to offer. And the students and I turned our classroom into a real science laboratory. I remember one day using an old Sparkletts water container to teach my class how to make clouds in a bottle. Another time in class, I used a gallon jug half-filled with water, vinegar, and baking soda and turned it into a homemade fire extinguisher to put out an intentionally set small fire in a wastepaper basket. I tried that experiment in another class, but I didn't have any vinegar. So I substituted hydrochloric acid. It worked— too well. I ended up creating an even more powerful homemade fire extinguisher that not only put out the fire in the wastepaper basket, it also "extinguished" all the students sitting in the first two rows.

That wasn't the only time one of our class experiments was a little too successful. One class project involved the construction of a working fifteen-inch volcano out of clay. When I say *working*, I mean flames and all. In fact, our volcano worked so well our entire classroom was filled with smoke. That day, my class and I took the phrase "science is about discovery" to a new level.

As a teacher, I always felt you don't learn if you don't try. As the saying goes: If you aim for nothing, you're bound to hit your target. I tried to create in my classroom an atmosphere that inspired students to ask, to seek, to explore, and to find. Isn't that the essence of education? As our connection grew between instructor and student—we learned from each other. Plato once said, "The power to learn is present in everybody's soul. And the instrument with which each learns is like an eye that cannot be turned around from darkness to light without turning the whole body." The philosophy of Vedanta says, "Within man is all knowledge—even in a boy, it is so—and it requires only an awakening. And that much is the work of a teacher."

There wasn't anything I wouldn't do as a teacher to try to keep my classes fun and interesting so that students would want to come back for more. One tool I used became very popular among my students, and it gave them the incentive to give nothing less than their very best in class. For students whose test scores were ranked in the highest 2 percent, I gave them an official "General Science Test Pass" which excused them from having to take the next regular exam.

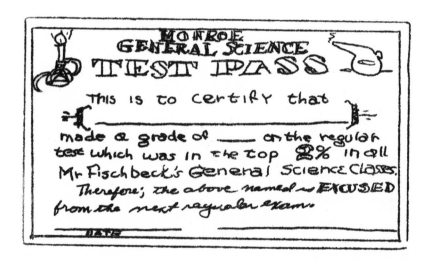

The test pass itself wasn't printed on anything fancy. I didn't have the money to go to a local print shop. So I created my own pass with pen and paper, writing in longhand that this was to certify the student named had Mr. Fischbeck's permission to be excused from the next test. I didn't know how this would be received by my bosses in the school's administration. To be honest, I never did hear anything from them. So in this case, I guess silence is golden. But the students'

response spoke volumes. Test scores rose dramatically. As their teacher, I found it to be a wonderful way to motivate "my kids" to do better.

The students and I also organized the first Monroe Science Fair, in which the entire student body was invited to enter their individual projects in various competitions. Once again, I used my limited talents in art and longhand to create a science award certificate to be given in recognition of "outstanding imagination, research, and diligence." I found competition is one of the best ways to maximize students' participation and reward them for their efforts. To get my students prepared for the rat race of the real world, we held what was called "The World Championship Rat Race of Monroe Junior High." The competition was fierce among all the classes. My students and I knew going in that the Fischbeck class didn't have the fastest rat. But in terms of motivating our rat, we were second to none. While the other classes put food at the finish line to get their rats to run fast, we let a gopher snake give our rat, shall we say, a little pep talk at the starting line. In the end, it was no contest. The Associated Press even ran a story on Monroe's rat racing on the national wire. In the teacher-student relationship, a little attention goes a long way.

I continued to search for ways to get my students into the fast lane of achievement. One year, I gave out S&H Green Stamps with report cards. Boy, did that pay dividends in class. Another time, I led my students on a door-to-door campaign for the March of Dimes. My kids set a national record for per capita participation. I parlayed all the attention we were getting into attracting some of the brightest minds in America to take part in our classroom's "Visiting Scientist Program." My students were able to meet top-flight men and women of science, business, engineering, medicine, law, and mathematics. And our class continued to grow as a forum for learning with academic values that are the key to life. As author Nora Roberts has said, "Knowledge is a great gift, and the thirst to seek it even greater."

When I look back at my career in education, I realize the road to becoming a teacher is a long journey that is never finished. From the very beginning, I wanted to help my students learn and grow. I had a desire and a commitment to make a positive contribution to their lives. And I was blessed with so many children and young people in the classroom that were a wonderful inspiration to me and validated the decision to dedicate my life to teaching and sharing with others. There is no finer recognition that teachers can possibly receive than to see their students go on and succeed in the challenges they choose with the foundation of education they were given in the classrooms where we serve. The two most powerful words in the English language are "thank you" when they are expressed from one's heart. I would like to share with you the highest honor that I have ever been given, by former students who wanted to say, "Thank you, teacher."

> *It was your class that started my interest in science. For the last 30 years, I have been a practicing clinical and forensic toxicologist for which you must share some of the blame! There are many things from that class I remember to this day. Thanks for your inspiration and dedication.*
>
> *~ Walter Blackwell*

> *What great memories. Really created my love for science.*
> *~ Michele Ungvarsky*

> *I remember he signed my Science Fair project at Eubank Elementary School. I have memories of him being not only a great teacher, but a real fun real person who laughed a lot.*
> *~ Cathi Thomas*

> *I was in one of the first graduating classes of the Head Start program. He was there to give us our diplomas with all the heartfelt support that any proud parent or grandparent could give. Thanks for such great memories, Dr. George.*
> *~ Amy Gutierrez*

> *Dr. Fischbeck came to my elementary school in the '60s. I have a certificate from him stating I was in his science club! All of us kids were sad when he left New Mexico. But I moved to California in the '80s and got to see him again! I have never forgotten you, Dr. Fischbeck. You are awesome!*
>
> *~ Paula Hernandez Stewart*

Dr. George taught my general science class the summer of 1959 at Highland High School, Albuquerque. I had never heard of him, but loved him and his way of teaching. He was great! I respected him so much, and more so as we both grew older . . . for his humor, his common sense, his weather teaching abilities, and his service helping the unfortunate. Thanks Dr. George for the "A-plus." I still have that report card. (Of course I kept it. It is the only "A-plus" that I ever got!)

Dr. George was my science teacher when I was in 6th grade at Monte Vista Elementary School in Albuquerque in the early '60s. I will never forget his signing the chalkboard in a fashion so that his name looked like a fish. The picture of a fish's back has kept his name in my memory all these years, not to mention his wonderful personality and ease with kids. I wish him the best. I am sure I am only one of thousands of his former students that remember him fondly. I will never forget him and how he made us feel good about ourselves and piqued our interest in science.

It's amazing how one person can make such an impression on an 8-year-old kid . . . that he still remembers him in his 50s. George, you were the best!

I remember Dr. Fischbeck somewhere in the middle to late '60s at our school in Artesia, New Mexico, at Yucca Elementary School when he visited us one day. I remember him being full of energy and excited and jumping up and down a couple of times . . . and explaining how the weather works.

(NOTE TO READERS FROM DR. GEORGE: The following letter was sent to me in the early 1960s from a little boy who had a special request. This is one of my all-time favorites!)

Dear Mr. Fischbeck,

I enjoy your science program a lot. My problem is that I have a crush on girls. What should I do to get a girl to like me? I hope you answer my problem.

Your friend,
"John"

As you can see, a teacher's job is never over! And in 1959, I was about to learn how teaching would expand my horizons in education with opportunities that would go far beyond the classroom.

My Classroom Expands

George Fischbeck is the Mark Twain and Will Rogers of the educational profession. People may laugh. But the humor is there for a purpose. People remember what they have been taught by him.

~ DR. ELDRED "DOC" HARRINGTON ~

Teacher

The late author and historian Henry Adams once said, "A teacher affects eternity. He can never tell where his influence stops." That sums up my feelings about Doc Harrington. He is my hero. Doc is primarily known for his teaching career at Albuquerque High School from 1932 to 1955, but he was also an author, a geologist, an engineer. And he was my friend and one of the biggest influences in my life. The beloved Doc took the time and had the patience to teach a young George Fischbeck how to be a teacher. Dr. Harrington had his priorities: students first, school second, teacher last. To Doc, a teacher had to remove self from the equation because there was nothing more important than the responsibility of shaping the educational lives of his ever-impressionable students. The lessons of Dr. Eldred Harrington have greatly enriched my career as an educator.

Words cannot possibly describe the joy and deep personal satisfaction you experience with the privilege of being a schoolteacher. But it also helps to have a loving and devoted wife because at $2,600 a year, I wasn't about to enrich Mrs. Fischbeck with just my paycheck. During all my years as a teacher, Sue had to work as well. In her words, it was necessary to keep the House of Fischbeck afloat financially. At first, Sue worked as a secretary for a local tractor company. She later served as an office manager for several real estate and insurance firms. When it came to paying the bills, it didn't take a Phi Beta Kappa to realize that two jobs are better than one.

At school, my classroom had expanded. While my primary assignment was Monroe Junior High School, I was also on staff teaching classes at two other junior high schools and a high school in Albuquerque. I never knew the meaning of summer vacation. I spent a number of summers on the faculties of New Mexico Highlands University, the University of New Mexico, and Adams State College in Colorado teaching elementary and secondary school science method courses. During one semester alone, I found myself teaching science classes for fifth, sixth, and ninth graders, as well as graduate students in college—sometimes all in the same day. One of my most rewarding experiences came when I was given the unique chance to teach at the tribal schools of the Navajo Indian Reservation.

Opportunity is a wonderful resource—you never know where it will lead you. One summer, a fellow teacher, Robert Smolich, and I were invited to serve as ranger-naturalists at Zion National Park in Utah. You couldn't ask for a better workplace, what with the park's stunning scenery, towering cliffs, and deep sandstone canyons. Zion National Park is a showcase of geology. Robert and I gave lectures and took park visitors on tours of this magnificent national treasure. That summer, it's estimated we gave sixty thousand visitors the first interpretive educational program ever offered at a national park or forest. And for teachers like Robert and me—what a classroom.

Now we did this on a volunteer basis, as in unpaid volunteers. We paid expenses out of our pockets. And as public schoolteachers, our pockets were not that deep. So we came up with a unique idea for fundraising with Uncle Sam as our partner. The U.S. Postal Service agreed to issue our own postage stamp featuring New Mexico's 10,678 foot

Sandia Crest. The stamp was quite popular, especially with collectors. Please don't think that Robert and I got rich from this—anything but. However, the stamp sales did pay for our expenses like gas. And what a summer we had, as a couple of small-town educators made a big-time investment in the public appreciation of our evolving history of nature and science.

Even though I continued my busy workload as a teacher, Albuquerque Public Schools added another job to my résumé—that of science consultant. Whenever I had some time free from the classroom, I was asked to speak to students in special assemblies at as many as four different schools in a single day. What a wonderful way to reach the young minds of our city! It also led to a deep friendship with teachers and principals throughout the entire school district.

Those friendships were formed because we were all members of one team. I certainly wasn't looking for any individual attention or praise. You won't find the letter *I* in the word team. That's because teamwork is more *we* than *me*. And after a number of teachers on our team asked me to share my lessons and classroom techniques from my years at Monroe Junior High, I decided to put it all on paper. Using my trusty old typewriter and a few illustrations that I drew longhand, I produced a sixteen-page guide called *Teach Your Science by the Side of the Road*. I chose the title because you can teach science anywhere: in the class, at a park, in the wilderness, even "by the side of the road." This guide for teachers included details of many of my lessons, experiments that students and I had conducted in class, and questions to ask students during classroom discussions to spark their interest and participation.

It was a forum for ideas. My guide certainly wasn't fancy—I used a simple mimeograph machine to make copies of my sixteen typewritten pages and a stapler to fasten the guides together. On a teacher's salary, I certainly couldn't afford high technology. And since I didn't have a publisher to market and distribute my guide, I handed it out myself to teachers on campus, at school events, at teacher-parent meetings, and at every gathering of educators that I could get to across the district. It was very well accepted. Teachers are creative, and they're so unselfish when it comes to sharing and bouncing ideas off each other. The dedicated teachers I served with would do anything to make their classes better and give students what they need to succeed. In the words of my idol, Doc Harrington, "If the student hasn't learned—the teacher hasn't taught." Doc never handed out a failing grade. And neither did I.

In 1959, I received a phone call that was to change the rest of my life, although I didn't know it at the time. The call was from one of the college professors I had taken a class with years before at the University of New Mexico. Dr. Wayne Bundy was now program director of a public educational television station in Albuquerque, KNME-TV (Channel 5). And he wanted to know if I would be interested in hosting a weekly thirty-minute science show for ninth graders on the channel. Dr. Bundy explained that it would be a low-budget production with very little pay. I jumped at the offer. And what I received in return was immeasurable.

At the time, the only thing I knew about television was how to turn a set on. But under the guidance of Dr. Bundy, it was just like going to class and doing what I love to do—teach. The small TV studio was set up like a classroom with a laboratory table in front where I stood and some shelves behind me where I put all of my science equipment. I prepared a lesson plan for each program, just like I did at school.

Dr. Bundy, ever the professor, was meticulous about every detail—especially my lesson plan. He was an educator at heart, who couldn't have cared more about me and our program. We would tape the science show one day a week. I would run over from school in the afternoon with my arms loaded with science equipment. We only had two cameras and a director in the control room. During the taping, if we made a mistake, "Professor" Bundy would have us do it again. A number of times we worked until midnight to get it right. This is one report card where our team had to really work to earn an A.

It was an absolute joy to be a part of. I wasn't nervous because it didn't seem like television. It was a classroom, and I was the teacher. Each week, we had a lesson with a beginning and an end. We did experiments. We did demonstrations. It may not have been a big production, but I learned quickly that you can do a lot of things on TV that you couldn't do at school. Our science program aired on a weekly basis on KNME-TV several times during the day. And Dr. Bundy arranged with Albuquerque Public Schools to show it in classrooms to ninth-grade students at every junior high in the city each week. As our science TV program continued to increase its viewing audience, we didn't have time to get a swelled head or become boastful about what was happening. When our team at KNME wasn't busy preparing to tape a show, we were busy sweeping the floors, changing the studio lights, and doing all sorts of odd jobs we couldn't afford to pay someone else to do. But my goodness, I was the happiest teacher on Earth.

None of this would have been remotely possible without the guiding light of Dr. Wayne Bundy. He was our beacon. The rest of my television career is directly connected to this visionary. He prepared me for everything. Edward Wayne Bundy has been hailed as the "godfather of New Mexico public television." A native of Utah, Wayne was a radio announcer who later taught at the University of Michigan, and then at the University of New Mexico. But first and foremost, Dr. Bundy was a pioneer in public television. In 1954, he served as executive secretary of the Louisiana Educational Television Commission. Dr. Bundy laid the foundation for public broadcasting at KNME in Albuquerque, where he produced and directed programming for many years. During a remarkable career that spanned more than five decades, Dr. Bundy also served on the New Mexico Commission on Public Broadcasting, and was the executive director of the Rocky Mountain Corporation for Public Broadcasting. He's been called "a real champion . . . dogged, determined, and focused. A relentless ambassador for the powerful role of public broadcasting . . . and an advocate for the needs of the diverse populations."

When it came to educational TV, Wayne Bundy was among the first in the nation to forge a relationship between teaching and television. In an article that appeared in the October 1962 edition of *New Mexico Magazine*, the writer said Dr. Bundy stressed, "Television cannot and was not meant to do the teacher's job. Tele-courses are designed to complement classroom teaching rather than supplement or replace it." In the words of Dr. Bundy, "The lesson isn't what goes on the television screen. It is what happens after the TV is turned off." Wayne Bundy taught me "Television is an aid, not a teacher." Over the years, he urged me to visit the individual classrooms at schools that were showing our program to find out firsthand what we can do at KNME to assist teachers in providing students with a well-rounded education.

At KNME-TV, Dr. Bundy was my coach and my cheerleader. When it came to George Fischbeck, Dr. Bundy didn't want a television performer. He hired me to be a teacher. And during all my years working for Wayne Bundy, I continued my work teaching in the classroom at Monroe Junior High School. I didn't ask for a lesser workload at school. I taught at Monroe, and I taught at KNME. Our science show on television was merely an extension of my classroom on campus. We didn't use cue cards. There was no teleprompter for me to read. Dr. Bundy wanted honesty from the heart to be the foundation of our courses on the air. If an experiment failed during the broadcast—it failed. Dr. Bundy didn't want any students sitting in our TV studio "classroom." He taught me that teaching and television should be a one-on-one experience. If I were to speak to students on the set, then everyone else (the television audience) would be merely eavesdropping. Dr. Bundy instructed me to look into that camera and make eye-to-eye contact with the students at home, just like I have for years with my students in class. And if it's a lesson that comes from the heart, it will be a lesson learned.

After our ninth-grade science program had been broadcast for one year, Dr. Bundy decided it was time to expand our television curriculum. And he ordered us into production for a second weekly science show on KNME, . . . this one for fifth- and sixth-grade students. We even had a title for our new program: "Science 5" (as in Channel 5). By now, our viewing audience had grown faster than any of us could have possibly imagined. Not only were both programs being seen in Albuquerque and in every public school throughout the city, we were now being broadcast across the entire state of New Mexico and in classes in every school district as well. What a balancing act this turned into! Both programs were each shown one night a week for our regular viewing audience. But we had to stagger the scheduled daytime showings for schools statewide during the week, so that each class could fit the programs into their schedules as well.

For example, if one of our programs was broadcast during a school's lunch hour, the students wouldn't be in class to see it. And you can imagine all the juggling that went on behind the scenes at KNME to make sure our two science shows were shown on the days and times requested at each school throughout all of New Mexico. But you know, it was great to be in demand. And just as Dr. Bundy had predicted when he first decided to merge teaching and television, we were filling a special need in the classroom. There were so many schools across the state, especially in small and rural cities, that couldn't afford to hire a science teacher for their students. And by turning on a television set and showing our two programs for fifth, sixth, and ninth graders in their classrooms, schools statewide taught the subject of science each week.

Of course, the increased schedule kept me on the run. Boy, did it ever. I worked it out with Monroe Junior High School so I could complete my in-classroom teaching duties by noon each day. Then, I would run over to KNME and teach in my television classroom. But my responsibilities didn't end there. I had to keep in constant touch with teachers and administrators at each school where our programs were being shown throughout the state. We exchanged lesson plans to make sure that what was being taught in the classroom and on television fit like a glove to enhance the learning capabilities and productivity of our students. The classroom teachers and I also coordinated our homework assignments so that we could help students improve in those areas in which they were at a disadvantage.

As our broadcast viewing audience expanded to include all of New Mexico, Dr. Bundy stressed the importance of making sure I visited each school around the state to meet my television students in an "up close and personal" way. Teaching someone on TV was one thing. But reaching out to them in person helped form a special bond between teacher and student. By doing this, Dr. Bundy said I was no longer just someone these children saw on television, but rather I became a real part of their teaching team. When you include the many community forums and parent-teacher meetings I was asked to speak at across New Mexico, it was a relationship that brought us all closer together to the benefit of our students.

Back at home, the family that I loved and cherished were my biggest supporters. Even though I was out on the road more and more, I was still a hit with Sue and our two adorable children. Little George and Nancy liked the idea of being able to see their father on television. Nancy was especially proud when she was able to watch our programs with her classmates at school and have Dad teach them another lesson from the world of science.

Now as the audience for our two science shows continued to grow, you might think we'd be rolling with success at the center for all of this— KNME-TV. But we were just a tiny public education station located in a very small house that used to be home for a college sorority. There wasn't room for ego. But we had big hearts. Dr. Wayne Bundy expanded our programming with a new show called *TV Kindergarten* featuring Joyce Marron as the teacher. One day Joyce called in sick. And I was literally thrown in as her replacement at the last minute, leading the way in singing and merriment for all the kids in TV Land. Live television is a challenge like no other. Joyce Marron found that out firsthand when she was a guest on one of our science shows, and a parrot with an attitude wouldn't let go of her on air. And by George, it was Fischbeck to the rescue "Live on 5."

I met another invaluable member of the KNME-TV team by accident as she was sitting in the lobby of our TV station in 1963. Kathleen McVicker was a local schoolteacher in Albuquerque, and she had just been offered a chance to host a music program for children on KNME. Kathleen was nervous and worried over whether to accept this new offer. I tried to reassure her that she wouldn't have been offered the job if she hadn't been the right person to fill that position. And I shared with her the same message that Dr. Wayne Bundy had shared with me four years earlier: "Don't be nervous. Just look directly into that camera and speak from your heart to the viewers as though they were one person." Kathleen McVicker went on to host *Sound Go Round* and *Sound Express* on KNME Channel 5 for nearly twenty years. To this day, Kathleen continues her tireless on-the-air fund-raising efforts to support programming for the station. What a teammate!

KNME was a founding father of public educational television in America. But it was also a launching pad for college students who dreamed of a career in broadcasting. Case in point—two of my former students at Monroe Junior High School who have gone on to post remarkable résumés in our industry. While they were both attending college, Ron Miziker and Tony Tiano also worked at KNME. Dr. Wayne Bundy had a policy that if you walked through the front door of his station, he was going to make it worth your while. Ron and Tony received on-the-job experience at KNME-TV they couldn't have gotten at any higher education institution in the entire world. They learned how to produce and direct. They worked as cameramen. They were taught how to light a studio. They were given the tools to build a television operation from the ground up. And if I may interject a personal note—these two young men helped make our science programs at KNME-TV even better. In fact, they made all of our station's programming a lot better.

My former students learned their lessons well. As a teacher, I couldn't have been prouder. Ron Miziker has gone on to become an award-winning giant in the entertainment world, having headed his own production company for nearly three decades now. Tony Tiano took his vision for broadcasting and became the president, general manager, and guiding force of the highly acclaimed public broadcasting station in San Francisco, KQED-TV. But then again, what else would you expect from graduates of the "University of Wayne Bundy"?

As you can see, there was no poverty of ideas at KNME. And in the mid-1960s, Dr. Bundy outdid even himself. Several years before the Public Broadcasting Service (PBS) was formed, Dr. Bundy decided to put together his own makeshift network to create a national audience for KNME's science shows for fifth, sixth, and ninth graders. He didn't have any money. He didn't have any satellite dishes. But Dr. Bundy had a dream. And he wouldn't take *no* for an answer. Since I didn't know any better, I followed. I will always be grateful for the rest of my life that I did.

Dr. Bundy started out by establishing his base of operations at the National Educational Television (NET). It was through NET that Dr. Bundy reached out one by one to TV stations across the country with his idea. Basically, Dr. Bundy would mail a videotape copy of our science show from KNME to another public education TV station and ask them to put it on the air in their city. When they got through with the tape, Dr. Bundy asked them to mail it to a second public TV station in another city so that our science program could be seen there. Dr. Bundy began to connect the dots across the nation. Station A would send our tape to station B, which would then send it on to station C, and so on. This form of communication is called *bicycling*. KNME couldn't afford satellite technology. So Dr. Bundy relied on each station bicycling our tape (as in mailing it) to another station. In the beginning, we had absolutely no idea if any stations were even airing our little program. Then the mail started coming in. We received thank-you notes from a TV station in one city and then a TV station in another—and they asked us to keep sending them more copies of our science shows so that we could become part of their regular programming each week.

Before long, Dr. Bundy had created a "network" of twenty-five stations coast to coast—from New York City to Los Angeles—that broadcast our science shows from the tiny studio at KNME-TV. We received tons of mail and phone calls from students, teachers, and even parents from across the entire country. For some reason, I don't think Dr. Wayne Bundy was surprised at our overwhelming success. He had that kind of vision. But as for me, I was flabbergasted!

I never was and never will be a television performer. I am just a humble schoolteacher who was grateful I had a classroom of students to reach out to. But thanks to Dr. Bundy and the dedicated and hardworking team at KNME, our "classroom" now extended across America. There is a Latin proverb that says, "He who teaches learns." I have been blessed to have a job that was created the first time a curious child in my class asked me a question. For I am a teacher. And I am so fortunate to carry on the tradition of those who cared enough to teach me.

In 1969, Dr. Wayne Bundy decided to bid farewell to his beloved KNME-TV. He went on to become executive director of the Rocky Mountain Corporation for Public Broadcasting. Dr. Bundy held this position for years while serving as a programming consultant for a number of stations and spearheading efforts to raise funds to support that programming as a passionate advocate for public education television.

Before he left our little station in Albuquerque, however, Dr. Bundy made some monumental decisions that greatly enhanced our broadcasts to the benefit of our loyal viewers. In 1966, a new transmitter was built atop Sandia Crest to boost KNME-TV's signal to maximum power. The next year, Dr. Bundy purchased a brand new camera that made it possible for KNME to broadcast our programs in color for the first time. In 1969, the station acquired its second color TV camera. And later that year, KNME-TV moved to its present location on University Boulevard in a new building. It was so big, you could have fit the entire sorority house where our old station was inside one of the spacious studios in the new place.

Under the exceptional leadership of Dr. Wayne Bundy, KNME-TV was named the National Educational Television's "Station of the Year" for our science programs. For my TV work in teaching science to the community, I received three of Ohio State University's "Awards for Excellence" in the Natural and Physical Sciences and the Education Television Award for the "best systematic televised school instruction in the United States." And our science shows for fifth, sixth, and ninth graders were the subject of articles that appeared in publications with a nationwide readership, including the *Saturday Evening Post*, *Life* magazine, *Reader's Digest*, and the *Lutheran* magazine.

There are no words that could possibly convey the deep appreciation and gratitude I have for Dr. Wayne Bundy. He has been the architect of my broadcasting career, my teacher, my mentor, and my beloved friend. He made a difference in my life by teaching me so much about life itself.

Wayne was also a fountain of wisdom and knowledge that continues to flow to this very day in so many lives that he touched. At the time, I had no idea what challenges and opportunities lay ahead of me in my lifelong journey. But I knew one thing—and that's the confidence that I would carry Dr. Wayne Bundy's lessons with me wherever I might go.

"Weathering" Local TV News

Everybody talks about the weather.
But nobody does anything about it.

~ MARK TWAIN ~

By the time I'd reached the tender age of forty-seven in 1970, I had far exceeded any possible dreams I had growing up as a young farm boy in rural New Jersey. I couldn't be happier doing what I always wanted to do—teaching a classroom full of students for twenty years in the Albuquerque public school system. I was in my twelfth year of teaching science on educational television, as our award-winning shows produced at KNME were being seen across New Mexico and in twenty-five cities throughout the United States. And when I wasn't in the classroom or at the TV station, I was home working on my lesson plans and cooking up science experiments for both teachers and students alike.

The motion picture *Love Story* starring Ali MacGraw and Ryan O'Neal was the box office champion of 1970. But the film's title couldn't be a better description of a real-life romance, one of the most romantic of all-time. The love story starring George and Sue Fischbeck was growing even stronger after two decades. To borrow a line from the silver screen, "Love means never having to say you're sorry." Our two children,

Nancy and George Junior, were now teenagers attending Sandia High School. The money from my two jobs wasn't all that great. But Sue continued to work as an office manager for an insurance company to help the House of Fischbeck balance its books. And even though we only had one car, Sue and her beloved teacher worked out a sharing agreement that we had "down to a science."

And then I got another one of those phone calls that was going to change the rest of my life. You know, for someone who later made a living off making forecasts, I never saw this coming. The call was from Jerry Danziger, who was the general manager of KOB-TV, the NBC television station in Albuquerque. Jerry asked me if I would like to "moonlight" as a weatherman on the Channel 4 local news each weekday night. The current weatherman on the station's Eyewitness News was about to leave. And Jerry thought that a schoolteacher who taught science would be a perfect fit.

The first thing that crossed my mind upon hearing the offer was that I was not willing to give up, or even reduce, my teaching assignments. And that was fine with Jerry. But I also had to make sure it was fine with the Fischbeck clan. "By George," I did have priorities—as in family first. But when Sue and the kids voted unanimously to accept the KOB offer, I signed on willing to try to "weather" the challenges that taking on a new job might present.

Of course, accepting a job is one thing. Doing the job is another. It didn't take me long to learn that this was a whole different ballgame than I was used to. KOB-TV is the second oldest television station between the Mississippi River and the West Coast. And since its inception in 1948, the station has always been an affiliate of the NBC Television Network. My primary assignment was to do the nightly weather forecast on KOB's Channel 4 Eyewitness News at 6 and 10 p.m. Johnny Morris and Gordon Sanders (who also served as news director) anchored our newscasts, which were running second in the Albuquerque news ratings behind number one KOAT-TV Channel 7 (ABC), but ahead of third place KGGM-TV Channel 13 (CBS—later named KRQE). Mike Roberts, who was the voice of University of New Mexico football and basketball for forty-one years, was our sportscaster. To be perfectly honest, I have never concerned myself with television news ratings. It's not that the issue wasn't important to me.

I was just way too busy doing the job that I was hired to do to worry about anything else.

We had a bigger technical team at KOB putting on the newscast than what I was used to working with at public educational TV KNME. In the Channel 4 studio, we had two camera people and a stage manager along with the anchors, sportscaster, and me. In the control booth, we had a director who was in charge of the live on-air product. A technical director pushed all the buttons on orders from the director. And we had a producer whose responsibility included the news content of the broadcast and making sure Eyewitness News was on time in terms of length. It was very important that our 10 p.m. news was off the air by 10:30 p.m. to make way for *The Tonight Show* starring Johnny Carson. I was given the last three minutes of each newscast to talk about the weather and give my forecast. I had no film or videotape to work with. But I was given some white paint and a brush so that I could draw the temperatures and the weather forecast on a blackboard for our viewers.

In terms of being qualified to do this job, I had worked in a weather department in the military during the Korean War, where I was trained to use the latest technology for meteorology. I was also a schoolteacher. I never claimed to be an expert on the subject of science. But I knew where the experts were. And there wasn't anything I wouldn't do to learn from those experts and then to share that knowledge and information with my students in class.

This formula had worked for twenty years for me at school. And so I decided to do what I do best—seek out the experts in weather each day and then share that information with our viewers. That's what a teacher does. And Channel 4 Eyewitness News became my latest "classroom." Now you might think since my weather forecast didn't air on the first newscast until 6:25 p.m., I might not have to show up at the KOB newsroom until late afternoon to get ready. But that's not how it worked—at least that's not how I worked. To be a good teacher, you have to prepare a lesson plan. And that takes homework.

From day one, I began my TV weather homework by showing up at the National Weather Service bureau in Albuquerque, where the real experts held their daily briefing at noon. These are the meteorologists who watch the weather twenty-four hours a day. They know what's happening. And they know why it's happening. Every day I went to the National Weather Service with a simple request: give me the knowledge—and I will share it. I promised to always give them credit during the newscast, and these wonderful meteorologists from that agency became my best friends. Anyone can take a weather update from the news wires and read it on the air. That's basically what the other TV stations in town did for their newscasts.

But I felt that weather was more important to our viewers than to just read a piece of wire copy to them. With my apologies to Denver, Albuquerque should be known as the "Mile High City" because its elevation is one mile above sea level. That means Albuquerque gets snow. It gets cold . . . real cold. Albuquerque can have severe windstorms. Tumbleweeds blowing in the wind can cause serious problems for people who have allergies. Weather is an important issue in the city I served. And you couldn't do it justice by reading a simple piece of wire copy. Our viewers deserved the latest updated information that I could gather for them.

That's why I went to the National Weather Service each day, sometimes several times a day. The experts there let me sit in with them as they developed their forecasts. These meteorologists graciously accepted me as one of their own. They took the time and had the patience to explain every detail of our current weather as well as what might be coming down the road in a day or two. I was smart enough to know just how much I didn't know when it came to weather. Confucius once said, "When you know a thing, to hold that you know it; and when you do not know a thing, to allow that you do not know it—this is knowledge." I will never forget the wise words of the late scholar William Arthur Ward: "The mediocre teacher tells. The good teacher explains." Mr. Ward also believed "before you speak . . . listen."

Before I ever set foot in the studio of Channel 4 Eyewitness News, I listened, and wrote, and absorbed everything I could from the dedicated men and women at the National Weather Service so that I could accurately report those findings every night to our audience. Finding and sharing—that's what I did in the classroom. And that's what I did on local TV news. Oh yes, there was one more thing you couldn't get from a news wire. Thanks to my new friends at the National Weather Service, nobody else in town had what we had—satellite photos. It's one thing to go on TV and give a forecast. But it's another to be able to share with our viewers pictures taken from space of the different weather systems that could affect our region in the coming hours and days.

I thoroughly enjoyed the responsibility of gathering this information and bringing it to the newsroom so that we could deliver the absolute latest on Eyewitness News. I loved doing what I was doing. And it was a team effort . . . not just from the folks who were on the air but from those invaluable people behind the scenes as well. No matter what you did—everybody played an important role in putting Channel 4 Eyewitness News on. And what a wonderful experience it was for me.

Now you may wonder what it was like to be on two entirely different television programs in the same day, teaching science on KNME and then forecasting the weather on local TV news. First of all, you have to understand that I wasn't portraying different characters like an actor. I am a teacher. As the saying goes: a leopard can't change its spots. When I agreed to do the weather on KOB-TV news, it was with the understanding that I would continue to teach science at Monroe Junior High School and on public educational television. Before I went to school each day and before I went to KNME, I would develop my lesson plan for that particular class or science show. And that's exactly how I prepared to do a weather segment for live local TV news. I would spend a good portion of the afternoon and evening gathering the information that I needed. I would draw up a lesson plan for my weather segment. And at 6:25 and 10:25 p.m., I would go on the air to share that information with our viewing audience.

I didn't have a script or use cue cards or a teleprompter. By the time Channel 4 Eyewitness News began, I had studied my material to the point that it was thoroughly ingrained in my head. And I used my teaching skills on the newscast to share what I had been taught that particular day and night by the experts at the National Weather Service. Someone once wrote that a good teacher is a consumer of knowledge. Be prepared. Do your homework. And you will always have what it takes to make the grade.

Now, there was just one problem. A teacher will always know when class is over when the school bell rings. There was no school bell at Eyewitness News. And since I never used a script during our newscast at KOB, I didn't always know when my allotted three minutes were up. And sometimes I went long—very long. The station's management liked what I was doing. And so the word went out that George can go as long as he needs. That was fine with me. But at 10:30 p.m., some viewers might be turning on Channel 4 to see Johnny Carson on *The Tonight Show*. And instead of "Heeere's Johnny," it was "Heeere's George" still doing the weather. We never heard any complaints from Johnny Carson about me going long. Because the ratings for Eyewitness News were going up, we never heard complaints from our bosses either. And that makes for a nice forecast.

When I was originally hired by Channel 4 in Albuquerque, KOB-TV management was hoping I would bring with me the loyal audience that had been watching my science shows for more than ten years on the public education channel KNME-TV. In fact, Eyewitness News announced my hiring with a huge advertising campaign with the slogan "Look who's coming!" In all my years doing the weather, I had absolutely no idea what it takes for a local TV news operation to become number one in the ratings. I had my hands full just trying to meet my responsibilities each day. But I can tell you this—it wasn't long before Channel 4 KOB shot past top-rated Channel 7 KOAT as the most popular newscast in town. It was a most gratifying feeling.

Whenever the family and I would have some free time, we'd love to go out and do something together. With Eyewitness News gaining increased popularity, more and more people were beginning to recognize me when the Fischbeck clan would venture out in public. Sue and the kids couldn't have been more patient when people would walk up to say "hi" and ask me to sign something. My devoted and loving family realized that we owed so much to the good folks who tuned in and watched my programs on television. After all, where would we be if it weren't for the loyal viewers I have always referred to as "my friends"? I always have time for my friends.

Of course, working three jobs as I was doing turned into quite a balancing act. But I was never more than ten to fifteen minutes away from our home. I was able to visit the home front several times each day no matter what I was doing. On a number of occasions, I even took George Junior and Nancy to work with me at KOB-TV. My job became even more enjoyable when I had my "little assistants" to lend a helping hand.

As Channel 4 Eyewitness News soared in the ratings, our newsroom continued to get more requests for its on-the-air personnel to make public appearances. I can't think of any social organization throughout Albuquerque—the Chamber of Commerce, the YMCA, the YWCA, the Kiwanis Club, the Elks Lodge, and the Loyal Order of Moose—I didn't appear before as an after-dinner speaker. Of course, the price was right; I was free. I would never accept money to speak to "my friends." I've always believed that if you took time to watch our newscast, then I should take time to help you.

In 1972, I received an invitation to be the master of ceremonies for an event that would become one of the genuine loves of my life. What was billed as a fiftieth birthday celebration for our sister radio station KOB-AM was going to culminate with a hot air balloon festival in the parking lot of a local shopping mall. It wasn't supposed to be that big of a deal. But thirteen balloonists from New Mexico, Arizona, California, Iowa, Michigan, Nevada, and Texas wanted to take part. Twenty thousand spectators jammed the event. And the sponsors had trouble finding room for the balloons to even take off.

I was the official meteorologist for that first festival. Weather is crucial in hot air ballooning as these "magnificent flying machines" go wherever the winds take them at an altitude of up to three thousand feet, although flights as high as ten thousand feet are possible. For the next twenty years, it was my honor and privilege to participate in the Albuquerque International Balloon Fiesta, which has now become the largest hot air balloon festival in the world with 750 balloons taking part annually. I developed a close friendship with famed balloonist Maxie Anderson, who was also my children's Sunday School teacher at our church. He was perhaps the bravest man I have ever known. Maxie asked me to serve as his on-ground weather forecaster for two historic flights: the first nonstop balloon crossing of the Atlantic Ocean and then a journey across the entire United States of America. Maxie Anderson lost his life when he and his co-pilot, Don Ida, were killed in a tragic balloon accident in Germany in 1983. But his legacy lives on. This pioneer helped place Albuquerque on the map as the balloon capital of the world. And the Anderson-Abruzzo Albuquerque International Balloon Museum is named in part after Maxie Anderson for his excellence in community involvement, leadership, and humanity.

Everything I do is directly linked to my love for teaching. It's been said that the secret of life is not to do what you like, but to like what you do. In the words of essayist Sydney J. Harris, "The whole purpose of education is to turn mirrors into windows." I will forever be grateful to God who has continually blessed me after I made the decision to put the occupation of "teacher" on my résumé of life. It's been estimated that by 1972, I had taught my courses on science to some 250,000 people in the state of New Mexico either in the classroom or on public television.

And that year, I was humbled by the surprise announcement that the University of Albuquerque had decided to award me an honorary doctorate in humanities at its graduation ceremonies. Humanities involve the academic pursuit of knowledge in literature, philosophy, history, and the fine arts. What a wonderful subject to be even remotely linked with. It's the study of ideas. Though I had earned a bachelor's degree in science and a master's degree in education years before, an honorary doctorate was far beyond any expectations I ever had for myself. From that point on, the folks at KOB-TV referred to me as "Dr. Fischbeck" in addition to "Uncle George." And to this very day, it reminds me of that remarkable afternoon when I was allowed to share the stage with the wonderful scholars and graduating students of a university that graciously honored me as well. Appreciation is the highest reward that a schoolteacher can ever receive.

CHAPTER 5

Los Angeles Comes Calling

Destiny is not a matter of chance. It is a matter of choice.
It is not a thing to be waited for. It is a thing to be achieved.
~ WILLIAM JENNINGS BRYAN ~

In 1940, Bing Crosby, Bob Hope, and Dorothy Lamour began a series of seven comedy films that became known as the *"Road"* pictures. Movies like *Road to Singapore*, *Road to Morocco*, and *Road to Rio* became box office hits featuring a formula of comedy, adventure, and romance. I mention this because the next chapter of my life could well be titled "Road to Los Angeles." But it has a real-life plot that you may believe is, shall we say, unbelievable. And it stars a television executive who embodied the famous quote from coaching great Vince Lombardi, "Winning isn't everything. It's the only thing."

For twenty-nine years, Max Sklower was general manager of KOAT-TV, the ABC network affiliate in Albuquerque. As you can imagine, Max was very good at his job. And his job was to make sure that KOAT's Channel 7 News was number one in the local ratings. An article in a magazine called *Outlook Business* described the battle over television ratings in the following manner: "The business of grabbing eyeballs appears to be a cut-throat business. More eyeballs means higher ratings, more ads, higher tariffs for those ads, and ultimately a healthier top line and bottom line." And the bottom line at KOAT-TV in Albuquerque was that Max Sklower liked to win. Quite simply, Max would take his efforts "to the max" in the quest to be number one.

In 1970, long before KOB-TV Channel 4 hired a local schoolteacher named George Fischbeck to be its weatherman, Sklower came knocking on my door. Talk about something that came completely out of left field . . . I never in my wildest dreams thought anyone would ever think of making that kind of an offer to me. At first glance, I thought that doing the weather on Channel 7 News in Albuquerque for Max Sklower would be a wonderful opportunity for a teacher like me to expand my horizons.

Teachers like to teach. And it appeared that I was about to have the best of all worlds in my educational landscape: teaching science in the classrooms of Monroe Junior High School, teaching science to my television students on KNME-TV, and now teaching the importance of weather to my fellow citizens of Albuquerque on the number one rated local TV newscast in town.

That's when I got hit hard with a cold dose of reality. Max Sklower told me that if I accepted his offer to join KOAT-TV news, there would be one condition. I guess it was like making sure I read the small print at the bottom of the contract. Max said if I wanted to do the weather each night on Channel 7 News, there was no way I could continue teaching my science programs on public educational television. A huge wave of disbelief immediately overwhelmed my initial feeling of exuberance. Giving up one of my classrooms was not only unacceptable, it was nonnegotiable. This was the only time I ever had a face-to-face meeting with Max Sklower. I guess very few people ever had the guts and the courage to stand up to this powerful TV executive and tell him, "No." But when it came to giving up my students—that's where I drew the line. And that's when I looked Max Sklower in the eye and said, "Don't you ever try to separate me from my kids."

Later that year, I did accept an offer to become a weatherman on the competing KOB-TV Channel 4 Eyewitness News. It was not about money. Even with me holding down three jobs at that point, my wife, Sue, had to keep working as well. Teaching and television didn't make you rich back in those days. But unlike Max Sklower, my new boss allowed me to continue teaching at school and on educational TV. I absolutely enjoyed what I was doing. And I hope it showed both in the classroom and on the news set. Within a matter of months, my new team at Channel 4 Eyewitness News had overtaken Channel 7 News to become number one in the Albuquerque local TV ratings. But I hadn't heard the last from Max Sklower. Stay tuned.

First, however, on the issue of ratings, please allow me to make this point. It's nice to be on the winning team. But it really didn't change anything in my life. The teachers who taught me over the years always let me know that I must give my all in anything that I do—no matter what. It didn't matter if Channel 4 Eyewitness News was number one in the ratings or dead last. The late author Og Mandino once said, "Always do your best. What you plant now, you will harvest later." I adhered to that every day I showed up for work at school or on TV. My bosses, my students, and our viewers deserved nothing less.

That being said, I always thought that our competition in Albuquerque local TV news did an excellent job as well. The hardworking journalists at KOAT (Channel 7) and KGGM (Channel 13) did their finest each and every day. And their newscasts were superb. I am so grateful that between 1970 and 1972 the television viewers of Albuquerque chose the Channel 4 Eyewitness News team that I served on as the most popular in the ratings. Believe me, our team tried even harder because we knew our audience had some excellent choices to turn to if we didn't give it our very best.

One of the greatest soldiers to ever serve this country, General Douglas MacArthur, once said, "There is no substitute for victory." And Max Sklower, the veteran general manager of KOAT-TV, couldn't stomach the thought of being number two in the news ratings. "Show me a good loser. And I'll show you a loser"—those words of coach Vince Lombardi could have easily come from Max Sklower, who regarded anything but being number one as utter failure. And for two years, after KOB-TV news knocked KOAT from its ratings perch, Sklower tried every trick in the general manager's toolbox to get Channel 7 News back as number one. Nothing he did worked. By this time, KOB's ratings had increased to the point that 55 percent of Albuquerque's viewers now watched our newscast. That's when Max Sklower added some new pages to his playbook. In March of 1972, Sklower tried once again to lure me over to KOAT-TV. If Max thought he had made an offer I couldn't refuse, he soon realized that this was anything but a scene from *The Godfather*. But Max had only just begun. Sklower then wrote a letter to the Albuquerque Public Schools' Board of Education, informing members that allowing me, a schoolteacher, to also perform what he suggested was lucrative work for a private company like KOB-TV Channel 4 Eyewitness News was a conflict of interest.

If my TV work was lucrative, it was news to my wife, who cashes the family paychecks (and knows better). But the conflict of interest allegation not only outraged the school board, one of our community's most highly respected (and powerful) citizens also got involved to answer Max Sklower by invoking the truth. On June 2, 1972, F. L. Nohl, one of the founding partners of the Albuquerque law firm of Nohl, McCulloch, and ReVeal, wrote a letter to KOB-TV general manager Jerry Danziger concerning Max Sklower and the company that owned KOAT-TV, Pulitzer Publishing Company. In the letter, attorney Nohl stated, "It is difficult to believe that a firm of that size would stoop to an attempt to coerce someone out of his job. You will note the bad faith on the part of Pulitzer Publishing Company in attempting to employ Mr. Fischbeck two and a half months before they undertook to embarrass him. They sought to employ him to do the same thing which he is now doing." As they say in court, "case closed." And this is one issue that went away for good.

But Max Sklower had one more "Hail Mary" pass to throw in his mission to get rid of me. At this point, Max figured if he couldn't force George Fischbeck off the air, he would try to get me shipped out of town altogether. What you are about to read was all done without my knowledge. Max Sklower taped my nightly weather forecasts on Channel 4 Eyewitness News. And then he sent a copy of those tapes to major market ABC television stations across America along with a message that basically said, "This is George Fischbeck. He does the weather here in Albuquerque. How would you like to have George doing the weather on your station?"

Well, I guess my performance on tape didn't impress too many people. I didn't exactly have television stations lined up eager to hire me. In fact, I only received one phone call, from a man named Bill Fyffe.

He was news director of the ABC network-owned station in Los Angeles, KABC-TV. Fyffe wanted to know if I would be interested in moving to L.A. and doing the weather on his local TV newscast. As grateful as I was to have been offered such an opportunity, I didn't even have to think about it for a moment. I told Fyffe that I loved New Mexico, I loved teaching in Albuquerque, and I was not interested in leaving the city that has a special place in my heart.

Bill Fyffe was not a man who takes *no* for an answer. During a remarkable forty-five year career in local television, Fyffe not only served as news director for the ABC stations in Detroit and Los Angeles, he also ran the ABC network-owned station in Chicago and the network's flagship station in New York City. Bill Fyffe knew how to do his job. And he wasn't about to give up until he had a schoolteacher named George Fischbeck on the job doing the weather at KABC-TV in the City of Angels. Fyffe kept calling me . . . and calling . . . and calling. Some people would describe Bill Fyffe as persistent. My wife, Sue, used the words "very pushy." But you had to admire his perseverance.

Fyffe was so committed to hiring me, he actually came to Albuquerque—not once, not twice, but three times in an effort to change my mind. He visited with my family, who thought he was very friendly. Fyffe toured our news operation at KOB-TV. And I took him all over Albuquerque to see the local sights. During Fyffe's third and final trip, I took him to the top of Sandia Crest for a ten-thousand-foot look at picturesque Albuquerque in all its magnificent beauty. That's where I asked, "Can you give me this in Los Angeles?" Fyffe replied, "I can double your salary." And I still said no. Bill Fyffe returned to Los Angeles, but he continued to call. That's when I decided to have a heart-to-heart talk with my family.

I told them right from the start that this new job offer was an extraordinary opportunity. But that didn't mean I wanted to go to Los Angeles. Swapping jobs doing the weather from KOB to KABC was one thing. But it would come with a deep and personal loss. I would have to give up my beloved science shows on public educational television, as well as my students and fellow teachers that I cherished at Monroe Junior High School. Yes, the increased salary would mean my wife wouldn't have to work anymore to help pay the bills. But my family and I loved living in Albuquerque. It was our home. In the end, Sue and the kids said it was up to me. This would have to be my decision. Whatever I decided, they would follow. After all, we were in this together. That's what family is all about.

I was at the crossroads of my life. I am also a man of faith. I've seen people facing tough decisions who would say, "I've done everything but pray to try to solve this." We should never use God as a last resort. Prayer should always be our first and only option. In Matthew 7 during the Sermon on the Mount, Jesus encouraged His disciples: "Ask, and it will be given to you. Seek, and you will find. Knock, and it will be opened to you." Keep asking, keep seeking, and keep knocking. The Bible—my family called it the Good Book—has taught me to always put God first, and He will take care of everything else. I will never meet someone who I can trust more.

During this personal and spiritual inventory, I decided to seek the wisdom and guidance of my mentor and teacher. I called Dr. Wayne Bundy to see if one of the wisest men I have ever been blessed to know could help point this humble schoolteacher in the right direction. There were signposts up ahead in this long journey we call life. I just wanted to make sure that I didn't get lost in confusion. It seemed like everybody in Albuquerque thought that I might be going to Los Angeles for the money. But I knew that wouldn't be the reason if I decided to go. And Dr. Bundy knew that as well.

This man who has meant more to my career than anyone else on Earth counseled me with these words: "The time to leave is when you're on top. This is a wonderful opportunity to take your teaching skills to a bigger classroom and a wider audience. They've already knocked on your door three times, but you haven't listened. And they may not come back." Dr. Bundy told me that while the Lord may close doors, He will open others. And my friend Wayne also said that if in my faith, I see myself being pointed in the direction of Los Angeles, then "I should see that light and take this chance." With that, an agonizing decision had been made. I broke the news first to my family. In the words of my loving wife, Sue: "If George wanted to do it, we'd give it a try." However, we also decided that Sue and the kids would remain in Albuquerque for the time being to give me time to see if this new job in Los Angeles was going to work out.

I promised to fly back home each and every weekend. I always believed that the family that stays together . . . well, it stays together. You don't think I wanted to spend lonely weekends all by myself in Los Angeles? The next person I called was Bill Fyffe at KABC-TV. Up to this point, he had been calling me. When I finally called him, Fyffe thought it was a negotiating ploy. "What do you want, George? More money and vacation time?" I thought of my conversation with Dr. Bundy when I told my new boss, "I just had to have a reason to come there. And now I do."

School was out for the summer. So I wasn't able to make any announcement to the students at Monroe Junior High School. But my fellow teachers, the administrators, and the school board members couldn't have been more supportive. After all, they were my friends. If something good happened to one of us, we were happy for each other. This wonderful institution had been my home for more than two decades. The lessons I taught my classes at Monroe were the same lessons I shared with my television students on public education KNME-TV. They were my students, and I was their teacher. A teacher never stops learning from his pupils.

While I was inside the studios of KOB-TV saying good-bye to my colleagues at Channel 4 Eyewitness News, a group of my students gave me a heartfelt thank-you note. They picketed outside the TV station with signs that read, "Please don't go." Voltaire once said: "Appreciation is a wonderful thing. It makes what is excellent in others belong to us as well." My news team at KOB made an on-the-air announcement about my departure. The local Albuquerque newspaper ran an article about it as well.

Much to my surprise, New Mexico Governor Bruce King even filmed a promotion for my new bosses at KABC-TV, informing Los Angeles viewers that "New Mexico's loss is Southern California's gain." Governor King also wrote a letter in which he stated: "I have known George for many, many years and consider him a fine friend. My son, Gary, a science major at New Mexico State University, gives great credit to Dr. Fischbeck in science learning. In fact, thousands of New Mexico students have had their education greatly enriched under Dr. Fischbeck as a science teacher." (By the way—the governor's son, Gary, has gone on to be elected to two terms as the State Attorney General of New Mexico. He also earned a PhD in organic chemistry.)

Nobody who has ever known me during all my years in Albuquerque can possibly comprehend just how hard it was to leave this city and "my friends" that I truly love. After I kissed Sue and our children good-bye at the airport with the promise "I'll be back to see you next weekend," I got on the airplane only to learn I would be flying to my new home with one of my former students as the pilot. I was one proud passenger!

In case you're wondering, I didn't learn about Max Sklower's "plot" to get me hired in another city until long after I had already arrived in Los Angeles. Max and I never had a conversation about it. To be honest, I didn't have a desire to talk with him about anything at this point. But I will say this again—Max Sklower was very good at his job. He continued as general manager of KOAT-TV for another fifteen years.

During that first flight to Los Angeles, I have to admit I was nervous—extremely nervous. I was facing the steepest challenge of my life. The city and the TV station where I would work were far bigger than anything I had ever experienced. It's the great unknown. The door was open. But I had no idea what was on the other side. That's why I walked through that door—to find out. At the age of fifty, here I was starting a new career.

California, Here We Come

Challenges are what make life interesting.
Overcoming them is what makes life meaningful.

~ JOSHUA J. MARINE ~

Writer Dorothy Parker once described Los Angeles as "seventy-two suburbs in search of a city." And as a small town school-teacher flying to his new home, I couldn't have possibly imagined the sheer magnitude of what lay ahead as my plane touched down at L.A. International Airport in October of 1972. Twenty-two million people now call Southern California their home. But I wasn't worried about having enough elbow room. My goodness, Los Angeles and Orange Counties alone encompass 5,700 square miles. That's bigger than three states: Connecticut, Delaware, and Rhode Island. In all, it took the House of Fischbeck more than nine months to make the complete move from Albuquerque to the Southland. I'm going to present this story in two parts. Later in this chapter, I'll tell you about the challenge of my new workplace at KABC-TV. But let's start out with how I survived the real-life drama involving my arrival in the nation's second largest city.

Unlike the emotional heartfelt farewell that my loved ones and friends gave as my plane took off from Albuquerque, there was absolutely no one waiting to greet me at the airport terminal after my flight arrived in Los Angeles. Quite simply, I was on my own. I humorously thought that perhaps my new boss, Bill Fyffe, had been "too busy" to tell anyone that I was coming. So I hailed a taxicab to take me to my new temporary home at the Sheraton Universal Hotel in Universal City. No, I didn't stay in one of the hotel's plush and lavish suites. KABC instead provided me with a standard room for the first month or so. I decided it was best not to tell hotel management about my pet skunk that I had brought from Albuquerque. I certainly didn't want to "raise a stink" at this point.

Now you can take George Fischbeck out of New Mexico. But you can't take this loving husband and father away from his family. Even though I went right to work doing the weather in Los Angeles for Channel 7 Eyewitness News, the skunk and I flew back to Albuquerque each weekend to be with Sue and the kids. The skunk alone should have made the Guinness Book of World Records for the frequent flier miles he earned. What a stinker!

By December of 1972, we had put our house in Albuquerque up for sale. Our daughter, Nancy, was in her senior year at Sandia High School, where she was a cheerleader. George Junior had moved out west to be with me in Southern California, where he attended Westchester High School. "Fritz" (my son's nickname) and I were now living in a small apartment in Marina del Rey. I had a rental car that I used to commute to work from the marina to KABC-TV in the Los Feliz area of Hollywood. Our family reunion was still months away. The Fischbecks were indeed a work in progress. But at least it was progress.

Six months later, we had finally sold our house in Albuquerque that we loved. George Junior was allowed to graduate with sister Nancy during ceremonies at Sandia High School. (Yes, Fritz and I flew in for this special occasion.) And then it was time to officially pull up stakes and head out west. What a caravan this was going to be! Nancy drove the family's Volkswagen bus, while Sue was behind the wheel of our Buick. The furniture (which included my rock collection that was years in the making) had gone ahead of them. It's one thing to fly to Los Angeles from Albuquerque within ninety minutes like I did.

It's another to make the 789-mile trip driving on Interstate 40 through the searing desert heat of New Mexico, Arizona, and California in the middle of summer. It's enough to make your blood boil. It took Sue and Nancy a long and wearisome two days to finally make their way to Southern California.

That's the good news. The bad news is that they arrived at five o'clock in the afternoon, just in time to get a firsthand look at a Southland tradition—the rush-hour traffic jam. Even though there are more than five hundred miles of freeways in Los Angeles County alone, it's not nearly enough to handle the volume of vehicles that use them each and every day. The typical motorist in Los Angeles spends an estimated ninety-three hours a year going absolutely nowhere in a freeway traffic jam. When Sue got her first look at the "parking lot" known as the Harbor Freeway in downtown L.A., she was shocked, stunned, and bewildered (to say the least). My wife had never seen anything like this in her entire life. I'm surprised that Sue and Nancy didn't pull a U-turn that day and head back to Albuquerque.

It was so wonderful to have my beloved family back together once again. Unfortunately, our tiny apartment in the marina wasn't exactly built for four people. We spent most of our time trying to keep from bumping into each other. Sue and I wanted to buy a house to be closer to the television station on the east side of Hollywood, but we couldn't afford it. Those homes were just too expensive. Someone at my work suggested we take a look at buying something in the San Fernando Valley. It took a couple of months. But we finally found a nice three-bedroom house in Woodland Hills close to the freeway for me to drive to my job.

Nancy and Fritz would be able to attend nearby Pierce College. My boss, Bill Fyffe, and his family also lived in Woodland Hills, and they introduced us to their church. Best of all, our new neighbors couldn't have been more outgoing and gracious. They even threw a block party to welcome us to the neighborhood. Four decades later, Sue and I still call it our home, as we have thoroughly enjoyed living in the "friendly confines" of Woodland Hills. However, the marathon project to move my family from Albuquerque to Southern California is only half of the story. Yes, it took quite an effort to pull up our small town roots from New Mexico and replant ourselves in one of the largest metropolitan areas of the world. But that challenge paled in comparison to my being thrown in the middle of a real-life "Adventureland" known as the local TV news wars of Los Angeles.

As they say, let's rewind the videotape back to October of 1972. I was out here all by myself, having checked into my new home in a small room at the Sheraton Universal Hotel. Nobody knew I was even here. I certainly hadn't been given the keys to the city. And I will never forget that fateful day when I got behind the wheel of my small rental car and nervously drove to my new workplace, where Channel 7 Eyewitness News was about to change the landscape of my life forever.

Up to that point, I had only worked for two television stations in my entire broadcasting career. And they were both small-time operations in Albuquerque. For ten years, our public education TV station was located in a tiny building that used to be a college sorority house. And the news center at KOB Channel 4 wasn't that much bigger. But we were all one small happy family. That was all I had ever known. But that was then, and this is now. As I drove into the parking lot of the facility where the network owned-and-operated KABC-TV is located, I knew instantly that my little career was about to undergo an extreme makeover.

Channel 7 in Los Angeles is not one building—or even one huge building. At the time, it was just one part of a mammoth twenty-three-acre palace of entertainment and broadcasting called the ABC Television Center. It is a sprawling complex of studios, offices, and sound stages built in the middle of a residential neighborhood at Prospect Avenue and Talmadge Street in the Los Feliz area. King Kong could have gotten lost here, not to mention an unassuming schoolteacher named George Fischbeck. And this is one piece of property that indeed has a fabled history right out of Hollywood.

The ABC Television Center was originally built on a twenty-nine-acre sheep ranch in 1915 as the home of Vitagraph Studios, which became the largest motion picture lot in the entire world. This was a silent movie plant that cranked out some of the most popular films of its time. I ought to know because my late uncle, Harry Fischbeck, served as a cameraman on 102 movies, including a number of Rudolph Valentino's movies that were made on the Vitagraph lot itself. Legend has it that several scenes for Lon Chaney's 1925 classic *Phantom of the Opera* were filmed on Stage 55. I've been told that if you walked across the Vitagraph lot in those days, you might have seen the likes of Mary Pickford, Cecil B. DeMille, or Norma Talmadge, who is said to have planted a pepper tree in 1920 in front of what later became the KABC-TV bungalows. Now you know how Talmadge Street got its name.

The Vitagraph Studios property was originally bought for just $20,000. By 1925, the price tag had skyrocketed to $1 million when it was purchased by Warner Brothers. The lot was renamed the Warner East Hollywood Annex. In 1927, parts of the first talking motion picture *The Jazz Singer*, starring Al Jolson, were filmed on Stage 5. Television was a mere infant in 1948, when the studios were bought by the American Broadcasting Company, which would use the lot as its West Coast headquarters for nearly fifty years. A number of programs that aired on the ABC network were actually produced (and some still are) at the ABC Television Center, which featured nine huge stages, a rehearsal hall, and state-of-the-art technology that would have made our space agency proud.

Popular shows like *Let's Make a Deal, Family Feud, General Hospital, Port Charles,* Dick Clark's *American Bandstand, The Lawrence Welk Show, Fridays, Into the Night with Rick Dees, Shindig!* (where both the Beatles and Rolling Stones performed live in the mid-1960s), and more recently, *Grey's Anatomy* were all taped or filmed at the ABC Television Center (which has now been renamed The Prospect Studios). The facility was broadcast headquarters for the network's coverage of the 1984 Summer Olympic Games in Los Angeles. And whenever the ABC network news or *Nightline* with Ted Koppel had to originate in Los Angeles, it was broadcast from the ABC News West Coast bureau at the ABC Television Center. A maze of studio audiences were always lined up throughout the day to attend the taping of one of their favorite programs. Over the years, the lot's stages were also rented out to other major networks and production companies for their shows as well. You never knew what star you might come across when you had lunch at the commissary.

Now in addition to its network operations, ABC also owned and ran five local TV stations in 1949. They were located in New York City, Chicago, Detroit, San Francisco, and Los Angeles. KABC-TV's original call letters were KECA, which signed on the air for the first time on

September 16, 1949. From the very beginning, Channel 7 was located at the ABC Television Center. In 1950, KECA began broadcasting a daily local news program called *The Southern California/Los Angeles Report*. Four years later on February 1, 1954, the station's call letters were officially changed to its present KABC.

You may wonder how what is perhaps the most recognized local TV station logo came into being—the Circle 7 logo I proudly wore on the air at Eyewitness News for two decades. In 1962, a man named G. Dean Smith ran his own graphic design company in San Francisco. The ABC owned-and-operated station (O&O) in that city, KGO-TV, hired Smith to design a logo. Smith created the Circle 7 logo, which was so liked, it was adopted by ABC's four other O&Os including KABC-TV in Los Angeles. G. Dean Smith also gained national attention for working on the AT&T globe corporate logo and for designing the Science and Industry stamp that the U.S. Postal Service issued in the early 1980s.

Also in 1962, KABC hired a veteran journalist who had spent six years running the news operation at crosstown KCOP-TV (Channel 13). Baxter Ward became the face at what would now be known as Channel 7 News. Ward was not only the anchorman of this broadcast, he was the news director as well. He had a long résumé in radio and television news in both Washington, D.C. and Baltimore before he moved to Los Angeles. Baxter Ward has been described as a hard-nosed yet sincere television anchor, who was exceptional at attention to detail. As news director, Ward was a strong advocate of investigative journalism.

This veteran journalist has also been hailed as a pioneer in the hiring of women for his newsroom staff. Ward believed that women were more reliable than men. Baxter was also a huge fan of Hollywood gossip. And in 1966, celebrity reporter Rona Barrett became a part of the KABC-TV newscast. Baxter Ward resigned from Channel 7 News in 1969 to run for mayor of Los Angeles. He was defeated. In 1972, Ward was elected to the Los Angeles County Board of Supervisors. In this public arena, Baxter was regarded as a political maverick. But he was a force to be reckoned with for two terms and eight years. Ward would later return to Channel 7 as a news commentator.

During the 1960s at KABC-TV, Baxter Ward's boss, general manager Elton Rule (who later became president and chief operating officer of ABC, Inc.) began appearing on the air to deliver station editorials. It provided Channel 7 with an influential voice on the important issues that faced Los Angeles and Southern California. And this policy continued with the executives who succeeded Rule as vice president and general manager of the station, including John J. McMahon in 1968, and most notably John Severino in 1974, who served two terms as head of KABC through the 1980s, as well as president of ABC-TV.

It has been said that the only thing that is constant in television news is change. And in the 1960s, a former copyboy and mailroom assistant invented a new format that revolutionized the way local TV news was delivered. Al Primo introduced his "Eyewitness News" concept in 1965 when he was a young and rising news director at a Philadelphia station. And the ratings for KYW-TV soared. Three years later when Primo took over the news operations for ABC's flagship station in New York City, WABC-TV, his Eyewitness News format gained national attention. Basically, Primo replaced a single anchor delivering the news one-on-one to the audience with a team of reporters on the set to discuss with the anchor or anchors the latest developments on the stories they had been covering as "eyewitnesses." At Channel 7 in New York, Eyewitness News became synonymous with team coverage.

The print media described the new format as "Happy Talk" because it took away the stiffness of a one-anchor newscast and allowed the anchors and reporters to chat with each other on the air—at times, in a more lighthearted manner. In the words of Al Primo, it was like having a "front row seat to life."

Channel 7 Eyewitness News soon became the highest rated newscast in New York City. ABC's other O&Os took note of this success. And in February of 1969, Eyewitness News was introduced on KABC-TV in Los Angeles. Bill Bonds, the highly regarded anchor of WXYZ-TV in Detroit who earned praise for his exceptional work during that city's 1967 riot, was brought to KABC to help launch the Eyewitness News format. (Bill Fyffe, as WXYZ news director, had originally hired Bonds.)

A new format also meant introducing new theme music to open the newscast. KABC chose to adopt the exact same music Al Primo had selected for Eyewitness News in New York. It was written by famed composer Lalo Schifrin, who has earned four Grammy Awards and six Oscar nominations during his remarkable career. The Eyewitness

News theme was originally written by Schifrin for the 1967 classic film *Cool Hand Luke* starring Paul Newman. The song "Tar Sequence" is featured in a scene where the shackled prison camp inmates work on a road. If you want to take a walk down memory lane, get the *Cool Hand Luke* DVD and go to 51:24 of the movie. And you will hear the original Eyewitness News theme that opened the Channel 7 newscast for twenty years beginning in 1969. The entire musical sequence in the movie runs from 49:39 to 51:38. When my wife, Sue, and I were watching *Cool Hand Luke* years later, I almost got up and went to work when that music came on! For his work on the film, Lalo Schifrin was nominated for an Academy Award for Best Music, Original Music Score.

Eyewitness News at KABC-TV had more to offer its viewers than just a new name and a catchy theme song. In December of 1969, a Channel 7 Eyewitness News reporter and camera crew scored one of the biggest scoops in the history of Los Angeles TV news involving one of the Southland's most infamous crimes. And this Channel 7 investigation played a pivotal role in cracking the case of the Manson family's Tate-LaBianca murders. At the time, Los Angeles police were searching for evidence in the brutal fatal stabbings of pregnant actress Sharon Tate and four others at the Tate home in Beverly Hills (one victim was shot to death). The next night, businessman Leno LaBianca and his wife, Rosemary, were murdered in a similar manner inside their Silver Lake home.

Eyewitness News reporter Al Wiman had a hunch. And he decided to check it out with a crew that included cameraman King Baggot. The Channel 7 crew began driving from the Tate residence down Benedict Canyon using the same route the killers used to make their escape. Wiman believed the killers may have taken off their bloody clothes and changed into clean clothes while driving away from the Tate home. So as the news crew drove from the Tate residence, Wiman took off his clothes in the car and then put them back on, timing the entire process with a stopwatch. It took six minutes and twenty seconds to complete. At that point, their car had reached the only spot on Benedict Canyon where you could pull off the road with no guardrail.

The crew pulled over and stopped. Wiman said they got out, looked over the edge of the hill, and found what appeared to be the bloody clothes that had been tossed. Los Angeles police officers came out and retrieved the evidence as Wiman's crew filmed a Channel 7 Eye-witness News exclusive. It was crucial evidence that led prosecutors to link cult leader Charles Manson and members of his so-called family to both the Tate and LaBianca murders. It was investigative journalism at its best. During the murder trial, cameraman King Baggot was called to testify and identify the bloody clothes.

By 1972, KABC-TV News Director Bill Fyffe had built a superb Eyewitness News team that included the finest anchors, reporters, producers, directors, camera crews, film editors, newswriters, studio technicians, and support staff. But in Los Angeles, you not only had to be the best—you had to be popular as well. In an effort to boost its ratings, Channel 7 sponsored a contest in which viewers were asked to write a letter explaining why they would like to have the 11 p.m. Eyewitness News broadcast from their home. The winner was a seventeen-year-old girl named Linda Jensen. And in June of 1972, the five-member Jensen family enjoyed their moment of fame when the Eyewitness News team turned their home into a news set. Anchors Joseph Benti and John Schubeck did the news segments sitting on a couch in the living room, the weather forecast was delivered from the kitchen, and all the sports and highlights were broadcast from the dining room. A beaming Jensen family was interviewed throughout the live newscast. It must have taken all night for an army of Channel 7 engineers to break down the cameras and transmitting equipment and haul it back to the television station. But this was one neighborhood that became Eyewitness News viewers for life.

My friends, the day finally came in October of 1972 when KABC-TV's newest employee—named George Fischbeck—drove onto the lot at the ABC Television Center for the very first time and reported for work at Channel 7 Eyewitness News. I had a desire and a passion to do a good job. To be honest, I still didn't understand why news director Bill Fyffe went to all that trouble to hire a fifty-year-old schoolteacher from a small town to forecast the weather on his newscast in the metropolis known as Los Angeles. But in the words of educator and diplomat Kingman Brewster Jr., "There is no greater challenge than to have someone relying upon you; no greater satisfaction than to vindicate his expectation."

There was just one problem. When I began at Eyewitness News, I don't think our audience quite knew what to make of me at first. No one watching our newscast knew that I had just spent twenty-three years in the classroom teaching science to students who were eager to learn. And now that I look back on it, I see my first appearance on Channel 7 must have hit viewers like a splash of cold water in the face. I certainly wasn't a professional announcer with a polished TV personality. When the live studio camera panned over to me during my first newscast, there I was on a table, pretending to be asleep. I introduced myself to Los Angeles by suddenly waking up, dressed in a bow tie and sneakers—and did the weather with as much energy, enthusiasm, and homespun humor as I could. I knew I was different—OK, a lot different. But as a teacher in a new "classroom" at KABC, I wanted to get everybody's attention so I could communicate with them. Anybody can give the viewers numbers. I wanted them to understand why weather is so important and how my forecast could affect their day.

The management at Channel 7 made sure it wasn't too long before Los Angeles got properly introduced to me. The station's top public relations man, Lloyd Peyton, and I got together one day. And Lloyd wanted to know everything about me. When I mentioned that I had received an honorary doctorate four months earlier, Lloyd got really excited and said, "From now on, you are Dr. George!" I didn't know exactly what that meant. But I soon found out. Lloyd Peyton launched a massive advertising campaign on television and in newspapers proclaiming: "Dr. George Fischbeck comes to Southern California!" My favorite ad showed a group of ducks watching me give the weather forecast on a TV set with a headline that read, "Anybody who cares if it rains or not turns on Dr. George." I didn't mind the title that Lloyd gave me. My doctorate may have been an honorary degree, but over the years, I had earned enough college units to qualify for two PhDs. When I was a kid, I always liked to going to school. It was certainly cheaper than going to the movies. Lloyd Peyton became one of my dearest friends. He dedicated thirty-three years of his life to serving Channel 7. Eyewitness News never had a better salesman.

It didn't take me long to realize that Los Angeles was a different playing field with, in some instances, a mean set of rules. A weatherman on a competing TV station in the Southland didn't like the way I did my job. And he was determined to teach the new kid on the block a lesson. His girlfriend just happened to work at the local office of the National Weather Service. And this weatherman instructed his girlfriend to make it "Mission Impossible" for me to get the latest weather updates from their forecasters. That made my job very tough in the beginning. If I couldn't talk with that agency's experts several times a day, I would be like a teacher going to class without a lesson plan. And I've never been unprepared. But once I sat down with these dedicated forecasters at the National Weather Service and expressed my deep appreciation of the job they did—we became best friends, just like in Albuquerque. I have never claimed to be an expert in meteorology. But I know where the experts are. And they graciously treated me like an equal, a part of their team in coming up with the latest weather information each day. My attitude was that if you, the viewer, invited Eyewitness News into your living room, you deserved nothing but the best from Dr. George.

But there was one more rocky road on my new journey in Los Angeles. Not long after I arrived, the former weatherman at Channel 7 was quoted by a local newspaper as saying that KABC-TV had dropped him because it wanted a clown . . . and that to the citizens of Albuquerque, Fischbeck was funnier than a snowstorm in August. It was a comment that deeply hurt me and my family.

I never came gunning for anyone's job. The job came chasing after me. News director Bill Fyffe flew to New Mexico three times to try to hire me. And I turned him down all three times until my cherished mentor, Dr. Wayne Bundy, told me I would be giving up a most wonderful opportunity as a teacher to bring my lessons into a new classroom. It became a challenging assignment that I couldn't turn down. As anchorman Tom Brokaw said, "It's easy to make a buck. It's a lot tougher to make a difference."

All in the Family

Our "Fisch" tank is full. These are two shots of the House of Fischbeck from the early 1960s. Dr. George, Sue, Nancy, and George Junior ("Fritz"). It's been said, "I don't care how poor a man is. If he has family, he's rich."

Teaching on Television

From 1959 to 1972, a junior high school teacher named George Fischbeck moonlighted by teaching science courses for fifth-, sixth-, and ninth-grade students on the public educational station KNME-TV in Albuquerque. My studio for the program resembled a garage in which I worked from a makeshift science laboratory. (Courtesy KNME)

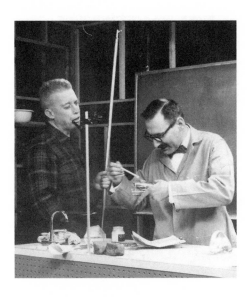

Above, left: On the set at KNME-TV with my boss, mentor, and beloved friend, Dr. Wayne Bundy, who plucked me out of a classroom and become the architect of my broadcast career.

Above, right: KNME's first home in the 1950s and '60s, which used to be a college sorority house. (Courtesy KNME)

In 1969, our KNME-TV team moved into this modern broadcast center, which, as a PBS station, is now capable of sending programs around the world with satellite technology in high definition. (Courtesy Lester F. Frolick, Jr.)

In the mid-1970s, I reunited with one of my former junior high school students and KNME alumnus Ron Miziker to put together a TV science program called *By George*, which went on to win an Emmy for Best Children's Show. As head of his own production company for nearly three decades, Ron is one of the real giants of entertainment.

This is one of our production assistants on *By George*, who apparently had a "bone" to pick with me!

EYEWITNESS NEWS

PROUDLY FEATURES George Fischbeck

MEMBER AMERICAN METEOROLOGICAL SOCIETY

TV Meteorologist on EYEWITNESS WEATHER
6:00 and 10:00 P.M. Nightly on Channel 4

Everyone is interested in the weather. Most television stations employ a weatherman, but in New Mexico only Channel 4's EYE-WITNESS WEATHER provides the viewer with a qualified meteorologist. George Fischbeck, Channel 4's meteorologist, is a widely known and highly respected scientist, educational television pioneer, humorist — but even more important, Fischbeck is known for the ability to reach out to the individual rather than merely address a vast and scattered audience.

In his many years at KNME-TV, Albuquerque's educational channel, Fischbeck has taught science to over one-fourth the population of New Mexico on his various science series. Several of his science programs are now distributed throughout the world. Three times Fischbeck has won National Educational Television's "Oscar" for the excellence of his TV teaching. Fischbeck is a proven success at reaching people.

In addition to receiving B. A. and M. A. degrees in science and education from the University of New Mexico, Fischbeck has completed course work at seven other leading universities. Fischbeck has received dozens of major civic, educational and scientific awards but we are especially proud that Channel 4's meteorologist, in a state which abounds with the highest per capita number of scientists in the nation, was one of only six New Mexico recipients of a special medallion struck in 1970 to commemorate the 100th anniversary of weather services in the United States and the 50th anniversary of the American Meteorological Society, of which he is a member.

See George Fischbeck, TV meteorologist, on EYEWITNESS WEATHER twice each evening on Channel 4.

George Fischbeck / TV Meteorologist  KOB 4 TV

BREAKING NEWS

In 1970, the NBC station in Albuquerque, KOB-TV, took out a full-page newspaper ad to announce that a local schoolteacher named Fischbeck would now be forecasting the weather on its 6 and 10 p.m. newscasts. (Courtesy of KOB-TV and KNME)

THE NUMBER ONE NEWS IN ALBUQUERQUE

On the air with top-rated KOB-TV Channel 4 Eyewitness News in 1972. *Left to right*: sportscaster Mike Roberts, anchorman Johnny Morris, anchorman Gordon Sanders (who also served as news director), and the weather guy who was nicknamed "Uncle George." (Courtesy KOB-TV Albuquerque-Santa Fe)

George Fischbeck and Blue Max
"I'm a Compulsive Teacher"

George Fischbeck Going to Coast

George Fischbeck, known to thousands of Albuquerqueans for his teaching, speaking appearances and television work, is leaving the city to work in Los Angeles.

Fischbeck has accepted a weathercasting position with KABC-TV in Los Angeles. His family will remain in Albuquerque and he will commute

CHANGE OF VENUE

This is an article in the *Albuquerque Journal* on September 24, 1972, reporting that I was leaving KOB-TV and my beloved "Duke City" to accept a job offer with KABC-TV in Los Angeles. It was one of the hardest decisions I ever had to make in my entire life. (Courtesy *Albuquerque Journal* and KOB-TV)

When it happens, the Eyewitness News Team is involved.

Pictured above are field reporters Chuck Henry, Dick Carlson, Henry Alfaro, Andy Park, Morgan Williams, Bob Banfield, Christine Lund, Bernard Morris, Fred Anderson, and Harold Greer

Benti Schubeck Nahan Fischbeck

Eyewitness in-depth reporting means more than just watching other people make things happen. It means getting involved yourself, on a warm, person-to-person level. Then rushing the facts back to the Channel 7 newsroom. Fresh, up-to-the-minute facts and film with that extra measure of understanding and insight that comes from really caring.

Eyewitness News ⑦

Experience it at 4:30, 6 and 11pm.

A Small Town Teacher Joins a Major League Team
In October of 1972, Channel 7 Eyewitness News introduced its new weatherman, by George, in a full-page ad that appeared in the *Los Angeles Times*. What a roster—the greatest teammates I could ever wish for. (Courtesy KABC-TV)

THE CHANNEL 7 EYEWITNESS NEWS TEAM—1972

This is how it all began for a "rookie" named Dr. George in Southern California in an article published by the *Alhambra Post-Advocate*. *Left to right:* anchors John Schubeck and Joseph Benti, sportscaster Stu Nahan, and your friendly neighborhood weatherman. (Courtesy Don Wanlass, Managing Editor, WAVE Newspapers)

"DRAWING" THE LINE

This is a sketch of Dr. George on the job at Channel 7 Eyewitness News in an advertisement that appeared in *TV Guide* on October 25, 1972. (Courtesy KABC-TV)

Anybody who cares if it rains or not turns on Dr. George Fischbeck.

Monsoons turn you on? Then watch our weather doctor. He'll give you all the highs and lows.

Plus some warm chuckles. Catch Dr. George along with Judd Hambrick, Barney Morris, John Schubeck and Stu Nahan on Channel 7. They'll turn you on.

⑦ The Eyewitness News Team
4:30, 6 and 11
People turn us on.

MY ALL-TIME FAVORITE

You might say things were quite "ducky" at Channel 7 Eyewitness News in a *TV Guide* ad from January 2, 1974. Who said Dr. George isn't what he was "quacked" up to be? (Courtesy KABC-TV)

"THIS IS CHANNEL 7—THE NUMBER ONE STATION FOR
NEWS AND INFORMATION IN SOUTHERN CALIFORNIA"

That was the intro to one of the most successful local newscasts in L.A. broadcast history . . . with Jerry Dunphy, Christine Lund, Dr. George, and the Channel 7 Eyewitness News team. (Courtesy Dianne Barone)

THE "TOAST" OF LOS ANGELES

This KABC-TV promo was shot in 1976 with anchors Chuck Henry, Christine Lund, Jerry Dunphy, and Dr. George with the champagne. (Courtesy KABC-TV)

EYEWITNESS TO SUCCESS

This ad appeared in the *Los Angeles Times* on December 29, 1975, after Channel 7 Eyewitness News won the Golden Mike Award for Best Television News Broadcast. *Left to right:* Stu Nahan, Regis Philbin, Jerry Dunphy, Christine Lund, John Hambrick and his brother Judd, Dr. George, and sportscaster "Fast Eddie" Alexander. (Courtesy KABC-TV)

"JUST THE TWO OF US"

As author Ken Kesey once said, "You've got to get out and pray to the sky to appreciate the sunshine; otherwise, you're just a lizard standing there with the sun shining on you."

Up, Up, and Away

Channel 7 restaurant and travel reporter Elmer Dills would go to the ends of the earth to do a good story for Eyewitness News. In 1984, he talked Mr. and Mrs. Fischbeck into joining him for a balloon ride for the cameras. This is one time Dr. George really was full of "hot air"! (Courtesy Martin Orozco)

A CELEBRATION OF LIFE

For nearly thirty years, Elmer Dills shared his vast knowledge of dining and travel with the viewers of Channel 7 Eyewitness News. Sue and I considered him one of our dearest friends. Elmer relished what he did. And it showed. In the words of Ralph Waldo Emerson, "Though we travel the world over to find the beautiful, we must carry it with us, or we find it not."

PROFILE IN COURAGE

Perhaps the bravest man I have ever known—famed balloonist Maxie Anderson— pays me a visit in the Eyewitness Newsroom in Los Angeles. Our close friendship dated back to my days in Albuquerque. Maxie died in a tragic balloon crash in 1983.

EYEWITNESS NEWS TEAMMATES

On assignment out in the field with one of the finest reporters to ever grace the airwaves of Los Angeles. The impeccable Bob Banfield served the viewers of Eyewitness News for forty-three years. (Courtesy Martin Orozco)

SPECIAL REPORT

One of the greatest privileges of being a member of the Channel 7 Eyewitness News team was being able to take part in a number of in-depth half-hour documentaries. This ad appeared in the *Los Angeles Times* for our report on the disasterous Long Beach earthquake that killed 120 people in 1933. (Courtesy KABC-TV)

"ANCHORS" AWEIGH

From one George to another. The legendary George Putnam, at one time the most influential TV anchorman in Los Angeles, shares one of his many Emmys with Dr. George and award-winning Eyewitness News cameraman Martin Orozco. (Courtesy Martin Orozco)

THE BEST OF TIMES

The photographic bookends of my blessed career at Channel 7 Eyewitness News in Southern California. The promo photo on the left was taken in 1972 . . . note the bold Circle 7 logo that we wore on our jackets back then. The picture on the right is from 1992. (Courtesy KABC-TV)

A "First" for All Times

Eyewitness News celebrates a Los Angeles ratings victory for all three time periods—5, 6, and 11 p.m.—for the second time in a row in 1979. *Left to right*: anchors Harold Greene and Christine Lund, sportscaster Ted Dawson, anchor Jerry Dunphy, sportscaster Ed Arnold, and Dr. George. (Courtesy KABC-TV)

Stuck on You

What would a book about Dr. George be without a Dr. George Eyewitness News vintage pin? Yes—they still exist. I'm told someone was actually trying to sell one on eBay recently for $7.99. My friends, I always gave them out for free! (Courtesy Rich Fischbeck)

CHAPTER 7

The Eyewitness News Team

Finding good players is easy.

Getting them to play as a team is another story.

~ CASEY STENGEL ~

Managed New York Yankees to ten pennants and seven World Series titles

Inquiring minds want to know. I can't even begin to count how many of our viewers over the years have asked me, "Is the Eyewitness News team really a team?" My honest answer is YES! Oh, we weren't the kind of team that went out and socialized together. We didn't attend picnics with each other or organize sleepovers with our families. But Channel 7 Eyewitness News was indeed a team. First of all, we looked like a team. And it all began with our news set. Gone was the one-anchor concept with a single anchor, usually a man, sitting behind a desk. When Eyewitness News came on, it opened with a wide shot of the entire set that delivered the message "team coverage." Viewers could see the expanded desk where the two anchors and sportscaster would be jotting down last-second notes on their scripts. To the right of the anchor desk, I would be busy at the weather wall writing my forecast numbers for the different Southland regions.

And Channel 7 didn't want its viewers to ever wonder what newscast they were watching. From the bold opening with a staff announcer proclaiming that it was Eyewitness News, we marketed our on-the-air product with team consistency. The walls of our news set sported rows of "Eyewitness News" with our Circle 7 logo in large blue lettering. Every reporter on the newscast was introduced as "Eyewitness News reporter." The reporters out in the field held a microphone that featured our station's Circle 7 logo. Each time we would use a chyron (text or graphics placed at the bottom of the screen) for a location or the reporter's name, that individual chyron would include a Circle 7 Eyewitness News on the second line. Of course, I was always introduced as "Dr. George with the Eyewitness News forecast." The format of our newscast allowed those on this expanded set to be able to talk with each other on the air—part of a team. The male anchors, sportscasters, reporters, and I wore jackets with the Circle 7 logo on the pocket. There was some very stiff competition in the local TV news ratings wars of Los Angeles. But no one in town marketed its newscast like Channel 7 Eyewitness News. We wanted to be the team you can count on.

Now for a team to be successful, you've got to have a very good roster. And I always thought I had the absolute best teammates. Anchorman Joseph Benti had an extensive résumé of anchoring for CBS News after working for both KTLA-TV (Channel 5) and KNXT-TV (Channel 2) in Los Angeles. Co-anchor John Schubeck came to KABC after anchoring for WABC-TV in New York City and before that, at WGN-TV in Chicago and KYW-TV in Philadelphia. I found John to be a brilliant man who had earned his law degree by day while anchoring at night. Stu Nahan began his sports reports for Channel 7 News in 1968. He was a former minor league hockey player who got into broadcasting by hosting a children's TV program in Sacramento ("Skipper Stu") and Philadelphia ("Captain Philadelphia"). Stu also did radio for baseball, hockey, and pro football before landing at KABC-TV. I think Stu knew every athlete in Los Angeles on a personal basis. He went on to enjoy a sports broadcasting career in Southern California that lasted more than thirty-five years.

Of course, to deliver high ratings, you've got to deliver the news. When I joined Channel 7 Eyewitness News in October of 1972, we had a team of reporters that was second to none. Bernard Morris (who was later known as Barney Morris) has been described as "one of the true treasures in Los Angeles broadcasting." He was originally hired by our news director, Bill Fyffe, at WXYZ-TV in Detroit. In 1972, Morris rejoined Fyffe at KABC-TV where he reported and co-anchored our newscast. In 1980, Morris ran the Eyewitness News Orange County Bureau for fifteen years. When it came to journalism, Barney Morris was a pro's pro.

Our Channel 7 reporting staff also included two of the most highly respected journalists who ever graced the Los Angeles airwaves. For forty-three years, Bob Banfield was a cornerstone in building the success of Eyewitness News. In addition to being an extraordinary reporter, Banfield served as news anchor for one of the best morning shows the Southland has ever enjoyed. In the early 1970s, *Ralph Story's A.M.* was live, local, and a forerunner of the ABC network's *A.M. America*, which later became *Good Morning America.*

But it all began in Southern California on Channel 7 with Ralph Story, who was the greatest human interest storyteller of all, his cohost, the bright witty and effervescent Stephanie Edwards (who had been Ralph's secretary at KNXT-TV for three years, and he had been her invaluable mentor), and of course Bob Banfield with the morning news. From 1980 until his retirement in 2010, Banfield served as the Inland Empire Bureau Chief of our news operation.

Henry Alfaro joined the Channel 7 Eyewitness News team in 1970 in a remarkable career that spanned thirty-five years. Alfaro was one of the first Mexican American TV reporters in the nation, becoming a role model and an inspiration. The National Association of Hispanic Journalists described Henry Alfaro as "a Los Angeles institution" and in 2006, inducted him into its Hall of Fame. When I say "remarkable career"—I think winning six Emmys, five Golden Mike Awards, and a coveted Peabody Award nomination more than qualifies for that distinction. In addition to his reporting duties for Eyewitness News, Henry also cohosted the Southland's first public affairs television program about Hispanics for English-speaking viewers, KABC's *Vista L.A.* For his excellence in serving the community, Henry Alfaro was named by *Hispanic* magazine as one of the one hundred most influential Latinos in the entire United States. My friend Henry is a pioneer and journalistic giant.

Channel 7 Eyewitness News also had three reporters who were not only among the finest ever in the field, but they also went on to become some of the best-known anchors in Southland television history. Christine Lund came to KABC-TV in 1972 from our sister station KGO-TV in San Francisco. Throughout much of her long career at Channel 7, Lund co-anchored Eyewitness News with Jerry Dunphy and helped catapult our newscast into number one in the ratings for years. Christine is one of the most talented and delightful people I have ever had the pleasure of working with.

Harold Greene was at one time the 6 p.m. producer of Channel 7 Eyewitness News. He went on to enjoy a career in television news most people in our business can't even dream about. Harold's reporting out in the field and in hard-hitting documentaries was impeccable. Greene is one of the finest news anchors I ever saw. Dr. George doesn't have his own star on the Hollywood Walk of Fame. But Harold Greene does, and deservedly so. Greene is an exceptional journalist and a superb broadcaster. There have been many instances that you don't get one with the other. But my teammate Harold Greene was the complete package. And it always showed.

Chuck Henry is well known as a longtime anchor of Channel 4 News at KNBC-TV in Los Angeles. But for a number of years, Chuck was an integral part and an invaluable member of the Channel 7 Eyewitness News team where he served as both a reporter and anchor. Wherever he was and whatever the story, Chuck Henry always made a difference. Henry was also a host of Channel 7's popular feature and lifestyle program called *Eye on L.A.*

Reporter Dick Carlson was in charge of investigative journalism on Eyewitness News. Dick was teamed with one of the legendary figures of Los Angeles TV news—producer Pete Noyes, who had been so instrumental in the success of KNXT-TV's *The Big News* on Channel 2 in the 1960s. Dick and Pete's investigative unit was housed in an old trailer outside our main newsroom. Pete Noyes was the greatest newsman I ever knew. During their tenure at Channel 7, Pete and Dick won television's highest award—the Peabody—for one of the superior investigations that they specialized in. Noyes can add that to his ten Emmys, seventeen Golden Mikes, and the prestigious Edward R. Murrow Award. (I told you he was good.) Dick Carlson went on to serve as director of the Voice of America and was later named U.S. Ambassador to the Seychelles by President George H. W. Bush. And to think I actually got to work with these guys!

When it came to versatility, Fred Anderson was your "go to" reporter. Fred was an original member of the Channel 7 Eyewitness News team in 1969. For decades, there wasn't an assignment he couldn't handle. And he did it all with excellence—from breaking news to the lighter stories, to which Fred added his own special touch. Anderson came to KABC-TV with a long résumé in radio—including an outstanding career at KNX Newsradio, where he was named Announcer of the Year in 1968 by the *Los Angeles Times*. For many years at Eyewitness News, Anderson teamed with restaurant critic Elmer Dills to produce highly popular travel pieces titled "Fred and Elmer." Fred Anderson was a talented, respected, and well-liked member of Channel 7 Eyewitness News. I'll never forget his deep voice and his sense of humor. He had an exceptional gift to make us laugh, especially in those trying times when it was needed. Fred was a great person to have as my teammate. He made our team a better team to be a part of.

Henry Ford once said, "Coming together is a beginning. Keeping together is progress. Working together is success." And a successful team must be composed of people who are united in a common goal supporting and encouraging each other as they transform individual sacrifice into collective excellence. In the words of Michael Jordan, "Talent wins games. But teamwork and intelligence win championships."

Behind every team there is a leader. At Eyewitness News, it was a visionary named Bill Fyffe. The viewers never saw this man during any of our newscasts. But as news director, Fyffe had a major role in what our audience did see. Bill Fyffe built the Channel 7 team from the ground up. Then he allowed them to do their jobs. Theodore Roosevelt said, "The best executive is the one who has sense enough to pick good people to do what he wants done, and self-restraint to keep from meddling with them while they do it."

Bill Fyffe knew how to run a big news operation. He was news director of the ABC stations in Detroit and Los Angeles, and he ran the network's stations in Chicago and New York City. Bill Fyffe was old school. And he was decisive. Fyffe once suspended anchorman Tom Snyder for a week without pay. Another time, Fyffe fired well-known and veteran New York anchor Roger Grimsby after eighteen years at the helm of WABC-TV's newscast. But first and foremost, Fyffe was a journalist—having earned the Peabody Award for his work in television news.

Bill Fyffe was adept at putting together anchors and reporters that had an on-the-air chemistry . . . a team that the audience could relate to . . . the Eyewitness News team. Fyffe wanted his reporters to be eyewitnesses at the scene, the link connecting that particular story with our viewers. Fyffe had an eye for talent. He brought reporter Ken Kashiwahara to KABC-TV from a Honolulu station and added another superb broadcast journalist named Bill Redeker—both of whom went on to have distinguished careers reporting from around the world for the ABC network news. Ken Kashiwahara was in the capital of South Vietnam on March 30, 1975, and filed a harrowing report for ABC that fateful day as Saigon fell. At KABC, Fyffe taught his reporters what's been described as old-fashioned journalism. When it comes to doing a story, you do it right, and you do it honestly. Then you follow it up by checking and rechecking. In 1972, Fyffe told the *Los Angeles Times*, "I like to leave the audience feeling that we've made intelligent choices, given them the stories they need information about, but also sure that the world is still going to be here tomorrow."

Now can you possibly imagine how I must have felt when I first reported to work at Channel 7 Eyewitness News and saw the major league lineup of talent that I was being asked to work with? It reminded me of the time comedian George Gobel appeared on *The Tonight Show*, only to come out on stage and see Bob Hope and Dean Martin sitting next to him. Gobel looked at them and then quipped to Johnny Carson, "Did you ever get the feeling that the world was a tuxedo, and you were a pair of brown shoes?" But then I thought about Bill Fyffe, the man who hired me. Fyffe thought I belonged here. I wasn't about to look at this challenge, give up, and head back to Albuquerque with my head down and my tail tucked between my legs. So I decided it was best I get to work.

My job was to give the weather forecast for Southern California on the 4:30, 6, and 11 p.m. newscasts. What I was being asked to do in Los Angeles wasn't any different than what I did for over twenty years in New Mexico. I'm a compulsive teacher. I love to teach and to impart knowledge. And at KABC, I needed to prepare for my assignment just like I did each day before stepping into my classroom at Monroe Junior High School—or on public educational TV. I remember the discipline I have been taught by my mentors that I cherish. At one of my very first teaching jobs at Ernie Pyle Junior High, Principal Adolfo Chavez wanted me to write out my lesson plans for him to read on a daily basis before I delivered it to my students in class. It was the same commitment to excellence that was instilled in me by Dr. Wayne Bundy during my years at KNME-TV. Dr. Bundy taught me that my science programs will only be as good as the homework that I did beforehand to help lay the foundation of their success. Perhaps the Boy Scouts said it best with their motto: Be Prepared.

Every day I worked for Channel 7 Eyewitness News, I began my homework by going to the National Weather Service located in the Federal Building in Westwood. And I went there at least twice a day: at noon to prepare for the afternoon newscasts and then in the evening to update my information for the 11 p.m. news. The experts in charge at the National Weather Service have a complete daily review of everything that's happening across Southern California. During this briefing, they would go over the maps of the past forty-eight hours. Only after absorbing information gathered from all over the world would they make their forecast for the Southland. The briefing was open to everybody in the media, but I was usually the only TV weatherman that showed up. I had to be there. I'd feel naked without the crucial information that I learned from these weather experts each day. I was hired at Channel 7 to give the most accurate forecast I could possibly put together for our viewers. In the words of Dr. George: you might as well submerge yourself in your subject. And as a wise man named John Cotton Dana once stated, "Who dares to teach must never cease to learn."

I was learning in a crash course that seemed like it would never end. Forecasting the weather for Albuquerque, which was only the 57th largest metropolitan area in the nation, was one thing. The Channel 7 viewing area in Southern California encompassed five counties and 176 cities. And one forecast doesn't even to begin to cover the whole area. It can be cloudy and foggy along the beach in Malibu yet at the same time sunny and hot in the San Fernando Valley. It can be fair and mild in downtown Los Angeles yet snowing with the best ski conditions in the San Bernardino Mountains. And as if that were not enough, the Southland has not one but two deserts, where the weather in both the high and low desert areas can be quite different from each other.

Now you know why I spent so much time at the National Weather Service each day. That's where I got the latest information for each region of Southern California. If you live in Long Beach, the forecast I have for Palm Springs isn't going to do you any good. On each newscast at Channel 7, I had to give an accurate weather forecast for every section of our area. But that's why Eyewitness News hired me—because I love the challenge of bringing our viewers my very best, even if it took me twelve to fourteen hours a day to get the job done.

Being an old farm boy from New Jersey, I'm used to hard work and long hours. My goodness, I was working three jobs at once my last couple of years in Albuquerque. But I really liked what I was doing. That makes a difference—because my work energizes me. And you know, I found that my work became even more interesting in Los Angeles. My daily schedule was a routine. After spending a couple of hours at home in Woodland Hills watching the morning news on TV, I left for the National Weather Service in Westwood around 11 a.m. I spent two hours there and then headed for Channel 7 in East Hollywood, stopping for a quick bite at a fast food restaurant along the way. I usually arrived at the Eyewitness Newsroom at 2:30 in the afternoon, and immediately began preparing my weather forecasts for the 4:30 and 6 p.m. news.

The moment the 6 p.m. newscast ended, I drove back home to Woodland Hills and ate dinner with my family. Then it was back to Westwood and the National Weather Service to get the needed updates firsthand from my best friends—the experts. By nine in the evening, I was at the newsroom again getting ready for our 11 p.m. news. My workday would normally end about ten minutes after midnight when I arrived back home in Woodland Hills and ate a bowl of Wheaties. By then, my wife, Sue, would be ready for bed after watching a TV show like *The Rockford Files.* I never could compete with actor James Garner. And while Susie dozed off, I'd usually read in bed for an hour before falling asleep and resting up for another day doing my job. I never shied away from the challenge of work. I heard someone say once there is no elevator to success—you have to take the stairs. Indira Gandhi had this to say about succeeding, "There are two kinds of people, those who do the work and those who take the credit. Try to be in the first group; there is less competition there."

Doing the weather for a major television station like Channel 7 certainly had its advantages. I was given far more tools to work with than I would have had in a smaller market. First of all, being a part of the ABC network meant we had access to news footage from sister stations and affiliates throughout the nation and around the world. Every day, KABC took in a feed that was called News One that featured video of breaking news, features, and weather-related items from other cities. Our engineering department recorded the News One feed on two-inch videotape. Each producer for the 4:30, 6, and 11 p.m. editions of Eyewitness News would decide which items he or she would use from the feed on their newscasts. And a newswriter would work with a videotape engineer to edit those items for use on air. For any weather stories that came down on the News One feed, the producer would consult with me as to whether I wanted to use any of the footage within my weather segments. The videotape would then be edited for me. And I would be given information about the story so that I could include it in my weather for that particular newscast.

Covering the weather in Southern California was another story. Each and every day, the Eyewitness News team had crews dispatched across a wide area of the Southland to cover news, sports, and weather stories. Our local weather could come in all shapes and sizes. It rained—sometimes very hard—and at times, that caused flooding. Heavy snow in our mountains could force the closure of roads—affecting motorists from the Los Angeles Basin who were looking forward to a weekend of skiing. Hot weather could make it absolutely miserable and caused power outages that could affect everyone. Then there's that infamous four-letter word that has been linked to Southern California for decades—smog. And dirty air is unhealthy for all.

When I first arrived on the scene at Channel 7 Eyewitness News in 1972, we shot all of our local stories on film. We didn't have minicam technology at the time. And film had its limitations. It couldn't be electronically transmitted immediately back to the television station from remote trucks like videotape. Once a story was shot, the film had to be driven back to KABC-TV in the Los Feliz area from the location. That could be extremely time-consuming. Once the film arrived in the newsroom, it had to be developed like any film. And that took time. When the film was developed, reporters or newswriters would look at the footage and then give instructions to our talented film editors to edit for use on air. If it was a weather-related story, then either I or a newswriter would work with the film editor. Because all of this took time, we had to allow for that in planning our newscast. For the 11 p.m. news, if the film wasn't shot by 9 p.m., there wasn't enough time to deliver the footage to the newsroom, develop the film, edit it, and make it on the air.

As you can see, doing a live newscast on Channel 7 in Los Angeles was a most challenging assignment. It was indeed a team effort: from the assignment desk to the reporters and crews out in the field . . . to the producers, newswriters, and film editors at the station . . . to the directors and technical staff in our studio . . . and to all the newsroom assistants who were so invaluable at airtime. Our small staff at KOB-TV in Albuquerque was microscopic compared to the army of people who teamed up to put Channel 7 Eyewitness News on the air in Southern California. And mere words cannot possibly even begin to describe the pressure we faced each day to make deadline. Talk about a rush job. We might get word of a breaking news story just one minute before airtime, or a last-minute script or an edited piece of film might be completed with just thirty seconds to go. The Channel 7 Eyewitness Newsroom could turn into a virtual track meet.

There's a scene in the 1987 comedy film *Broadcast News* in which famed director James L. Brooks brilliantly captured the pressure cooker of a television news operation. In the scene, a producer and videotape editor finish a taped report that is scheduled to be shown on the evening news in just fifty-two seconds. It was hilarious to watch the frantic foot race that ensued to get the edited videotape into the playback machine clear across the entire newsroom and get it on the air. It made it—just barely. The viewers at home had no idea of the miracle that it took to get the report they were watching on the newscast. As for the out-of-breath news staffers who looked at each other in exhaustion afterward, it was a job well done. That is a scene that I have seen played out at Channel 7 Eyewitness News time and time again. If you cared enough and if you ran fast enough, it would make air. Thomas Edison said, "Genius is 1 percent inspiration and 99 percent perspiration."

The physical layout of KABC-TV made that challenge even more daunting. The Eyewitness Newsroom and the studio where we did the actual live newscast were not located in the same building. They were not even close. If you've ever wondered why I wore sneakers while doing my weather segments, I'm about to tell you why.

Channel 7 was just a small part of the twenty-three-acre lot known as the ABC Television Center. Our newsroom was located on the second floor of a building situated on the eastern end of the lot. The studio where we did the newscasts was in another building to the west about two hundred yards away. So many times I would be in the newsroom working frantically to get the latest information about a breaking weather story—when I would be told I had one minute to get to the studio to go on live. My friends, it was off to the races. I would run out of the newsroom and down the stairs to the first floor. But once I got outside of the building, the studio audience for the game show *Let's Make a Deal* would be lined up there waiting to be let in to that program. And oh my, I had to run through that crowd in order to make it to our news studio two hundred yards away. And I could never say "no" to those folks who wanted to shake hands, get a hug, or have something signed. If I ever seemed out of breath on Eyewitness News when the anchors tossed it to me, it was because I had just set a world record for fifty-year-old men in the two-hundred-yard dash. Those sneakers I wore always came in handy.

Now a lot of things were written about me in the local newspapers when I first began forecasting the weather on Channel 7 Eyewitness News in Los Angeles. I wouldn't be honest with you if I didn't tell you some critics didn't care for my enthusiasm or lack of polish on the air. One columnist even printed this reaction to me from one of his readers: "He overdoes the humor and goofs around too much." In response, let me say . . . I'm human. Going in, I knew I couldn't please everyone. But my philosophy of life can be summed up this way: If you want to be a success, double your rate of failure. Don't be afraid to fail. Take that chance. You'll never know if you could have done something unless you try.

I take my weather reports very seriously. In my entire career in the classroom and on television news, I never went to my job unprepared. I did my homework like someone in my position should do every day. I couldn't stand to give out misinformation. In my weather segments, the humor is there for a purpose. And the purpose is for the viewers to remember what is being said. During all my years as a schoolteacher, I found out that if you can get children to smile, you can teach them anything. It's been estimated that I taught 25 percent of the population in the entire state of New Mexico at least one full year of science either in school or on public television. And as a weatherman at KOB-TV in Albuquerque, I was given the coveted Seal of Approval of the American Meteorological Society. And that's after undergoing the scrutiny and meeting the high standards of a national panel of experts and professional meteorologists.

Yes, I like to do "weather with a smile." But communication is my job. I would have used smoke signals if they would have helped. During my twenty years at Channel 7 in Los Angeles, I tried my best to show our viewers the importance of weather and how they could use my forecast to plan their tomorrows. And along the way, I hope we shared a smile, my friends. I've always liked this quote from the author Colette: "You will do many foolish things in the world. But always do them with enthusiasm."

One of the highest compliments I ever received came from newspaper columnist Bob Martin of the *Long Beach Press-Telegram:* "It has been said that Dr. George doesn't so much give the weather . . . but teaches it." A professor named Leo Buscaglia shared this thought: "I can plant a seed. And it becomes a flower. Share a bit of knowledge . . . and it becomes another's." But the education of George Fischbeck at Channel 7 Eyewitness News was a never-ending process. My boss, news director Bill Fyffe, told me that I had to learn all about Los Angeles. And he meant every single city from Ventura to San Juan Capistrano. In Fyffe's words, "You've got to know them all. Each town has to know that you're talking about them . . . the one-on-one process with our viewers. You've got to establish a relationship with them."

And as the ratings for Eyewitness News started to rise, I began to receive number of invitations to visit communities all across Southern California. I appeared before youth groups, service clubs, local churches, and professional organizations. It was my civic duty. And I tried to fulfill my obligations with fervor. I worked with the Boy Scouts. At one point, I was deeply honored and humbled to receive the Silver Beaver for my efforts—the highest award in Scouting at the council level. I became an honorary Girl Scout, an honorary Den Mother, and an honorary Campfire Girl. Whatever I did in Albuquerque, I was going to do in Los Angeles. If you invited Dr. George into your living room each night, then I needed to come to your community and say "thank you." I owed that to our local viewers. One night, I was a part of the Channel 7 Eyewitness News basketball team that played the Harlem Globetrotters at the Forum. As you can imagine, challenging the Globetrotters is a "no-win" situation. But despite our lopsided loss, we scored with the fans. And that is what really counts.

As I continued my tour of the Southland, it was the schools that got my special attention. It was a chance for me to revisit my first love—teaching and sharing with young students. In these classrooms, my subject was science and the weather. I probably had more experiments flop than anybody around. But the kids loved it. I always tried to teach these children the importance of education, saying, "Every day, some part of what I learned helps me. None of it was wasted."

At one elementary school in Carson, I helped students release balloons with postcards attached, in hopes the recipients would mail them back so that the class could determine how far and in what direction their balloons had traveled. This student project met with incredible success. It's an annual event at Carson Street School in which one fourth-grade class sent a nine-inch helium-filled balloon that was found on a farm in Leonardville, Kansas—fifteen hundred miles away! The farmer and his wife wrote back and invited the students to visit their farm if they were ever in Kansas.

Now we believe in teamwork at Channel 7 Eyewitness News. And Dr. George believes in teamwork during my visits to classrooms across Southern California. I never went to a school without my favorite teammate—a skunk. Matilda the skunk was a teaching tool. The children loved Matilda. Once we got their attention, Matilda and I could begin presenting our lesson plan. Like a sponge, these students would absorb a potpourri of information. Educator Helen Peters once wrote, "Teacher appreciation makes the world of education go round." I've never felt more appreciated than when I received special handwritten thank-you notes from many of the young students I visited.

> *Dear Dr. George,*
> *Thank you for teaching us about the animals and the weather. I hope you will come again to teach us more. You are a very good scientist.*
>
> *Love, Roxana*

> *Dear Dr. George,*
> *I hope your skunk will not run away. Sometimes skunks stink. But Matilda does not stink.*
>
> *Love, Brigid*

> *Dear Dr. George,*
> *I like your show on TV. I like how you wigill your mutas. And your skunk is kut.*
>
> *From Leo*

(NOTE: I think Leo means "wiggle your mustache." And yes, I think my skunk is "kut" too!)

> *Dear Dr. George,*
> *I'm 48 inches tall . . . weigh 67 pounds . . . and watch you with all my might.*

You know, my friends, sometimes the best gifts indeed come in the smallest packages!

CHAPTER 8

"From the Desert to the Sea, to All of Southern California"

~ JERRY DUNPHY ~

O ver the years, there have been countless claims from TV stations to being number one in Los Angeles. But no one has enjoyed such overwhelming success on a consistent basis for decades as Channel 7 Eyewitness News. Since 1997, KABC-TV has been known as ABC7. And today, it remains by far the top-rated newscast in the Southland. What a tradition.

But that hasn't always been the case. I know. I was there. In 1974, Eyewitness News was a distant third in the local ratings. Anchorman Joseph Benti had moved on. Co-anchor John Schubeck signed a deal with KNBC-TV, where Tom Snyder's 6 p.m. news on Channel 4 was the most popular with L.A. viewers. A future anchor named Kelly Lange did the weather on that newscast. But things change—especially in the landscape of TV news. I'm about to tell you a story of how one of the savviest executives I've ever seen lured perhaps L.A.'s best-known anchorman in a high-stakes poker game with a competing station . . . and changed the face of broadcast journalism in the City of Angels.

It all started when John Severino was named vice president and general manager of KABC-TV in 1974. Severino came to Channel 7 from Chicago where he ran the ABC network owned-and-operated station WLS-TV. He was highly successful in the Windy City. Severino had a reputation for hiring veteran anchors from other stations and then surrounding them with a younger staff on the air. It paid off richly in the ratings. When Severino arrived in Los Angeles, he figured Channel 7 needed a marquee anchor to give Eyewitness News a needed ratings boost. Severino set his sights on anchorman Jerry Dunphy, who was still under contract with KNXT-TV (now KCBS). Dunphy had been the cornerstone of Channel 2's groundbreaking *The Big News*, the nation's first one-hour local newscast in the 1960s, which literally owned the market when it came to ratings. But by the mid-1970s, Channel 2's newscast had fallen on hard times. *The Big News* with Dunphy still at the helm had slid to second place in the ratings. KNXT management tried all sorts of game plans to try to reverse the trend. They paired Dunphy with a number of different co-anchors and even introduced a brand new news set. But nothing worked.

John Severino figured if he could lure Jerry Dunphy to Channel 7 and team him with a younger co-anchor, Eyewitness News would rise to the top. "Sev" (as we called him) believed that if his formula of "stealing" anchors worked in Chicago, it might work in Los Angeles as well. So in 1975, Severino quietly called Dunphy and asked to talk with him over dinner. And the plot was about to intensify. At dinner, Dunphy admitted to Severino that he wasn't happy at Channel 2. Severino suggested the veteran anchorman go tell that to KNXT general manager Russ Barry and then ask for a letter allowing Dunphy to shop his services elsewhere.

During his entire career, Jerry Dunphy never had an agent or lawyer represent him in contract talks. Dunphy always handled his own business dealings. And Jerry went in alone to see Channel 2 GM Barry and asked for the letter Severino had suggested. Several days later, Barry and Severino played a friendly tennis match as they would do from time to time. Not knowing Severino had talked with Dunphy, Barry asked the Channel 7 head if he had any interest in hiring Jerry. Severino said "no," adding that he thought Dunphy was too old and over the hill. Satisfied that KNXT wouldn't lose its top anchorman to competitor

KABC, Barry gave Dunphy the letter he was seeking. And Severino quickly signed Dunphy to a deal, even agreeing to continue to lease the expensive Rolls-Royce that Channel 2 had been paying for for Dunphy's use. After learning what had happened, a stunned Russ Barry called KABC-TV to ask Severino why he had claimed to have no interest in Dunphy. Sev replied, "I lied."

But even though Jerry Dunphy was now on the Channel 7 Eyewitness News team, our ratings went nowhere. And it remained that way for awhile. Dunphy was teamed with different co-anchors, including Chuck Henry and John Hambrick (whose brother Judd had also anchored our newscast). We even changed the opening of Eyewitness News to one in which the on-the-air people walked onto the news set in a wide shot (to emphasize "team coverage") after Dunphy had read the headlines. But nothing we did gave our ratings the shot in the arm that we needed.

Back in the weather department, it was business as usual. Our newscast schedule had changed somewhat at this point. The 4:30 p.m. news had been replaced by the *3:30 Movie*. And we were now doing one-hour newscasts at 5 and 6 p.m., with a half hour at 11 p.m. My daily routine was still the same. I continued to visit the National Weather Service in Westwood at least twice a day. I have found that you can never do enough homework to prepare for that which is important. And our viewers have always been that important to me. I also never tired of going out into our communities to meet and greet our audience . . . with a hug, a smile, and a wiggle of the nose and mustache. Winston Churchill said, "We make a living by what we get. We make a life by what we give."

When a baseball team isn't doing well in the standings, it may be time to shake things up. The manager will likely make changes to his lineup, move the batting order around, or even allow a reserve on the bench to get a chance to start. To have more of an impact, the front office could sign a free agent. And in 1975, John Severino added a talented free agent to the Channel 7 lineup. It was a move that would pay dividends for years to come.

Regis Philbin was signed to be the entertainment reporter for Eyewitness News as well as host a one-hour local morning show called *A.M. Los Angeles*. Earlier in his career, Regis had hosted his own local TV talk show in San Diego and St. Louis. In 1967, Philbin got his first national exposure when he was picked to be the sidekick on the ABC network's late night program *The Joey Bishop Show*. Thanks to Johnny Carson and *The Tonight Show*, Joey Bishop never had a chance to succeed ratings-wise. The program was cancelled after two years on air.

On *A.M. Los Angeles*, Philbin was paired with a delightful cohost, Sarah Purcell, and later, with Cyndy Garvey. But with Regis at the helm, the ratings soared to number one. *A.M. Los Angeles* was shown live in Southern California. And it was Regis Philbin at his best, as he playfully dueled with his cohosts and celebrity guests on a daily basis—live and local. It was a highly successful morning talk show formula that in the mid-1980s led Philbin to host the nationally syndicated *Live with Regis and Kathie Lee*, a New York-based program that would replace *A.M. Los Angeles* on KABC-TV in 1991. Whether it was Kathie Lee Gifford or Kelly Ripa as cohost, it was still "Live with Regis," just like it was on *A.M. Los Angeles*. Nobody in the history of television has ever logged in more time in front of a camera. The *Guinness World Records* says Philbin's mark is now at more than seventeen thousand hours. And to think "Rege" was once my teammate at Eyewitness News.

Whether he was hosting a talk show or doing a movie review for our local newscast, Regis was still Regis. And for me, he was always a delight to watch because in the tradition of Frank Sinatra, Philbin always did it "My Way." He was certainly unconventional, to say the least. Whenever Regis would go out with one of our news crews at night to cover a movie premiere, he would shoot a series of, shall we say, "schticks" with the arriving celebrities. Each one was hilarious. Regis would then bring the unedited footage back to the Eyewitness Newsroom and ask one of our talented newswriters to work with an editor, and put some of the best schticks together for his piece on the 11 p.m. news. It was something our staff looked forward to seeing every night. Regis Philbin was wonderful to have as a colleague. He made going to work fun. It still wasn't enough to make Eyewitness News number one in the ratings. But we were getting close.

KABC-TV's top management continued to look for an anchor formula that would work and push Channel 7 Eyewitness News higher in the ratings. Television stations have a wealth of information to look at in their efforts to reach such a decision. They hire consultants. They look at the latest research. They even have screenings with a test audience selected from a cross-section of viewers to gauge reaction. But sometimes it comes down to just trusting your own instincts. And when it comes to local TV news, I don't know if there's ever been anyone with better instincts than the man who succeeded Bill Fyffe as news director at Channel 7—Dennis Swanson. At one pivotal point, Swanson and John Severino decided to pair Jerry Dunphy with another co-anchor to see how that worked. You must understand that in this business when you make a decision—there are no guarantees. But when Dunphy and Christine Lund began anchoring Channel 7 Eyewitness News together—it worked like a charm.

I will be the first to admit I am anything but a genius when it comes to ratings. And when the Dunphy-Lund Eyewitness News team shot to number one, I was the last to know. My work load had me going back and forth between KABC and the National Weather Service in Westwood each day to prepare my lesson plans for our newscast. I had absolutely no idea what was happening with the ratings. But I will say this: The mood around the TV station did seem to be a lot brighter after Dunphy and Lund began anchoring our news. I vividly remember one happy executive who greeted me one day by saying, "Wonderful things are happening, George." I didn't know what he was talking about. But I certainly didn't want to ruin his spirit. So I replied with a smile: "That's nice."

Jerry and Christine were great people to work with. But we never so-cialized away from work. I was so busy preparing for my weather segments, I'm not even really sure where their individual offices were in the newsroom. On the set, we'd talk about the issues of the day just before and after the newscast. And on the air during the weather, if I got real excited about a ten-foot wave in Newport Beach, that was just fine with Jerry and Christine. If you look at the ratings, I guess we bonded with our audience pretty well. Management looked at Dunphy, Lund, and Fischbeck as a team. And when I say this, I'm certainly not trying to elevate my importance. My friends, I just do the weather. But Severino and Swanson always said that when it comes to Jerry, Christine, and Dr. George, Channel 7 Eyewitness News would have never reached first place without one or the other.

I know one thing—what a joy I was having going to work each day. I didn't know what tomorrow would bring. You know how weathermen are—they can't see more than five days ahead anyway. But let me share with you my formula for career happiness. Find a job you like so much that you would do it for nothing. Then do it.

When it comes to success, the noted philosopher and essayist Ralph Waldo Emerson had this advice: "Do not go where the path may lead. Go instead where there is no path and leave a trail." If you ever wanted to get on the road to success, you couldn't do better than to follow in the footsteps of Dennis Swanson. You talk about someone with vision. Dennis would go in a direction that others dared not go. And then he would blaze a trail to success.

For more than four decades, Swanson has achieved success in one of the most extraordinary careers television has ever seen. Ever since Swanson arrived at KABC-TV in 1976, he made things happen. At Channel 7 Eyewitness News, Dennis Swanson was the architect of its meteoric rise, laying a foundation of success that would affect our newscast for years to come. Swanson led the technological revolution that brought Eyewitness News from the film era to the modern age of mini-cams and live remotes that radically changed how we do the news.

Dennis Swanson was a disciplined former Marine captain. He was always the first to show up at the newsroom each morning—and I mean early in the morning. There were never enough hours in the day for this hard-charging executive. Swanson did things that our competition didn't have the capacity to think of first. Dennis had a favorite saying: "When others zig . . . I zag." Swanson was an innovative risk-taker when it came to knowing in his gut what stories Channel 7 needed to cover. It was Swanson who ordered reporter Wayne Satz to investigate three shootings of unarmed people by the Los Angeles Police Department, who had aroused the news director's suspicions by refusing to release information. Satz's special report on LAPD shootings and alleged racism within the department included a dramatic interview with a masked L.A. police officer who talked about cops he claimed were "extremely eager to be in a shooting." The police chief called it yellow journalism. Swanson, Satz, and his producer John Babcock (one of the Southland's finest broadcast journalists ever) earned the prestigious Peabody Award for KABC-TV.

In 1978, when Proposition 13 (the property tax initiative) ignited a volatile political debate, Dennis Swanson saw a unique opportunity.

He invited the initiative's author, the outspoken Howard Jarvis, to debate all comers on Eyewitness News each night. Swanson knew what he was doing. All of Los Angeles tuned in to watch this war of words. Our news director also invited noted political activists as Bruce Herschensohn, former Senator John Tunney, Bill Press, Al Julius, and former anchorman-turned-politician Baxter Ward to engage in lively debates and commentaries on the issues of the day. Unlike some of today's cable channels that flaunt opinions and bias as "journalism," Eyewitness News under Swanson's leadership clearly labeled the debates and commentaries so that there would be no misunderstanding with our audience as to what they were.

Wherever Dennis Swanson went, he made a difference. Following his success in Los Angeles, ABC asked Swanson to run its TV station in Chicago. And that's where Dennis discovered Oprah Winfrey. In a bold move, he gave Oprah her first daytime talk show. As president of ABC Sports, Swanson was the driving force behind one of TV sports programming's most dramatic and historic moves—convincing the Olympics to stagger its Winter and Summer Games every two years instead of four. Under his watch at WNBC-TV as president and general manager, the NBC network-owned station in New York City catapulted to number one in short order. And after overseeing operations for the entire Viacom Television group in which he revamped its forty CBS and UPN stations, Swanson is now president of station operations for Fox, where he manages the network's twenty-seven owned-and-operated stations across America including Los Angeles, New York City, Chicago, Philadelphia, Boston, and Washington, D.C. Dennis Swanson never met a challenge he didn't like. Channel 7 Eyewitness News was number three in the Los Angeles ratings when Dennis first came on board. By the time he left, KABC-TV was the top-rated newscast in Southern California—and stayed that way. His methods work. They always have. Believe me, I'm an eyewitness.

May 17, 1974, marked the dawning of a new era for local TV news. More than one hundred officers of the LAPD and SWAT team surrounded a house on 54th Street in South Central Los Angeles where soldiers of the revolutionary group the Symbionese Liberation Army (SLA) were barricaded. Three months earlier, the SLA had kidnapped newspaper heiress Patty Hearst. For several hours, police and the

SLA shot it out in an urban gunfight in which officers, the news media, and neighbors were pinned down by flying bullets. KNXT-TV was the only station that was able to get a live signal out from 54th Street with its experimental mini-cam unit. And for the next two hours, Channel 2 reporters Bill Deiz and Bob Simmons provided live dramatic coverage of one of the largest police shootouts in history. Nine thousand rounds were fired as the nation watched the remote pictures beamed back by the courageous KNXT crew of Rich Brito and Rey Hernandez.

All six SLA members in the house died in the shootout and fire. It was the first time any television station had covered a breaking news story live as it was happening by using the new mini-cam. This technology would revolutionize the way we cover news, weather, and sports. Al Primo, who pioneered the format of Eyewitness News in the 1960s, said Electronic News Gathering (ENG) allows crews to go live from more places and do it faster—right up against deadline. It gives TV newscasts the immediacy of a breaking story that newspapers can't provide.

At Channel 7 Eyewitness News, we began experimenting with mini-cams back in 1973. But this new technology was just in its infancy. We were not yet able to use it to do live remotes. The new cameras with a bulky battery weighed about forty to fifty pounds, far heavier than the 16-millimeter film cameras we were using. And the ENG camera had to be hooked to a tape deck that weighed another thirty-five pounds. A two-person crew was needed to run the camera and tape deck. And they were loaded down with a tripod and a bag that carried several five-pound batteries (the crews called them "bricks").

In the beginning, we not only couldn't electronically feed the video-tape shot in the field back to the newsroom, but our mini-cam trucks were also not equipped to edit any tape. So that meant either the crews had to drive the cassette tapes back to the Eyewitness Newsroom . . . or messengers were sent to the locations to pick up the field tapes and bring them back. Either was time-consuming. But once the cassette tapes arrived, they didn't have to be developed like film. They could be edited immediately with one of our ENG tape editors. And that saved a lot of time in getting our stories ready for air. The new mini-cam technology was also of immense help for my weather segments on Eyewitness News. Most of the footage I used in weather was still being shot on film. And that took a great deal of time delivering, processing, and editing the footage for use on air. But as we relied more on our mini-cam technology, we could actually shoot videotape of a storm at 10:30 p.m. And if the location of our mini-cam truck was close enough to the newsroom, we could still get tape of the storm on our 11 p.m. newscast. That made a big difference to me . . . and more importantly, for our viewers as well. It was so nice to be able to say on the air, "My friends, I want you to look at what we just shot for Eyewitness News."

The transformation of our news operation from all film to all tape with live capability was years in the making. It took a lot of patience, training, retraining, and dedication. Along the way, Eyewitness News got better, faster, and far more technically advanced. By the time Dennis Swanson signed on to be our news director, we had learned that the new boss doesn't like to stand still. After all, a turtle makes progress only when he sticks his neck out. And if Eyewitness News was to be live and local, Dennis Swanson couldn't wait to get there. After an initial modest investment of two mini-cam trucks with live capability, Channel 7 soon added six more to its growing remote caravan. It was a technological overhaul in which everyone on our staff—including Dr. George— had to sprint to keep up. Speed is the essence of what we do in television news. And live coverage makes it even more compelling. I'm about to tell you about the coordinated teamwork it took behind the scenes at Eyewitness News so that folks like me could say, "You are looking live."

A fully equipped mini-cam truck is designed to do live remotes from any destination where you can get a signal out to a transmitter. By now, most of our trucks had tape-editing bays so that the reporter and crew could do all of their videotape editing right there in the field. The newer ENG cameras had also been streamlined, incorporating the tape deck right into the camera. Once the reporter and the cameraperson had shot the videotape needed for the story, either the cameraperson or a second engineer would edit the tape with the reporter on the editing bay inside the truck. The completed story would then be electronically fed back to the newsroom for use within the reporter's live remote from the scene. And you can take Dr. George's word for it—that is easier said than done.

Attempting to connect a live signal from the mini-cam truck to a transmitter is like trying to insert thread through the eye of a needle. It has to be accurate. It has to be exact. And both the people in the truck and at the newsroom have to be highly trained at what they are doing. In order to establish a live signal, the truck's mast, which is equipped with a microwave transmitter, has to be extended up about forty feet. When extended, the mast kind of looks like a telephone pole. The engineer inside the truck turns the mast and its transmitter around—trying to find a mountaintop transmitter with which to connect the live signal from the mini-cam unit. KABC-TV had more mountaintop sites than any other station in Los Angeles. Having more mountaintop sites gives the mini-cam crews more targets and more flexibility in trying to connect the live signal from their trucks. News director Dennis Swanson and his team of managers had the foresight to place numerous mountaintop transmitters across the Southland near areas you would want to be able to do live remotes from. In time, our transmitters included Mount Wilson, Santiago (just north of San Diego), Palos Verdes, Point Mugu, Verdugo (near La Crescenta), and another one in the Hollywood Hills that we called "KJOI" (pronounced "k-joy") because our transmitter and receiver for that location was installed on a tower owned by a radio station with those call letters.

The engineer inside the mini-cam truck would communicate by radio with the transmission engineer in the newsroom to coordinate hooking the ENG live signal with a mountaintop transmitter. Once that connection was locked in place, the mini-cam truck would then feed its videotape to the newsroom for use in the reporter's live remote from the scene. Getting ready for the actual remote was another steep challenge in and of itself. Even though the live signal had been established, the mini-cam crew then had to connect the camera with the truck by cable. And that could mean using hundreds of feet of cable to make that connection. There were countless times in which the mini-cam truck itself could not be driven to an inaccessible location for the remote. But if you could pull enough cable from the truck to reach that location by foot . . . anything was possible. In the words of legendary coach John Wooden, "Don't let what you cannot do interfere with what you can do."

I cannot tell you how many times during my years at Channel 7 Eyewitness News I have seen our brave ENG crews and reporters do the seemingly impossible in broadcasting remotes from raging wildfires, massive floods, and other breaking emergencies. Instead of merely telling you what was happening—they wanted to show you. Sometimes our Eyewitness News crews had to do it under intolerable conditions, having to pull cable through rugged terrain, in adverse weather, or in dangerous situations. But if it meant being able to get their camera close enough to an out-of-control fire so that our viewers could be an eyewitness to the drama that was unfolding live, it was a risk worth taking. And there have been some very close calls.

It was indeed a team effort. Our live remote pictures let threatened homeowners see just how close flames were burning in their neighborhoods. Our reporters were able to inform wildfire victims where evacuation centers were being set up. These journalists out in the field were supported by assignment editors and writers in our newsroom making sure we had the latest information to share with the viewing audience. We had to be accurate. And yet, we had to be fast. Each one of us knew that these emergencies could become a matter of life and death.

Weather was a crucial part of our coverage at Channel 7. In a wildfire that is threatening homes, high winds can carry burning embers onto houses a good distance from the main fire. And the information that we gathered as a team was vital not only to potential victims, but also to the heroes on the scene trying to keep an emergency situation from becoming a deadly tragedy.

I would like to share with you a letter we received from a fire weather forecaster and disaster preparedness meteorologist after one massive fire in Southern California. The work Sylvia Graff did was invaluable to the courageous firefighters who risk their lives to protect you and me. In reading this letter, please understand that even though Sylvia mentions me by name, this is a thank-you note to each and every member of the Channel 7 Eyewitness News team. My friends, I'm not being humble. I'm just proud to have the honor of calling them my teammates.

> *Dr. George has been of tremendous help to me while I was assigned to some of the many Southern California forest fires. There have been numerous occasions when the equipment has failed . . . leaving me without a current*

500 millibar chart for guidance. But Dr. George, bless his heart, comes to the rescue. I have taken a small TV with me to fires in the hope of being able to receive Channel 7.

And for approximately 75 percent of the time, I have been successful in getting Dr. George, the 500 millibar chart, and his in-depth coverage . . . and the plus of seeing the satellite pictures.

In particular, I would like to mention the Sage Fire of September 1979. My equipment failed. And Dr. George gave me the necessary information that allowed me to provide a correct forecast for the firefighters. I almost made an incorrect forecast based on no data. I shudder at the thought of lives that could be lost because of the firefighters planning an attack based on an incorrect forecast because of little or no data.

Dr. George's presentations have been invaluable. I thank you for your programming . . . and most of all, for having a TV weathercaster that really cares.

Sylvia K. Graff
Fire Weather Forecaster
Disaster Preparedness Meteorologist
National Weather Service Forecast Office

I hope that in this chapter I have been able to take you beyond what you saw on Eyewitness News for a look at the dedicated people that make up the roster of our team. I have never worked alongside anyone that has cared so much. I'm supposed to be a teacher. But I will carry the lessons I have learned from these teammates for the rest of my life. If you ever wondered why I sometimes appeared to be so excited during our newscasts at Channel 7—now you know. I had a lot to be excited about. I was so blessed to be a part of the team at Channel 7 Eyewitness News. A wise person named Ryunosuke Satoro once said, "Individually, we are one drop. Together, we are an ocean."

Porterville—A Love Story

A smile is the light in your window that tells others
that there is a caring, sharing person inside.
~ DENIS WAITLEY ~

I want to share with you the greatest success story I have had the privilege of seeing unfold before my very eyes. It is about a blessing that is located far from the big city, nestled in the foothills of the San Joaquin Valley, fifty miles north of Bakersfield. What happens there won't make banner headlines in your morning metropolitan newspaper. It won't be breaking news on the evening local TV newscast. But the people who work there perform miracles on a daily basis, making a difference for those desperately in need, who would have otherwise been lost and forgotten.

It's been said that the worth of society is measured by how it treats its weakest and most vulnerable. And I want to tell you about a community asset—a civic treasure—that has become a beacon in the harbor of hopelessness. I have seen firsthand the compassion and tireless dedication of visionaries who took the time to light a candle in the darkness of life for those who are helpless. The Porterville State Hospital (now called the Porterville Developmental Center) has been home to nine thousand severely mentally and physically challenged people with permanent disabilities. For twenty years, I had the honor of taking part in a most worthy cause—Dr. George's Toys for Porterville campaign for KABC-TV in Los Angeles. It was a Christmas program that brought joy and happiness to the residents of Porterville year-round. But Channel 7's participation in this cherished project started long before our viewers across Southern California even knew that I existed.

This special partnership began in December of 1962. The news director and anchor of Channel 7 News, Baxter Ward, may have had a seemingly gruff exterior, but inside that man beat the heart of a humanitarian. Baxter had a friend whose child was developmentally disabled and had been admitted to the residential treatment program at Porterville State Hospital. One day, Ward decided to pay a visit to this six-hundred-acre facility near the Sierra Nevada Mountains in Tulare County.

What this veteran journalist saw that day touched his heart in an immeasurable way. Baxter Ward was an eyewitness to several thousand profoundly disabled people who might have had little hope for the future had it not been for a staff of caring and loving individuals dedicated to bringing them back into the mainstream with productive lives—against all odds. Even though the patients (called "residents") ranged in age from babies to seniors, most of them had the mental capacity of three years in age. It was Christmas time. And Baxter couldn't help notice that the residents had no toys to play with. A facility funded by the state budget could only go so far. Baxter Ward decided to open a door and create a program that would become a Christmas tradition at KABC-TV for three decades. And the Toys for Porterville campaign was born.

Now in any partnership, you have to have partners. Baxter knew he couldn't do it alone. But he also knew where to go for help—and did Channel 7 News viewers ever respond. Each year by the time Baxter Ward had delivered his month-long Christmas message for Porterville on his newscast, the station had collected enough toys to fill an entire moving van. An inspirational woman named Sally

Koch had this food for thought: "Great opportunities to help others seldom come. But small ones surround us every day."

When I signed on to be a member of the Eyewitness News team in 1972, I was asked to fill Baxter Ward's shoes in the Toys for Porterville program. At first, it was a challenge that seemed daunting to me because Baxter had been such a godsend to the residents of Porterville. Then again, I saw it as a wonderful opportunity to spread the word: "Be a giver, not a taker." Goodness knows, the world needs it. And our viewers' response continued in such an amazing way that perhaps even Ripley wouldn't have believed it! I was a mere part of the teamwork that came together during the holiday season to make Toys for Porterville a success. Each December, Channel 7 Eyewitness News unselfishly devoted airtime on every newscast to promoting the Porterville campaign during the entire month. And this investment by KABC-TV brought returns to those in need that were priceless.

Porterville may be located in Central California, but thanks to our station's corporate partners, we brought it as close as your local McDonald's restaurants and later, hundreds of Baskin-Robbins ice cream shops throughout the Southland. That's where huge boxes were set up so that our viewers could bring a new and unwrapped toy and drop it off for our special friends at Porterville. The generosity of our Channel 7 audience defied description. You talk about a network of angels—our viewers donated every kind of toy you could conceivably think of. They gave bicycles, roller skates, balls, recreational equipment, dolls, radios, musical instruments, clothing, room decorations, coloring books, tape machines, and records. The Cub Scouts of Pack 81 in Brentwood actually made their own toys for Porterville, and hundreds of Scouts throughout Greater Los Angeles followed suit.

A group of caring architecture students at Cal Poly Pomona took the time and the love to make specially designed toys for our beloved family at Porterville. And when their instructor transferred to Cal Poly San Luis Obispo, his students there designed and created toys to donate as well. Channel 7 Eyewitness News reporter/anchor Warren Olney remembers mentioning on the air one morning about a need for a piano at Porterville. And our viewers enthusiastically responded with fifteen pianos and organs. The wonderful folks who watch Eyewitness News never let us down when it was time to give from their hearts. Someone even donated two horses, which brought such delight to the residents through the equestrian therapy program at Porterville and helped teach them balance and coordination.

Now of course, giving was a vital part of our Toys for Porterville program. Collecting all the donated toys was another story. I don't know what we would have done if it hadn't been for members of the citizens band radio group REACT, who went out across the Southland and picked up all of our collection boxes and brought them to the parking lot of KABC-TV the last weekend just before Christmas each year. We had enough toys to fill not one but three moving vans for the trip to Porterville. And we had a "Santa Claus" named Bill Maxwell, the owner of Ace Moving in Long Beach, who provided the moving vans and drivers for more than twenty years to transport our toys all the way to Porterville.

I will never forget my very first Christmas at the Porterville State Hospital in 1972, when I had the honor of delivering our viewers' many presents to these most wonderful residents who I will always cherish and love. My friends, all of you who gave and gave taught me a most important lesson during my initial Toys for Porterville campaign. Life is indeed a gift that should be celebrated each day. And our viewers— you're heroes in my book—are proof that there are no limits to what the human spirit can truly achieve.

Two days after Christmas in 1972, I received a heartwarming letter from the man who represented the 5th District on the Los Angeles County Board of Supervisors. You may remember him as the Good Samaritan who started the Toys for Porterville campaign years before. He was so gracious.

> *Dear Dr. Fischbeck,*
>
> *I am in your debt because of the handsome manner in which you and your people responded to the need of the patients at Porterville State Hospital. You were spectacularly successful.*
>
> *And I share the enthusiasm of the staff there for a remarkable success in a task that used to take me twice as long . . . and still gather only half as many toys.*

Please accept my best wishes for the year ahead.

Sincerely,
Baxter Ward

Then there is the unsung hero who was indeed the most valuable teammate of the "Toys for Porterville" campaign over the years. You never saw him on the air at Channel 7 Eyewitness News. In fact, you probably wouldn't recognize him in a police lineup wearing a name tag. But you know his work. You have seen his love. And you have been touched by his unwavering dedication to this project.

His name is Steve Skootsky. As this book is being written, Steve is still making a difference at ABC7 Eyewitness News in Los Angeles, where he has been the best newswriter that I've ever seen for some forty years now. And "Skoots" poured his heart and soul into bringing the story of Porterville to our audience for so many years. In order to ask our viewers to give to our toys campaign, we had have to give them a reason. Steve Skootsky gave them that reason. He was my producer. Each year, Steve would bring an Eyewitness News camera crew to Porterville. And he captured the story of Porterville on film with touching images that made such an indelible impression.

Steve's mini-documentaries on Porterville State Hospital were presented on Channel 7 throughout the month of December and were not aimed at bringing in high ratings. This wasn't journalism that was "fair and balanced." When it came to Porterville, we were as biased as we could be. There was only one side to this issue: the courageous story of permanently disabled patients who had developed such a zest to succeed and not allow their downward spiral to become even steeper and darker. Through Steve Skootsky's efforts each year, we were able to show our audience the small victories that are achieved every day at Porterville . . . so that our viewers and their generosity could help connect the dots and turn those victories into miracles.

You see, being disabled doesn't mean that you don't have the ability to learn. And Porterville staff members have worked with the residents for years on end to find the key to tap into their hidden potential. There was one resident I remember named James who couldn't talk. But through the use of a language machine, a speech therapist was able to teach James to respond by punching a button to create images. I was there when James actually learned to communicate with others through these images that he chose on the language machine.

And how about the success story involving a patient named Gary who not only couldn't talk, he could only respond to someone by making sounds. But I was there when speech pathologist Marge Purbin had the time and patience to try to teach Gary how he could turn those sounds into a single word. Yes—the progress can be painstakingly slow. But Marge Purbin's loving efforts—this hero—helped Gary earn a great victory in his battle to communicate. Marge said she tried and tried and tried so hard to teach Gary to speak. And finally, Gary looked at Marge and said "nuts." Marge Purbin was overjoyed! It may have been just one word, but it was a start. My goodness—Marge called it earth-shattering! And that's a win I was able to celebrate with the good folks who watch Eyewitness News.

My friends, let me tell you about another achievement at Porterville State Hospital that the audience of Channel 7 made possible. Our viewers donated so many animals to Porterville, the staff was able to set up a place of joy called Camp Vandalia. That's where the residents could visit an enclosed petting zoo with horses, ponies, turkeys, sheep, and a donkey. An aviary center was also established. During one of my visits, a mother hen and her baby chicks had just moved in. The residents not only learned how to take care of the animals, they were also able to go fishing at a pond. A greenhouse was built where the residents grew plants that could be sold to the public. The more they could touch and feel, the more they could experience and grow. The residents get paid for doing this work. And it teaches them to be self-proficient. That's why Camp Vandalia became such a wonderful part of the on-going therapy at Porterville.

There are so many things in life that you and I take for granted—abilities that for the residents at Porterville have become a steep challenge they are forced to deal with every moment of every day. But love can move mountains at Porterville, especially on those days when the impossible is transformed into a rewarding experience. I was there when the blind were taught to run with the help of a guide rope in preparation for the Special Olympics, where everyone who takes part is a winner. In the beginning, many of the blind residents would sit huddled in a corner, refusing to come out. The blind can have such a fear of taking chances—afraid of falling down. But staff members work endlessly with the blind to build self-confidence. It can take months, even years to accomplish. But you can't help but be touched by the smiles on their faces and the glow of their spirit as they run. Recreational therapist Linda Stevens said there is such a great reward in being able to teach the residents a new skill that they had never before even had a chance to learn. And once they learned it, the residents had the enjoyment of being able to say, "Hey, I can do it too!"

There wasn't a dry eye in the newsroom at Channel 7 when we aired a heartfelt segment on the littlest of Porterville patients who will never escape being held captive in a life rubbed raw by their disabilities. I visited Porterville's baby ward where the children command constant attention. I walked over to one bed where an infant girl lay motionless amid her beloved stuffed animals that our viewers had donated. This little treasure didn't have the physical ability or strength to move her head and look at me. A loving nurse had to gently do it for her. And I got to shake her tiny hand. It was a touching scene that reminded me no matter how far down any of us are on the ladder of achievement . . . there is a spirit that will always guide us into reaching for that next rung. At Porterville, I was so proud at how often these residents would make it.

Then there was the miracle of little Tessie. She, too, will never know what it's like to be a healthy child. Her sunshine has been dimmed by a disability that will probably entrap her for the rest of her life. But there's never been a shortage of tender loving care at Porterville. I was there when teacher Joyce Christiansen worked so patiently with this bedridden infant to see if she could hit a small ball for Dr. George. Tessie was able to tap the ball with her little hand in a giant victory that put a smile on my face that will never leave my heart. And my friends, guess where that ball came from? These are your gifts that keep on giving. It's been said that the real secret of happiness is not what you have or what you receive. It's what you share.

Someone once asked me if I could describe our greatest accomplishment during all the years Channel 7 Eyewitness News sponsored the Toys for Porterville campaign. You know, it hasn't got anything to do with what we at Channel 7 may have accomplished. We were merely reporting on the victories that were being won by the real heroes of Porterville. One major figure in this success story is Gary Johnson, who retired as Porterville's program director after devoting thirty-nine years of his life toward making the developmental center a happy home for its residents. Johnson says KABC-TV through its Toys for Porterville campaign sent a positive message to our viewing audience about people with disabilities . . . and how they can be treated and embraced so their lives can be made better.

You want to talk about heroes? How about Ruth Butler, who gave from her heart to serving the Porterville facility for forty-five years. Ruth can tell you what motivates someone to stay year after year, caring so much to reach out and give hope to the hopeless. Ruth says it touches your heart to see a little child who is disabled take that first step—and smile at you. What a connection! As Ruth told me, it's a feeling that is indescribable, like seeing a baby's reaction to a beautiful flower. That's why Ruth Butler fell in love with Porterville and stayed for four and a half decades.

But there are other reasons for this everlasting dedication. Music therapist Carol Robinson says faith led her to form a very special relationship with the residents. Carol gives all the credit to the Lord, saying she came to Porterville because that's where God wanted her to be. Lydia Brumley, who served as the assistant director of Camp Vandalia, retired after working more than a quarter of a century at Porterville. Lydia described it as a very rewarding occupation, because you learn to love the children. But it's mutual. As Lydia told me—the kids never forget you.

So many helping hands contributed to the success of this developmental center. A group of local women called the Council of Volunteers opened a thrift store in Porterville. It raised more than $20,000 a year that helped pay for items like draperies in the residential buildings, things the hospital's budget just couldn't afford. And those of us at Channel 7 never knew who might be watching our coverage of the Porterville story. A college sorority in San Jose was so deeply touched, the students decided to sponsor an entire building of the hospital with a generous financial donation each year to help pay the cost of living quarters for a number of the residents. And then there was the young man who never forgot the images of Porterville that he saw as a child watching Eyewitness News. And he decided to make an enduring investment. For more than a decade, Dr. Sean Fleming has practiced medicine at the Porterville Developmental Center. A man named Norman B. Rice who devoted his life to seeking solutions said, "Dare to reach out your hand into the darkness, to pull another hand into the light."

Thanks to the people who cared at Porterville, thousands upon thousands of severely disabled patients have been able to return to their communities with productive lives guided by supervision. For some two decades, I had a front row seat to watch the Porterville team reach out to those who have been abandoned by society with a life in confusion and a résumé of despair. They are nothing less than miracle workers who believe that for anyone to achieve, they must first be given the opportunity to try. I know what I've seen. And I am in awe. I have a special place in my heart for the viewers of Eyewitness News who always answered our plea for help with compassion.

My friends, I would like to share with you a benediction that symbolizes the love and spirit of Porterville, and the most valuable human beings who turned certain defeat into the greatest victory of all. "May God bless you with tears to shed for those who suffer pain, rejection, starvation, and want . . . so that you may reach out your hand to comfort them, and to turn their pain into joy. And may God bless you with enough foolishness to believe that you can make a difference in this world . . . so that you can do what others claim cannot be done."

Under the Weather—
Taking L.A. by Storm

I've never seen Dr. George blasé about anything.
Not only does he read the weather . . . he lives it.

~ ARTHUR LESSARD ~

National Weather Service

I was once quoted by *People* magazine as saying that I love my job doing the weather so much, it's embarrassing to get paid for it. But it does have a downside. Every time someone wants to make fun of local TV news, it seems the weather person is usually their first target. Maybe it dates back to comedian George Carlin and his take on the Hippy Dippy Weatherman. "Tonight's forecast: dark. Continued dark throughout most of the evening . . . with some widely scattered light toward morning." Legendary talk show host David Letterman began his career as a weatherman on an Indianapolis TV station—where he would humorously congratulate a tropical storm for being promoted to a hurricane. A couple of famous actresses got their start in television weather. Jackie Joseph, who played the love interest of Ernest T. Bass on *The Andy Griffith Show*, was one of the KTTV "Weather Girls" on its Channel 11 News in 1961. Jackie was "Miss Monday." And a former La Jolla High School cheerleader named Raquel Tejada worked as a "weather girl" for News 8 in San Diego at the age of eighteen. She went on to become better known as Raquel Welch.

In Los Angeles, a stand-up comedian (Fritz Coleman) and a rock and roll disc jockey (Garth Kemp) have both become popular weathermen in local TV news. Another Southland weather forecaster (Pat Sajak) has gone on to host the longest-running syndicated game show in television history. Did you know that one of the most highly respected journalists in the world—ABC News anchor Diane Sawyer—got her start in TV news by doing the weather for WLKY Channel 32 in Louisville, Kentucky? In 2004 and 2009, one Southern California TV station held well-publicized auditions for viewers to do the weather, with the winner being given a short on-the-air contract. And you may have thought the weather forecast was going to the dogs on one local TV newscast in Texas. That's where Stormy the Weather Dog was trained to walk over and press a button that activated a graphic detailing the latest weather for the viewing audience. And if I'm going to poke fun at others, I might as well point at myself. In the mid-1970s when I went on vacation for one week, I was replaced on the Channel 7 Eyewitness News Weather by such celebrities as Mr. Blackwell, comedians Rich Little and Louis Nye, and famed ventriloquist Paul Winchell. I rushed back from vacation after learning that someone named "Knucklehead" was doing my job!

You know, after spending twenty-three years as an instructor in public schools, I found that humor is an excellent teaching device. When I first appeared on Channel 7 Eyewitness News in 1972, many of our viewers in Los Angeles thought I was putting on an act with my outbursts of enthusiasm. That was no act. It's the same thing that I did in the classroom all those years. I always believed that if I could put some fun in my lesson plans, it would help my students pay attention. Never underestimate the power of a smile. And even when I was doing the weather at KABC-TV, I was an educator at heart. I considered my role to be that of teacher to student, looking into the camera and making that one-on-one connection.

You could say I was just moonlighting when I did the weather. My real profession was teaching—a science teacher for school kids. But weather and science are connected. Weather forecasting is the scientific study of our atmosphere. Even though I tried to be a breath of fresh air on the news, I took my duties of gathering information about the weather very seriously. As a teacher, I wanted our Eyewitness News viewers to know why weather is important and how it could affect their personal lives. Like any class I have ever taught, I needed to prepare a lesson plan for my weather segments. And that meant doing my homework—and lots of it. There wasn't a single day on the job at Channel 7 that I didn't visit the National Weather Service in Westwood at least twice daily—and make frequent checks by phone as well, especially late at night. My attitude was no one should have warmed-over 6 p.m. weather on the news at 11.

Mark Twain once said, "If you don't like the weather in New England, just wait a few minutes." But to many people, the weather in Los Angeles is boring. Yes, many days my weather segments on Channel 7 would be nestled in the middle of the newscast with a mild forecast that might look like a repeat of the day before. No drama there, my friends. But that was not always the case. There are days when Southern California has to brace for heavy rain that can trigger massive flooding and mudslides . . . or strong winds that can rip roofs off buildings and homes, uproot huge trees, and topple big rigs. And coastal residents are rendered absolutely helpless when the ocean moves in. I've seen high waves destroy homes and ruin lives from Malibu to Newport Beach.

Bad weather does not discriminate. It doesn't matter if you're rich or poor, famous or unknown. It is equal opportunity. Everyone is affected. And our ratings soared when the weather made news. It was our responsibility to inform our viewers about any impending problems. And whenever my weather segment was moved to the top of our newscast, our Channel 7 Eyewitness News camera crews were able to show you live pictures from the areas that were heavily affected. We shared the latest information from our reporters at the scene and our superb news-gathering staff in the newsroom.

Weather is made up of changes in the atmosphere that surrounds us. Some changes are slow and can take months or even years to develop. But it's that relationship . . . the atmosphere around us . . . that affects our daily and future lives. All things—the sun, the air, and water—go into making up our weather. And they are always in motion and changing. Sunshine changes liquid water in the oceans and lakes into humidity in the air. As the air rises and cools, clouds are formed. The moisture in the air clings to particles and forms drops. And we have rain—which falls only to be reevaporated. Then the cycle begins again.

Because we live in this atmosphere, we are affected by all changes, small and large. It affects our daily lives—everything from what we do for a living, to our housing, and even to how we dress our children for school. As a forecaster on TV, I was always asked questions by our viewers about how the weather might affect some special event they were planning, if it would be cold, hot, or rainy on their wedding day, graduation day, or family picnic. They would want to know if the weather would allow them to go sailing, surfing, flying, or engage in other outdoor activities. I was even been asked on a number of occasions if the grunion would be running on a certain night.

In the Los Angeles area, you can have vastly different weather conditions depending on where you live. For example, the weather along the coast usually varies a great deal from what's happening in downtown L.A., the San Fernando Valley, and the deserts. The on-shore, off-shore flow where the ocean weather meets the inland areas changes constantly. It can be cloudy, foggy, and downright cold along Southland beaches. However, the World Meteorological Organization has officially declared Death Valley in the Mojave Desert as the hottest place on Earth.

During my long career at Channel 7 Eyewitness News, I regularly wrote a "Dr. George Newsletter" to youngsters who had dreams of growing up to become weather forecasters. To a teacher like me, it was a special classroom in which I could share my lessons with our younger viewers. One of my favorite subjects in my newsletter: what is meteorology? This may surprise you. But meteorology is not a study of the weather but rather of the changes in the Earth's atmosphere that happen to produce our weather. The sky can be divided into two areas: Astronomy studies space above the atmosphere and its objects, and meteorology studies the atmosphere and its appearance due to clouds, impurities, and phenomena such as wind pressure and temperatures.

To be completely honest, you and I are really just amateur meteorologists (unlike the experts at the National Weather Service), depending upon our understanding and enthusiasm. But, my friends, you can begin enhancing your knowledge of meteorology just by observing the beauty of a sunset or the awe of a thundercloud. Watch our weather's changing patterns. Photography can be of immense help, as can utilizing simple weather instruments. Take notes and keep records, so that when someone says, "It's cold today," you can reply, "It's nothing compared to what it was on April second." That's when you start becoming a real meteorologist.

Now let's take a few moments to raise your weather IQ. Air pressure is one of the most highly influential aspects of our weather. In forecasting weather changes, air pressure is important in making those predictions. Our atmosphere is a blanket of air that goes all around the earth. Gravity is the force that keeps the air in our atmosphere close to earth. For example, if there were no gravity, you and I would be weightless, floating above the ground like our astronauts in space. Gravity pulls things back to earth. As the gravity pulls air down, the changes in air pressure bring changes to our weather. It's important to note that air pressure is not the same across the earth.

High pressure systems will usually produce mostly clear skies and dry weather. The change in temperature between day and night is normally greater in high pressure because there are no clouds to trap the heat when the sun goes down. Therefore, it gets a lot cooler at night. A low pressure system will mean we will have more clouds and a higher chance of rain. Meteorologists use a scientific instrument called a barometer to measure the atmospheric pressure. You can buy a good barometer for prices ranging between $50 and $250. When the barometer is rising, air pressure is increasing, which will usually indicate fair weather and winds that are calmer. When the barometer is falling, air pressure is decreasing, which will result in more clouds, stronger winds, and an increased chance of rain. So to my fellow forecasters—if your barometer reading is higher, we should have dry pleasant weather. If your barometer reading is lower, clouds and stormy weather could be on the way. But if your barometer reading is steady, you shouldn't expect any immediate changes in your local weather.

Most professional meteorologists use a mercury barometer, which is considered far more accurate than an aneroid barometer.

Here on earth, weather is a never-ending show. There are several things that are vital in producing Earth's weather. The sun is our energy source. In fact, scientists say the sun is the biggest supplier of energy to our planet's surface. The sun's radiation moves across space. When it strikes the molecules of gas that surround earth, the energy causes them to move faster. And that gives us moving weather, like storm fronts, hurricanes, and winds.

But have you ever wondered why there isn't any weather on the moon? In order to have weather, you must have an atmosphere. No air? No weather. The moon receives sunshine from the sun. But it doesn't have an atmosphere. Because there isn't any air, the moon has no weather. The moon is basically a satellite of rock and dust that orbits Earth. However, our moon is the fifth largest in the entire solar system. Even though the moon has no weather, you could describe its conditions as sunny, dry, hot, and cold—with no air, which means there's also no wind. When our Apollo astronauts walked on the moon, they left footprints that will remain for thousands of years. Since the moon has no weather, there is nothing like wind gusts that could erase those footprints. But even though there is no weather on the moon, it can still get as hot as 250 degrees during the day and as cold as 385 degrees below zero at night. That's because the moon has no atmosphere that can block any of the sun's rays in daytime or help trap some of that heat when it turns to night. In case you're thinking of making a trip to the moon in hopes of becoming the first space meteorologist—be advised that only twelve people have ever walked on the moon in the history of humankind. And that's one exclusive club.

In the film *L.A. Story*, Steve Martin portrayed a television weatherman who videotaped his forecast several days in advance acting on the thought that Los Angeles basically has no change in the weather. That made for a very funny movie. But that is a world of make-believe and not reality. Over the years, weather forecasting has advanced with modern technology. And television meteorologists need a wealth of knowledge, the smartest computers, radar, and satellites to keep a station's ever-changing weather reports up-to-date and accurate around the clock in Southern California.

At KABC-TV, the presentation of the weather has a long and rich tradition at Eyewitness News. For twenty years, I was so blessed to have a job where I could teach our Los Angeles viewers about the 500-millibar chart, what a coastal eddy might bring to our area, and how an ever-persistent inversion layer could affect the forecast. But it took a real team to cover our local weather at Channel 7. And I formed a special partnership with two of the finest meteorologists who have ever graced the airwaves. They both became signature weather personalities so well-known and popular among our viewers, you only have to say their first names—Dallas and Johnny—to know who I'm talking about. They were my teammates. They became my friends. We learned from each other. And the individual willingness to share and encourage paid collective dividends. As author Margaret Carty once said, "The nice thing about teamwork is that you always have others on your side."

In the year 1978, I was asked to visit our sister ABC station in Chicago and appear as a guest meteorologist on its local newscast. When I walked onto the news set, I met a young man who was about to become my friend for life. His name was Johnny Mountain. He was the station's weatherman, and he'd come to Chicago after years working on television in his native Tennessee. Johnny and I bonded almost immediately. During a private conversation, Johnny told me that he was unhappy with changes that had been taking place at the Chicago station. I suggested that a change of scenery might give his weather career a more positive forecast. And I promised to keep in touch.

Once I arrived back in Los Angeles, I put in a good word for Johnny with KABC-TV's top management. He may have already been on their radar because it wasn't long before Johnny Mountain became a member of our Eyewitness News weather team. He didn't know it at the time, but Johnny was about to begin a journey at Channel 7 that was going to last twenty-seven years in one of the most enduring careers in Los Angeles television history. And there is a reason—Johnny is an extremely likeable person. What viewers saw on the air is the way Johnny is off the air as well. He is funny, laid-back, generous in spirit, and a joy to work with. Johnny was the ultimate team player, willing to do whatever job the team wanted him to do. Wherever there was a need, Johnny Mountain filled that need. He did the weather for every shift around the clock, weekdays and weekends, night and day.

Johnny has a wonderful personality. He was also called on to help fill in as host of the morning show *A.M. Los Angeles*, a new afternoon talk show called *330*, and a number of local magazine shows that KABC-TV produced and aired. In a word, Johnny Mountain was invaluable.

Johnny was finally given a regular work shift that really wasn't "regular." Monday through Friday, Johnny would do the weather for Eyewitness News at 6 a.m. (which in time became 5 and 6 a.m.), the news at 11:30 a.m., and then return for the 5 p.m. news that evening. He did it for years and years. But Johnny never complained. He was such a delight in our workplace. On one early morning newscast, Johnny did his live weather reports in a remote broadcast from the Los Angeles Zoo. During one segment, Johnny allowed zoo officials to wrap an entire snake around him. The producer in the control booth back at the station was scared of snakes, so he hid his eyes during Johnny's "snake" remote. At one point, the producer asked, "What are Johnny and the snake doing now?" And the director said, "They're looking at each other." As you can see, Johnny got along with everybody.

In 2005, Johnny Mountain "retired" from KABC-TV—only to re-surface at crosstown KCBS, where he finished a nearly unprecedented thirty-two year career doing the weather on Los Angeles television news. Johnny loved working at Channel 7 Eyewitness News. But at Channel 2, he was assigned to do his forecasting on the evening 5, 6, and 11 p.m. newscasts. My longtime friend looked like a man with a new lease on life as he was finally able to sleep in for the first time in years.

On January 24, 2009, I was honored by the Radio and Television News Association of Southern California at its 59th Annual Golden Mike ceremonies. And Johnny Mountain was selected to be my pre-senter as I received the prestigious Lifetime Achievement Award. Having Johnny there made one of the most cherished moments in my life even more meaningful. My goodness, it was so special. It's been said that truly great friends are hard to find, difficult to leave, and impossible to forget.

When it comes to forecasting weather, I guess you could say that Johnny Mountain and I are kind of from the "old school" of broadcast-ing. And in the mid-1980s, the management of KABC-TV went look-ing for someone a bit younger who would be able to carry the weather torch for Eyewitness News into the twenty-first century and beyond. The year was 1984 when a personable young man named Dallas Raines first reported for work in the Channel 7 weather department. He was bright, friendly, and a heck of a lot more handsome than Johnny and me. Dallas came to us from Cable News Network (CNN). Several years earlier, the ABC network had come calling wanting to hire Dallas away. But Ted Turner, with all the persuasion he could muster, personally convinced Dallas to stay at CNN. When his contract was up, Dallas came to Los Angeles. And a new chapter was about to begin at KABC-TV.

In the beginning, Dallas Raines was assigned to work weekends on Eyewitness News. And you couldn't help but like him. Dallas told the *Los Angeles Times* he was down in the dumps one day in the weather department. But he says I came in with my hand over my heart and gave a "Dr. George" pep talk about the weather. Dallas told *Times* media columnist James Rainey, "I thought, if this man can get that excited . . . then at 28, I can get excited and put some enthusiasm into it too."

It was obvious that KABC management was preparing Dallas for bigger and better things. And I've been asked how I felt watching him possibly being groomed as my heir apparent doing the weather on Eyewitness News. I was sixty-two when Dallas first came on board. At the time, our anchor, Jerry Dunphy, was regarded as the elder statesman of local TV news in Los Angeles. And I was only one year and twenty-one days younger than Jerry. So I figured it was only natural that Channel 7 would have a younger relief pitcher warming up in the weather bullpen.

In all honesty, I do admit that it would have deeply bothered me if I saw that I was being succeeded down the road by someone who didn't have the proper weather credentials. But that's not what happened. Are you kidding me? Dallas Raines is more qualified to do the weather than anyone else who has ever attempted to give a forecast in Los Angeles TV news. Dallas is a graduate of Florida State University (oh, does he love the Seminoles football team!), where he studied earth science and meteorology. He has completed a vast landscape of graduate level work in climatology. And "Professor" Dallas has even taught a number of meteorology classes at Cal State Northridge.

Yes, I noticed that the KABC-TV website asked Eyewitness News viewers to vote for their favorite Dallas Raines on-the-air signature body moves when doing the weather, like the "Pump," the "Swing," and the "Whirl." I think it's fun! And if it gets viewers involved—that's even better. I remember one time bringing in a real live lion cub and a lamb into the studio to feature in my weather segment because I wanted to get our viewers' attention. And in doing so, I could teach them some important weather information that day. As a teacher and as a weatherman, I worked hard each day to prepare my lesson plan. But I needed our audience's attention when I delivered my lesson. And it worked—the ratings bear me out. And for more than a quarter of a century, Dallas Raines has continued this success. Boy, has he ever! Dallas has that unique combination of knowledge, technology, and personality in presenting a weather report that is both entertaining and informative. His segments on ABC7 are watched by far more viewers than any other station in Los Angeles. I was a proud part of that tradition. And my friends, it couldn't be in better hands.

I cannot possibly write a chapter about doing the weather without sharing one of my most rewarding experiences at Channel 7. And it involves someone in our weather department that you never saw on the air at Eyewitness News. Then again, you couldn't have helped but see this person's oh-so-valuable contributions to what I did. In 1981, a young woman who had been working as a page for the ABC network was assigned to be my assistant in the newsroom. Dianne Barone was twenty-one at the time, and she was attending college majoring in art design. When Dianne reported for work that first day, she had absolutely no background in television news or the weather. In the beginning, this bright assistant did whatever she could to try to help. She handled my mail and phone calls. She ran errands for the weather department throughout the station. Whatever odds and ends there were to do—Dianne Barone did them with enthusiasm. And she couldn't have been more loyal.

But at some point during our six years together, the small office that Dianne and I shared with Dallas and Johnny became a classroom. In Dianne's words, I was the teacher, and she was the "sponge." A man of knowledge named Anthony J. D'Angelo said, "Develop a passion for learning. If you do, you will never cease to grow." And over time, Dianne grew by leaps and bounds at Eyewitness News, going from being my assistant to becoming my virtual producer. There wasn't anything in the world of broadcast weather that she didn't absorb.

Dianne had an insatiable thirst for expanding her education as well. She studied oceanography at Glendale College (later renamed Glendale Community College), climatology at Los Angeles City College, and meteorology at UCLA. And just like Dr. George, Dianne learned the value of going to the National Weather Service office in Westwood, where the experts taught her how to put a forecast together from the ground up. Dianne was more than capable of doing everything even the most veteran of TV meteorologists had to do in putting an entire weather segment together. At Eyewitness News, she made us better— a whole lot better.

And that's when Dianne Barone decided to take the most important step in her young career and pursue a dream. Armed with a half-dozen audition tapes and a huge book with the address and phone number of every television station in the nation, Dianne left Los Angeles, the only home she had ever known. And she went job hunting across America with no agent to represent her. First stop—Harlingen, Texas, the 117th biggest TV market in the country. Dianne was hired to do the weather at a station where the pay was so low, she had to moonlight ironing shirts to make ends meet. But this rookie was now laying a foundation for success with a personal forecast that was bright and sunny.

Ten months later, Dianne moved to a bigger market in Spokane, Washington—where her hard work on local TV news paved the way for a spot on the Weather Channel in Atlanta, and a national audience of up to 57 million viewers. But who says you can't go home again? In 1991, KCAL-TV News in Los Angeles was looking for a new weather forecaster. And Jerry Dunphy, who was now anchoring Channel 9's news, told news director Bob Henry about a former assistant to Dr. George at Channel 7 Eyewitness News who might be perfect for the job. And from 1991 to 1998, Dianne Barone became an award-winning meteorologist for KCAL-TV in Southern California, earning a well-deserved two Emmys and three Golden Mike Awards for her remarkable work.

I cannot possibly convey through mere words how proud I am to see my former "assistant" become so accomplished. During our time together at Channel 7 Eyewitness News, I hope I was able to be an encouragement so that her dreams and aspirations might come true. When Dianne learned that I was writing this book, she asked if she could share her thoughts as well:

One would always walk away from watching a Dr. George weather segment knowing a little bit of something. And it was mostly something interesting. His excitement and enthusiasm is contagious. What does Dr. George mean to me? Opportunity . . . inspiration . . . motivation . . . passion. What he taught me, I utilized everyday on the air. No ego. The weather was always the star.

~ Dianne Barone

As you can see, Dianne is so gracious. And let me tell you one more thing about her—she is indeed a pioneer. When Dianne Barone decided to depart Channel 7 Eyewitness News in the mid-1980s and seek a career forecasting the weather on the air, it was an occupation that was completely male-dominated. At the time, you didn't see women doing the weather on TV. It took courage for someone like Dianne to try to walk through that door. She didn't have an agent leading the way. But Dianne had the guts and unwavering determination to do it. There are now a number of female weather forecasters across the dial throughout the Southland. And each one of them owes a deep debt of gratitude to Dianne for opening that door ahead of them.

Pulitzer Prize–winning journalist Al Martinez wrote in the *Los Angeles Times* in praise of Dianne's work: " . . . shepherding us through drought and storm with an equanimity of spirit rare among weather reporters. She gave us rain and sunshine without judgment in a manner that concealed no secret desire to be either a stand-up comic or a circus clown." And in another Al Martinez column: "Barone loves weather the way a boy loves his puppy. She never wearies of talking about it . . . sometimes to strangers in supermarkets who approach her and ask whether it's OK to plan a golf date Sunday in Palm Springs."

No one can ever take away the special memories I will always cherish having been a part of the Eyewitness News weather team. There's an old saying that epitomizes what I learned working with teammates like Dallas, Johnny, and Dianne: "A job worth doing is worth doing together."

Together Again

What I do you cannot do; but what you do, I cannot do.
The needs are great . . . and together we can do something wonderful.
~ MOTHER TERESA ~

Throughout my life, I have been so blessed by God to be surrounded by heroes who have been such an inspiration to me. They have been a tremendous source of motivation . . . always willing to go the extra mile in lending a helping hand, and doing so with enthusiasm and humility. Althea Gibson, who has been called the "Jackie Robinson of tennis" for overcoming racism and breaking the color barrier to win eleven Grand Slam titles, once said: "No matter what accomplishments you make—somebody helped you." And I want to tell you about someone special who reached out to me after years of separation and guided Dr. George into becoming an asset through achievement.

His name is Ron Miziker. And I first met him when he was a ninth-grade student of mine at Monroe Junior High School in Albuquerque. I can't remember how good Ron was on the subject of science. But he had an unwavering desire to go into television production. And while Ron was attending classes at the University of New Mexico, he also worked at our public education TV station KNME. Ron Miziker was no college intern just trying to learn the ropes. He became an integral part of our entire operation. Ron worked on each show that was broadcast on KNME-TV. He was a cameraman, a stagehand, an engineer. He was a director and a producer. My goodness, there wasn't anything this genius couldn't do. At college, Ron was the homecoming chairman. He was the "fiesta" director for the school. He was even president of his fraternity.

But television was Ron's first love. As both producer and director of my science shows at KNME, Ron guided us to success that I never dreamed was even remotely possible. What started out as a little production in a small studio that was seen only locally in Albuquerque was soon being broadcast in every city and school throughout the state of New Mexico, and later in twenty-five markets across the nation. Ron Miziker had indeed made his mark. But he was just getting started. And what a résumé it was going to be.

Upon graduation, Ron moved to Southern California, got married, had a baby, and started looking for a job. Using a college placement manual, Ron began sending letters to companies starting with the letter "A". He didn't have to go very far down the list. Ron was hired by the Armstrong flooring company to do advertising and rose to vice president. But success on Madison Avenue couldn't keep Ron from returning to television and carving out a career emphasizing the "show" in show business. Talk about baptism by fire—Ron produced a live ninety-minute daily TV variety program in Cincinnati called *The 50-50 Club*. It featured entertainment, interviews, and news before a studio audience of 450 people. Even the commercials were done live. Every day was a challenge for this young producer. But a local TV station in the Midwest was the minor leagues for someone with major league talent like Ron Miziker.

A cartoonist-turned-visionary named Walter Elias Disney once said, "All your dreams can come true if you have the courage to pursue them." And Ron followed his dream to the Magic Kingdom known as the Walt Disney Company. As director of entertainment and show development, Ron was given the unique opportunity of planning and producing every live show, parade, and extravaganza at each Disney theme park around the world. He was in charge of it all. Do you remember the dazzling Main Street Electrical Parade enjoyed by over a billion people for more than a quarter of a century? Ron Miziker was its co-creator. What Walt Disney said about Disneyland can certainly be applied to Ron's career: "It will continue to grow as long as there is imagination left in the world."

At the Disney Studios, Ron produced the popular TV show *The Wonderful World of Disney*. And he helped launch the Disney Channel, where Ron guided dozens of TV series, specials, and movies onto the air for a nationwide audience to enjoy. Ron has been and will always be the consummate showman who epitomizes what author Karen Ravn once wrote: "Only as high as I reach can I grow. Only as far as I seek can I go. Only as deep as I look can I see. Only as much as I dream can I be." And it's a dream that knows no boundaries. For nearly three decades, Ron's Miziker & Company, which expanded into the Miziker Entertainment Group, has produced and staged spectacular events across America and in seventeen countries. There is no stage too big for Ron's award-winning team to take the center-stage spotlight for its gala shows. His list of clients reads like a Who's Who of entertainment—from the Super Bowl to the World Cup to the Olympics, from Universal Studios to Radio City Music Hall, from presidents to kings and queens and even a sultan. His work has brought Ron fame and fortune. But to this day, he insists that his greatest reward is "listening to the cheers and applause after one of my shows."

As an old schoolteacher, I can't tell you how rewarding it is to see one of my former students become such a success story in the field that he has chosen. But there is something else on Ron Miziker's résumé that means even more to me. He is my friend. When Sue and I moved to Southern California from Albuquerque, Ron couldn't have been more gracious in making sure that the welcome mat had been rolled out. We didn't know anyone in Los Angeles. But Ron took the time and the care in making us feel right at home. That was so special. It made such a difference. To Sue and me . . . our friend Ron is a treasure.

By the time I arrived in the Southland, the science programs that Ron Miziker and I had put together at KNME-TV were no longer being broadcast in Albuquerque or across the nation. But apparently we were missed. A number of people wrote letters. One television station that aired the science shows received this handwritten request from one of our littlest viewers.

Dear Sir,
    Would you please put George Fischbeck back on your
program soon. Thank you.

Yours truly,
"Larry"
6 years old

I was deeply touched. Now Ron Miziker and I remained in contact . . . you know, having dinner together and calling each other. Once
he even came over to KABC-TV to see Channel 7 Eyewitness News in
person. I can't remember how the subject came up. Ron being a top-
notch producer, I'm sure it was his idea. But he and I began discussing
the possibility of doing a limited number of new science shows for air-
ing in television markets across the country so that even six-year-old
Larry could watch. And we decided to put together a plan: I was to
handle the program's content. My beloved mentor from KNME-TV,
Dr. Wayne Bundy, agreed to come on board as consultant. And as producer, Ron Miziker would be in charge of everything else. Ron has
likened the job of a producer to that of the president of a company.
The producer hires all the key people. He budgets the money. And he
manages the project. I saw my job as basically staying out of Ron's way
so that he could do his job. Believe me, that was the key.

After forming our own production company called Trike Productions, Ron and I had a meeting with my boss at KABC-TV, general manager John Severino, where we presented our proposal. Sev liked the
plan. He was extremely impressed with Ron Miziker's credentials. He
said: "OK, let's do some shows." The series was named *By George*. And
it would consist of five half-hour programs that would teach children
different science principles. The shows would be shown not only on
Channel 7 in Los Angeles, but also on all of the ABC network owned-
and-operated stations throughout the country.

Ron arranged for the funding. He put together a technical team
that was second to none, pulling in a lot of favors in doing so. For
example, Ron hired the incomparable Bob Dickinson, who is the king
of lighting live events on television. Bob has worked on the Academy

Awards, the Grammys, the Tonys, and the Super Bowl halftime show, as well as opening and closing ceremonies for three Olympics. Ron Miziker has a deep desire to work with only the best. And who could say "no" to this man? Even though Dr. Bundy and I were in charge of the program's content, Ron pushed to make it more contemporary. We shot the various series episodes on location throughout Southern California including Griffith Park, the beach, even a cave. Ron always had an ingenious idea on how to make each segment even better. For example, for the opening shot of a segment called "It's About Time" (which explored the subject of time), Ron decided to have me sit inside a tire that was connected by cable to a huge crane. At one point, the crane hoisted the cable and tire (along with me) high off the ground—and began swinging us back and forth like the pendulum on a clock. It was a sensational shot. But there were moments up there in that tire that I worried perhaps my "time" was running out! I never did ask Ron if he had taken out an insurance policy on his host. *By George* was a complete success. And we ended up winning an Emmy from the Academy of Television Arts & Sciences for Best Children's Show.

Ron Miziker and I would later reunite for another series of science shows called *Back to Basics*. This was a program that was designed for adults, showing viewers how they could make everyday products like soap and facial cream out of items you find around the house. It was a wonderful concept. Ron and I were able to come up with four weekly episodes of *Back to Basics*, which also ran on all of the ABC network O&Os. I am humbled my former student would care enough about his old science professor to come back into my life so that, together, we could enjoy victory through accomplishment. As a producer, Ron has no peer. And he's an even better human being. Eleanor Roosevelt said, "Many people will walk in and out of your life. But only true friends will leave footprints in your heart."

The dictionary describes the word *mentor* as a wise and trusted counselor or teacher. I've also heard it described as someone whose hindsight can become your foresight. That so aptly describes the mentor in my life, Dr. Wayne Bundy. It was Dr. Bundy who reached out in 1959 and plucked an unknown schoolteacher named George Fischbeck out of a classroom to fulfill a dream of devoting an entire television channel to public education. And it was Dr. Bundy who in 1972 talked that same teacher into accepting the challenge of another "classroom" of opportunity . . . forecasting the weather for KABC-TV in Los Angeles, as he transformed my fears into courage.

By the late 1970s, Dr. Bundy had become a strong and influential voice for noncommercial educational TV, serving as executive director of the Rocky Mountain Corporation for Public Broadcasting. He fought for funding. He opened the doors for informative programing. He made a difference. And one day, opportunity came knocking on my door in the form of a proposed project that would reunite Dr. Bundy and me with KNME-TV and its viewers that I had served for thirteen years as a television science teacher in Albuquerque. Dr. Bundy asked me to host a five-part series called *The Energy Store*, dealing with one of the most crucial issues facing America—energy. We had the money to fund the program, thanks to a sizeable grant from the U.S. Department of Energy to the State of New Mexico's Energy and Minerals Department.

The producers of the series worked it out so that I could fly to Albuquerque and shoot everything that was required of me in just two days. But they were long days—marathon work days that ended at four o'clock in the morning. The studio setting for the program was shot at KNME-TV. And it resembled an old-fashioned hardware store featuring energy conservation materials. But we also went out and did some shooting at various locations throughout Albuquerque. In each of the five programs, we covered different facets of home weatherization, ways to conserve energy, and how to harness the sun's energy through solar power to help cut expensive utility bills in half. I called it "news you can use." Our message was timeless. And its information on alternative energy is certainly relevant to this very day. *The Energy Store* was not only broadcast on five successive nights on KNME, but it was also seen on public television throughout the entire state of New Mexico.

The average American spends four hours each day watching television. And when you add children to the equation, the TV set is turned on at least seven hours a day in the typical household. The great journalist Edward R. Murrow said television can teach, illuminate, and inspire. "But it can do so only to the extent that humans are determined to use it to those ends. Otherwise, it's nothing but wires and lights in a box."

To be honest, much of what we watch on television today has been criticized as seemingly mindless. Dr. Wayne Bundy would fight for our right to watch such shows. But he also wanted to give us a choice with thoughtful, educational programming that can instruct, enlighten, and be used as a weapon against ignorance and indifference. Dr. Bundy dedicated his life to giving viewers that choice. Edward Wayne Bundy died in 2007 at the age of eighty-seven. But his dream lives on.

KNME-TV is a full-fledged member of the highly acclaimed Public Broadcasting Service (PBS). Dr. Bundy's daughter, Heidi Brown, served as an invaluable member of station management for ten years. Channel 5 is not limited as it once was to televising only a few hours a day, instead broadcasting 24/7. KNME is no longer housed in a converted college sorority house—but in a modern broadcast center capable of high definition with satellite technology that can send programs around the world at the speed of light.

But there is one thing that has not changed over fifty years of broadcasting at KNME-TV—Dr. Wayne Bundy's commitment to quality programming that continues to be an asset to its loyal viewers and the community. Dr. Bundy believed in that mission. And he never compromised. This man of vision affected my life and my career like no other. It's been said no person who achieves success in their life can do so without acknowledging the help they received from others. In the words of philosopher James Allen: "No duty is more urgent than that of returning thanks."

Eyewitness to the Eighties

Because there's more to life than news, weather, and sports.
~ EYEWITNESS NEWS SLOGAN (1982) ~

Paddy Chayefsky, the American playwright and screenwriter who wrote a critically acclaimed scathing attack on the television medium called *Network*, had this to say about the little box we watch each day: "It's the menace that everyone loves to hate but can't seem to live without." Frank Lloyd Wright once described television as "chewing gum for the eyes." And perhaps the legendary writer and producer Larry Gelbart put it best when he commented on the TV viewing habits of America: "Today's audience knows more about what's on television than what's in life."

The news that is presented on TV has been roundly criticized in some circles. There are critics who call it sensationalized and biased . . . with an overserving of tabloid celebrity, murders, shootings, and live police chases. There was a newspaper column on the subject of TV news with a headline that read: "If it bleeds, it leads." I guess when you open a window to the world—it can get ugly.

But I will say this to those critics out there. In the twenty years that I worked for Channel 7 in Los Angeles, I never once saw management in any way try to slant the news that it was presenting. Not once. And while our newscasts did feature strongly opinionated commentaries and debates, they were clearly labeled as such so that our audience would not confuse bias for news. I wish some of today's so-called cable "news" channels would abide by the same strict guidelines. In terms of news coverage, I think all channels in Los Angeles do their fair share of crime and celebrity stories. News operations live and die by the ratings. And if you want to be successful, you've got to attract viewers. For example, let's say actress Lindsay Lohan is due in court on a particular day. You would be wise to send a reporter and camera crew to the courthouse. It's a story that the viewers watching your newscast will probably want to see.

I think what people really want is information—the latest news that is given to them fast and accurately. At Eyewitness News, we wanted the audience to have confidence in our team and to feel that we made intelligent choices in the stories we covered. We owed our viewers nothing less. When news breaks across Southern California, such as a fire threatening homes and neighborhoods, live television coverage can give these stories an immediacy that newspapers can't touch. When news happens, people will watch.

Of course, there are times when we in the journalism business are faced with slow news days when absolutely nothing is happening. There is a wonderful story about a radio announcer who discovered one night that there was not even one piece of news worth talking about. And he decided to be completely honest with his listeners. It was Good Friday in 1930, when a BBC reporter signed on for the evening news and simply announced, "There is no news tonight." The rest of his newscast was filled with recorded piano music.

With the dawning of the 1980s, there was plenty of news to report each day in the City of Los Angeles. And the landscape in reporting that news was about to change dramatically. Channel 7 Eyewitness News was number one in the ratings at 5 and 6 p.m. But one of its competitors was beginning to make inroads. KNXT-TV decided to get a jump on both KABC-TV and KNBC-TV by starting its afternoon news a half hour earlier with a 4:30 p.m. newscast anchored by Connie Chung (truly, one of the nicest people in our business). Channel 7 was still air-ing a movie from 3:30 to 5 p.m. But with Channel 2 News now coming on at 4:30 p.m., KNXT was able to attract more viewers to its 5 p.m. newscast as well. And Channel 2 started creeping up on KABC in the news ratings at 5 and 6.

But with general manager John Severino and news director Dennis Swanson at the helm, KABC-TV made a decision that radically changed local television news in Southern California. And it dealt a decisive blow to Channel 2. In September of 1980, Channel 7 Eyewitness News introduced a new one-hour newscast at 4 p.m. And KABC became one of the first stations in the entire country to feature a three-hour block of local news on its afternoon and evening slots (4 to 7 p.m.). Using Severino's successful formula of pairing a veteran anchor with a younger co-anchor, Jerry Dunphy was teamed with Tawny Little (who was Miss America in 1976) to do our 4 p.m. news. At the time, Tawny had served three years as a general assignment reporter for Channel 7. Another veteran anchor, Paul Moyer, who had come to KABC-TV from KNBC-TV a year earlier, was assigned to do Eyewitness News at 5 p.m. with Ann Martin. It was an anchor team that would remain intact for nearly twelve years. Jerry Dunphy and Christine Lund would continue to anchor the Channel 7 newscasts at 6 and 11.

But there were some major lineup changes to our roster at 11 p.m.—anchors Paul Moyer, Ann Martin, and Tawny Little became street reporters. In the words of one station executive: "We just dominated. It was magic television." Eyewitness News had superb talent both in the studio and out in the field. Our dayside reporting staff had already been bolstered by three of the finest and most respected journalists to ever work in Los Angeles television—John North, Gene Gleeson, and Mark Coogan. And our producers, camera crews, writers, editors, and technical staff were simply impeccable. Every day, I always realized just how lucky and fortunate I was to work alongside these people I called my teammates.

Of course, I didn't have any free time on my hands to just sit there and smell the roses. My goodness, I was now doing the weather on the 4, 5, 6, and 11 p.m. editions of Channel 7 Eyewitness News. I had to arrive at the newsroom one hour earlier to get ready for the expanded newscasts. And that meant I had to leave the house even earlier in the morning to make my way to the National Weather Service in West-wood each day. I still went home to Woodland Hills after the 6 p.m. news to eat dinner with my family. But then it was back to Westwood and KABC-TV to update the weather at 11. You know, I will always re-gret not negotiating my contract so I could be paid by the mileage!

You may remember the advertising slogan that was used to promote Eyewitness News in the early 1980s: "Because there's more to life than news, weather, and sports." With three hours of news to fill each weekday, Channel 7 added sixteen people to our production staff. They included a number of lifestyle reporters: psychologist Dr. Irene Kassorla, psychi-atrist Dr. William Rader (who was married to actress Sally Struthers at the time), medical expert Dr. Art Ulene, communication specialist Dr. Lillian Glass, senior citizen reporter Doris Winkler, consumer spe-cialist Russ Nichols with "Seven on Your Side," and auto safety expert Byron Bloch. As you can imagine, we had a busy newsroom at Chan-nel 7. Just like my old station KOB-TV in Albuquerque, Eyewitness News was the top-rated newscast in town. And with loyal viewers inviting us into their homes each day, it sure was nice to be liked.

My friends, there is another side to doing live television news—a darker side that I will try my best to address here. I can't imagine that anyone who has ever worked in our business hasn't worried about safety on the news set or in the field. And when I say safety, I mean from someone in the public who might want to harm a person doing the news. It's not something those of us in TV news talked about openly. But there has always been concern.

Security is an issue. Television management pays a steep cost in providing security at its stations—and even in the field when it's war-ranted. But it's not fail-safe. I remember one day when a man carrying what looked like a gun walked onto the set at Channel 4 in Burbank during a live newscast, pointed the weapon at the back of consumer reporter David Horowitz, and ordered him to read a statement. At that point, KNBC immediately broke to a commercial. But the anchors pre-tended they were still on the air. After Horowitz read the rambling statement, the man placed the weapon on the desk. Anchor John Beard quickly grabbed it. And police hauled the man off and arrested him. The weapon turned out to be an unloaded pellet gun. Ironically, the man had been invited by another anchor to come watch the news after being told he was the son of a former KNBC-TV employee. The man was hospitalized a number of times for alleged mental problems.

On October 24, 1983 . . . our worst fears were realized at Channel 7 Eyewitness News. And every person who was in the newsroom that fateful night will never forget this horrifying incident. Shortly after 10 p.m., anchor Jerry Dunphy was driving back to our station for the eleven o'clock newscast along with KABC makeup artist (and later his wife) Sandra Marshall. At a stop sign at the corner of Prospect Avenue and Talmadge Street outside the ABC Television Center in a residential neighborhood, a car full of assailants pulled up alongside Dunphy's Rolls-Royce and opened fire. Both Dunphy and Marshall were hit and seriously wounded. Jerry was shot in the neck and arm. Sandra was hit in her right arm and suffered a fractured jaw and a neck injury when the couple's out of control car crashed into a corner house. The two victims bolted from the vehicle and ran for their lives, collapsing a half-block away on the driveway of Channel 7's main gate.

About 10:15 p.m. in the Eyewitness Newsroom, we received a frantic call from the main gate that Jerry Dunphy had just been shot outside our station. It was a frightening moment. At first, we all thought that someone may have gotten upset at something that had been said on our newscast, and after shooting Dunphy, the gunman might next be heading to the newsroom. Mere words cannot possibly describe the wave of fear and panic that swept us instantly as everyone ran and hid. Minutes later when we realized that any immediate danger had passed, we rushed outside to the main gate only to find a wounded Jerry Dunphy lying on the driveway. It seemed like the entire Los Angeles Police Department was already on the scene with its helicopters flying overhead and Chief Daryl Gates leading the intense investigation.

The Eyewitness News staff was in a state of shock. And I can in no way overstate this. At that particular moment, we didn't know if Jerry and Sandra were going to survive. Our hearts were heavy, burdened with grief. News director Terry Crofoot rushed to the station from his home. As our leader, Terry knew exactly what we were going through. Someone had just gunned down two of our teammates. And with only a half hour to go until the 11 p.m. news went on the air, Crofoot called in while he was driving to KABC and ordered us to delay the newscast until 11:30. Our workplace had now become a crime scene. Everyone was in tears. And our boss truly understood just how hard our job was going to be that night under the most trying of circumstances. And I will always have a deep appreciation and respect for a news director who had the courage and the thoughtfulness to make that decision, perhaps knowing full well that it might be criticized later in the media. Every member of our staff that was there that night dug down deep and did their very best to put on a newscast. I know. I was there. The man who anchored Eyewitness News had become the lead story, shot along with his girlfriend just seconds from work. Our job couldn't have been tougher. But apparently, our best wasn't good enough for the *Los Angeles Times*.

On October 26, *Times* television critic Howard Rosenberg lashed out at Eyewitness News for "getting scooped" by our competitors in covering Dunphy's shooting. Even though Rosenberg admitted in his column that Channel 7 may have been thrown into "chaos" by the shooting, he criticized the decision to delay our newscast . . . saying KABC-TV "temporarily ignored" the story. Perhaps worst of all was the headline for Rosenberg's column that in bold letters proclaimed: "After Dunphy shooting, KABC fires a blank." I expected far more from one of America's great newspapers and a columnist who would later in his career go on to win a Pulitzer Prize. Maybe Eyewitness News wasn't at its best that night. But there was a reason. Like I said . . . I was there. I saw the pain and the heartbreak. I saw the unwavering dedication to try to work through our tears and get Channel 7 Eyewitness News on the air—no matter what. All things being equal—I don't think Channel 2, Channel 4, or a certain columnist at the *Los Angeles Times* could have done any better.

After Jerry Dunphy was released from the hospital, the station moved him out of his house and into a Beverly Hills hotel for his protection. And KABC-TV replaced the Rolls-Royce it had been leasing for Dunphy with a less conspicuous Mercedes-Benz. The shooting left Jerry with limited use of his left arm for a while, which hampered his ability to type news scripts. Four suspects were later arrested. And one was granted immunity in exchange for his testimony. At the trial, Dunphy told jurors that he saw three weapons pointed at him during the attack. Prosecutors accused the defendants of taking part in a robbery spree from Gardena to Hollywood the night Dunphy and

Marshall were shot. In its verdict, the jury convicted one man in the shootings . . . but acquitted the two others. The jury foreman was quoted as saying he believed that the fourth suspect who was granted immunity actually shot Dunphy. Jerry was outraged at the jurors' decision to free two of the defendants.

When Channel 7 entered the 1980s with an expanded three-hour newscast in the afternoon and early evening, our staff got to move to a brand new newsroom as well. No longer would the Eyewitness Newsroom be located in a different building from the news studio two hundred yards from each other. The new newsroom was built on the second floor of the same building where we did the actual newscast. That was good news for a nearly "sixty-something" weatherman like me who was getting worn out from years of sprinting hundreds of yards from one building to the other in a frantic race to get on the air. In fact, I was no longer wearing sneakers but my favorite cowboy boots. I did have a new obstacle course to conquer—running down the stairs from the second floor to the first floor studios as fast as my cowboy boots could go. Thank goodness I never ran into anybody on the way. But to be honest, I had some close calls!

Our new weather office in the newsroom was another challenge. It was really just a regular size room that Dallas, Johnny, and I had to share. And it was crammed full of desks, a file cabinet, a bookcase, a credenza, a television set, and a big machine that kept spitting out weather maps. We also had a huge window the news staff could look through to see how much fun "The Three Musketeers" of weather were having with no elbow room. And in 1985, our close quarters became even closer. That's when a communications company called Capital Cities bought the entire ABC network and all of its owned-and-operated TV stations.

It wasn't long before two high-tech experts from Cap Cities showed up at the weather office and took up the rest of our space by installing new computers. They said Cap Cities wanted to modernize our on-the-air weather graphics. There was just one problem. Once the high-tech experts left, nobody in our office knew how to work these computers—especially when they broke down. I'm just an old-fashioned schoolteacher who was quite happy getting by with nineteenth-century technology. I don't know what any of us would have done if

Dallas Raines and Dianne Barone hadn't been such quick learners in figuring out how to make these newfangled machines work. In all honesty, these sophisticated computers allowed us to do an even better job. They provided us with the latest satellite maps twenty-four hours a day to bring our viewers the most accurate weather in town. But I always had my old chalkboard on standby just in case.

On September 8, 1986, we got a new teammate at Channel 7 in Los Angeles. And it's a partnership that paid off handsomely for KABC-TV during the next quarter of a century. That's when the nationally seen *Oprah Winfrey Show* was first broadcast at three in the afternoon as the lead-in for Eyewitness News at four. It became the most popular daytime television program in America. And through the magic of cross promotion, Channel 7 was able to persuade much of Oprah's huge audience to stay tuned for Channel 7 Eyewitness News. It's a formula that became a ratings success story for two and a half decades.

Our anchor lineup went through some changes in the mid-to-late 1980s. Christine Lund left in 1986 to spend some more time with her family (eventually returning in 1990). But with anchor talent like Jerry Dunphy, Paul Moyer, Ann Martin, Harold Greene, Laura Diaz (who joined the Eyewitness News team in 1983), and Tawny Little, we always gave viewers friendly, familiar, and reliable people to be their source for news and information each day.

While our on-the-air talent remained a rock of stability, the technology of gathering news was growing by leaps and bounds. Covering breaking news as quickly as possible from wherever we can is of the utmost importance. When I first arrived at Eyewitness News, we were shooting everything on film. Now we were about to enter the Space Age.

KABC-TV became one of the first stations in the entire country to have a satellite truck in its remote arsenal. This $500,000 communications center on wheels allowed Channel 7 to do live remotes from anywhere. It came equipped with a satellite dish, camera, its own generator, and a tape editing system, along with satellite and cell phones. A mini-cam truck's live capability is limited to those areas in Southern California where it can link a microwave signal with one of our station's transmitting points. But with a satellite truck—the sky is the limit, literally. You can be anyplace in the world. As long as you can send a signal from the truck to a satellite twenty thousand miles in space, a TV station can receive that signal after it has linked up with the same satellite.

To do so, engineers at Channel 7 had to book time on a particular satellite with the ABC coordinating office in New York City. Because such satellite links are expensive, you would normally book the time in five- to ten-minute windows. But as long as the satellite truck and the receiving TV station were synced up with info on the satellite link and the time window . . . you were in business. Not only could our reporters do live satellite remotes for Channel 7 Eyewitness News, but also for our sister ABC stations across the nation. My friends, excuse me for saying this. But this is technology that is "out of this world"!

I've seen a lot of technological breakthroughs in television news during my long career in broadcast journalism, but there's nothing more exciting than watching live breaking news from a helicopter. At KABC-TV, we even had a slogan: "News on the fly with Channel 7's Eye in the Sky." When Eyewitness News first contracted with a helicopter company to provide choppers for our camera crews to cover stories from the air, they didn't have the capability to go live. So when the story was completed, the helicopter would transport our camera-person with tape (and reporter, if the story warranted one) back to Channel 7, where a landing pad was located on the east side of our parking lot. The major reason KABC leased a helicopter from another company instead of buying one was the issue of liability. It was easier for the helicopter company to obtain the insurance that was required.

But it wasn't long before Eyewitness News was able to go live from the skies over Los Angeles with the introduction of a $750,000 Bell Jet Ranger that we called Newscopter 7. Quite simply, it was a virtual flying television station. And did it ever give our viewers a bird's-eye view of the news! Newscopter 7 was equipped with its own transmitter, located on the bottom of the craft. One small TV camera was mounted on the helicopter's instrument panel so that the viewers could see the pilot/reporter on air. An engineer on board operated a second camera from the chopper's side door for shots of the scene below.

One of the most enjoyable assignments I was ever given at Eyewitness News was to take our viewers behind the scenes to see how we covered the news with Newscopter 7. It takes real teamwork to cover breaking news in the skies of Southern California. It's no place for rookies.

The two veteran members of the Newscopter 7 team I profiled were confronted with stress and pressure each and every day as they worked against the clock to make deadline several times each newscast.

Cameraman Marco Robalino has one of the most remarkable stories within the Eyewitness News family. You want to talk about the American dream—Marco immigrated to the United States from Ecuador in the early 1970s. And he has been an eyewitness to some of the biggest news stories as they dramatically unfolded before his camera. Marco Robalino was on the scene for Channel 7 Eyewitness News in 1975 when kidnapped newspaper heiress and accused bank robber Patty Hearst was arrested in San Francisco. In 1976, an entire school bus of twenty-six children and their driver were kidnapped in Chowchilla, California. You may remember the gripping pictures of the victims as they were successfully rescued after they had been buried in a moving van. That footage was taken by Marco Robalino of Eyewitness News, who was the first cameraman to arrive at this breaking story. As this book is being written, Marco is still serving the viewers of Channel 7 and is now in his thirty-eighth year as a cameraman covering news as it happens.

Shooting stories on board Newscopter 7 was a challenge unlike any other, where Marco had to perform a balancing act with unrelenting perseverance. When the helicopter would arrive on the scene of a breaking story, it was Marco's job to link the chopper's transmitter with one of KABC-TV's receiving sites on the ground. Marco had to manually aim the signal to the station's receiving site through a radio tracking system. Once the transmitting signal was set up, Marco would then strap himself securely to the helicopter . . . open the chopper's side door . . . position a camera on his shoulder (and it was a heavy camera) . . . and shoot pictures of the scene as he sat in the open door with his legs hanging out, his feet on a footrest attached to one of the landing skids. During a live remote from Newscopter 7, Marco could control with the push of a button which picture he wanted to transmit—either a shot of the scene below or a shot of the pilot/ reporter from the second camera mounted on the helicopter's instrument panel. As you can imagine, communication between pilot and camera operator is crucial. And Marco Robalino couldn't have asked for a better teammate in the pilot's seat on Newscopter 7.

He was known to our viewers as "Captain Ron". His name was Ron Bodholdt. And he was the first member of the Eyewitness News team to serve as pilot and reporter on Newscopter 7. Over the years, a number of men and women pilots have worked on television news for the various stations in the Los Angeles market. But no one had the résumé or expertise of Ron Bodholdt. And I'm about to tell you why Captain Ron made a difference.

Ron served our country as a military combat helicopter pilot during the Vietnam War. He was highly decorated, having won the Distinguished Flying Cross, the Bronze Star, and two Medals of Valor. After returning home from war, Ron Bodholdt dedicated thirty-four years of his life serving the public as a Los Angeles County Sheriff's Deputy. And it was a courageous act of bravery as a helicopter rescue pilot that earned him the department's highest honor.

On March 3, 1983, Deputy Bodholdt and his partner flew in harsh storm conditions to the rain-swollen San Gabriel River in Whittier. A young boy had been swept downriver by raging waters after his boat had capsized. Ron carefully navigated his sheriff's rescue helicopter just above the powerful river where the child was hanging onto a vine for his life. Ron told me he got so close that he could look directly into the boy's eyes . . . and saw an unbelievable look of determination. That's when the boy let go of the vine and grabbed onto the helicopter's landing skids. And Ron plucked the victim from the raging river and saved his life.

My friends, we were able to obtain the dramatic footage of this rescue for our use in profiling Ron Bodholdt on Eyewitness News. And I am in awe of how Deputy Bodholdt and his partner put their own lives on the line in a fierce storm to save this little boy from certain death. On August 12, 1983, these two heroes were given the Medal of Valor by Sheriff Sherman Block for this extraordinary rescue.

During all the years Captain Ron served Channel 7 Eyewitness News covering breaking stories from the Southland skies, he continued his work as a deputy. Ron would work in the morning and early afternoon for the Sheriff's Department and then spend the late afternoon and early evening flying Newscopter 7. Whenever our viewers would see Ron's live helicopter reports, they were watching these dramatic developments through the eyes of a seasoned law enforcement pilot and decorated combat veteran who logged ten thousand flight hours in a distinguished career that spanned three and a half decades.

On December 27, 2008, Ron Bodholdt passed away after a prolonged illness at the age of sixty-two. He served his country and the county with bravery, courage, and humility. In the words of Leonardo da Vinci, "For once you have tasted flight, you will forever walk the earth with your eyes turned skyward, for there you have been, and there you will always long to return."

THE CHANNEL 7 DREAM TEAM

Try beating this lineup that Eyewitness News fielded in 1980. As one of our station executives put it, "We just dominated. It was magic television." *Left to right*: Tawny Little, Dr. George, Christine Lund, Jerry Dunphy, Ann Martin, and Paul Moyer. (Courtesy KABC-TV)

WHO SAYS IT NEVER "RAINES" IN SOUTHERN CALIFORNIA?

He is the most qualified, knowledgeable, talented (and handsomest) meteorologist who has ever given a weather forecast in the annals of Los Angeles TV news. Oh yes—the guy standing next to him is Dr. George. (Courtesy Dianne Barone)

Taking L.A. by Storm

These "Dr. George Umbrellas" that Channel 7 gave to our viewers made even a wet forecast seem bright. There's a saying, "And when it rains on your parade, look up rather than down. Without the rain, there would be no rainbow." (Courtesy KABC-TV)

Tight Quarters

You might say things were a little cozy in the Eyewitness News weather department in 1985. This was the entire office that the four of us had to share. Dianne Barone, Dr. George, Johnny Mountain, and Dallas Raines weren't kidding when we told everyone that we had a "close" working relationship! (Courtesy Dianne Barone)

"THREE'S COMPANY"

On the set of Channel 7 Eyewitness News with two teammates that made going to work so enjoyable for me—Dallas Raines and my assistant Dianne Barone, who went on to become a two-time Emmy-winning meteorologist at KCAL-TV in Los Angeles. (Courtesy Dianne Barone)

A FORECAST THAT'S "OUT OF THIS WORLD"

We had some fun for a special project Eyewitness News produced for the Griffith Park Observatory in Los Angeles. This is what the forecast would look like if Dr. George was doing the weather on another planet. (Courtesy KABC-TV)

Channel 7's "Eye in the Sky"

In 1992, I climbed into the cockpit of Newscopter 7 and showed viewers how Eyewitness News covered live breaking stories in Los Angeles from a helicopter that became a virtual flying television station. (Courtesy KABC-TV)

"Don't Rain on My Parade"

Displaying a lot of "horsepower" as I took part in the Monrovia Day Parade. I always believed that if you, the viewer, took part of your day to watch Channel 7 Eyewitness News, then I needed to spend some time with "my friends" to say thank you. (Courtesy Keith Johnson and Gem City Images)

PORTERVILLE—THE GIFT
OF GIVING
For twenty years, I had the honor
and privilege of taking part in
KABC-TV's Toys for Porterville
Christmas campaign . . . as our
generous viewers donated gifts,
joy, and happiness to the young
residents of the Porterville State
Hospital. Channel 7 collection
boxes were set up throughout
Southern California.
(Courtesy Dianne Barone)

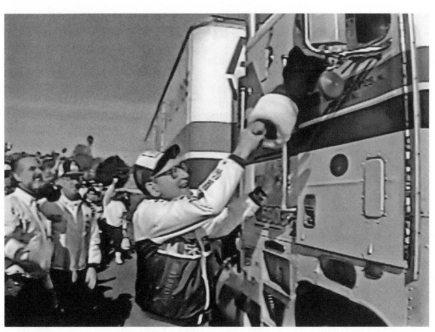

SPECIAL DELIVERY
My friends, this is why I call Porterville the greatest success story I have ever seen.
Each Christmas season, the viewers of Channel 7 Eyewitness News donated so many
toys for the severely mentally and physically challenged that it took several moving
vans to transport these gifts from KABC-TV in Hollywood to the Porterville State
Hospital fifty miles north of Bakersfield. (Courtesy KABC-TV)

DR. GEORGE AT THE "ANIMAL HOUSE"
Moonlighting at the Los Angeles Zoo. For twelve wonderful years, I served the zoo as a volunteer docent. That means I gave public tours of the zoo, entertained children from schools across Southern California, and got to know some eleven hundred animals, many of whom remain my dear friends to this very day! (Courtesy Los Angeles Zoo)

GREAT MOMENTS WITH "LINCOLN"
The Lincoln Training Center teaches job skills to nearly six hundred people with disabilities and places them at more than fifty job sites throughout California annually (as it has since 1964). For a number of years, I was honored to help this marvelous team with fundraising, promotional videos, and loving encouragement. (Courtesy Tobi Jabson/Lincoln Training Center)

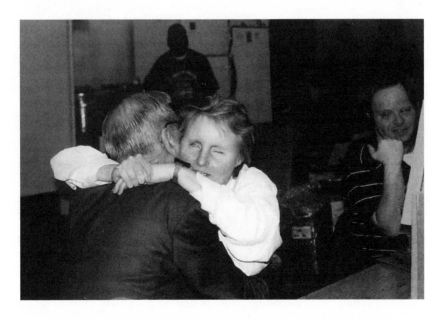

LINCOLN'S MISSION: "TURNING DISABILITIES INTO POSSIBILITIES"
It's been said, "The high road to service is traveled with integrity, compassion, and understanding . . . people don't care how much we know until they know how much we care." (Courtesy Tobi Jabson/Lincoln Training Center)

Alisa Ann Ruch
Burn Foundation

Heroes, Healing, and Hope

Formed as a living memorial to a little girl who died in a tragic fire at the age of eight, the Alisa Ann Ruch Burn Foundation has raised millions and millions of dollars over forty years to help burn survivors in need. Since 1985, I have taken part in the foundation's annual burn relay, a caravan of firefighters and volunteers that travels statewide to pick up checks with a mission: "We make a life by what we give." (Courtesy Alisa Ann Ruch Burn Foundation)

A "QUEST" OF COMPASSION

Channel 7 Eyewitness News anchors Gene Gleeson, Kathy Vara (now at KNBC-TV), and Phillip Palmer join me at the 2003 rally for Firefighters Quest for Burn Survivors. This annual fundraising caravan covers twelve hundred miles across Southern California to help restore lives. Quest's motto: "Together we will make a difference." (Courtesy Firefighters Quest for Burn Survivors)

NEVER GIVE UP—WHERE DEFEAT IS NOT AN OPTION

Here is bravery and courage that is truly heroic. *Left*: My wife Sue with Glendale firefighter Bill Jensen, whose fight for life and monumental will to live helped inspire Quest. (Courtesy Firefighters Quest for Burn Survivors) *Right*: A severely burned little boy for whom the Alisa Ann Ruch Burn Foundation is a lifeline of support and love that knows no limits. (Courtesy Alisa Ann Ruch Burn Foundation)

Golden Mike Awards®

— R T N A —

59th Annual Ceremonies

Dr. George Fischbeck

Lifetime Achievement Award

January 24, 2009

(Courtesy Radio & Television News Association of Southern California and Henk Friezer)

A "Golden" Opportunity

This is one of my most cherished moments. Here I am receiving the Lifetime Achievement Award at the 59th Annual Golden Mikes in 2009. And to make it even more special, my beloved friend and teammate Johnny Mountain was selected to be my presenter. (Courtesy Rich Fischbeck)

The Golden Mikes: "Under the Weather"

There was no shortage of forecasters the night I was given the Lifetime Achievement Award. *Left to right*: Kyle Hunter (who on this evening was awarded the Golden Mike for Best Television Weather Segment), Dr. George, Dallas Raines, and Johnny Mountain. (Courtesy Kyle Hunter)

A Touching Act of Kindness and Class
This is the full-page ad that my family at ABC7 placed in the Official
Program of the 59th Annual Golden Mike Awards. (Courtesy KABC-TV)

BACKSTAGE AT THE GOLDEN MIKES—TOGETHER AGAIN

On a night that I was given a Lifetime award . . . I couldn't have achieved it without three special people who were also in attendance at the ceremonies. *Above*: My former Eyewitness News teammate and lifelong friend Ed Arnold. *Below*: I'm standing with two reasons Channel 7 News was always number one in weather (and still is)—Dianne Barone and the incomparable Dallas Raines. (Courtesy Rich Fischbeck)

55th Annual Los Angeles Area Emmy Awards

The Governors Award

September 6, 2003

THE EMMYS: A MOST EXCLUSIVE CLUB

An ordinary man receives an extraordinary honor. And as I am given the prestigious Governors Award from the Academy of Television Arts & Sciences, I am humbled to be joined on stage by a group of L.A.'s best-known TV meteorologists, including Mark Thompson of KTTV and Mark Kriski of KTLA. (Courtesy Rich Fischbeck)

A "FAMILY AFFAIR" AT THE EMMYS

Sharing a special night with my favorite Fischbecks—Rich, Nancy, Cristy (Rich's wife), Spring, and Sue—along with the best boss I ever worked for, former KABC-TV president, general manager, and news director Terry Crofoot with wife Beth. (Courtesy Rich Fischbeck)

A Note of Thanks to Two Giants of Broadcast News
In 2010, Sue and I attended a retirement party at KABC-TV for Bob Banfield (*above*) and Gene Gleeson (*below*). During their combined seventy-three years of service, these legendary journalists helped put Channel 7 Eyewitness News on the map in Los Angeles, leaving an indelible mark that time can't erase. Bob and Gene were also first-class teammates and human beings, which only enriches their remarkable legacy. (Courtesy Martin Orozco)

A WALK DOWN MEMORY LANE

How's this for an Eyewitness News reunion? *Left to right*: Ric Romero, Bob Banfield, Henry Alfaro, Gene Gleeson—and by George, "Me." You know, we could start a pretty good news operation with this bunch! (Courtesy Martin Orozco)

A LICENSE TO LAUGH

Nothing like being a name-dropper! (Courtesy Rich Fischbeck)

FOLLOWING IN HER FATHER'S FOOTSTEPS

My daughter Nancy's curiosity and love of life led her to a job in television at public education station KETC-TV in St. Louis. Nancy's proud Dad paid her a visit at the studios of Channel 9 along with Sue and George Junior.

OUR FAMILY: MY CELEBRATION

Left to right: granddaugher Leilani "Spring," daughter Nancy, and wife Sue. They are my gift. Someone once said, "What you do today is important because you are exchanging a day of your life for it. When tomorrow comes, this day will be gone forever. In its place is something that you have left behind. Let it be something good."

CHAPTER 13

Behind the Scenes—To Tell the Truth

I'm not the smartest fellow in the world,

but I can sure pick smart colleagues.

~ FRANKLIN DELANO ROOSEVELT ~

I would have liked to call this chapter "Stories I Only Tell My Friends." But that's the title actor Rob Lowe chose for his memoir that became a bestseller. I may not be a successful actor like Lowe, but we do have one thing in common. Rob and I have both been blessed with the opportunity to work with some wonderful and interesting people in our respective careers. And like Rob Lowe, I have stories to share from over the years as well. So let me take you behind the scenes of Eyewitness News and tell you some anecdotes about my colleagues that I would only tell "my friends."

First of all, if I'm going to poke fun at someone, I might as well start with me. The year was 1981 when a twenty-year-old stocky baseball pitcher from Mexico took Los Angeles by storm as Fernando Valenzuela led the Dodgers to the World Series championship. He didn't speak a word of English. But his charm was infectious and ignited a craze that swept the City of Angels called "Fernandomania." So you can imagine the hysteria that overtook our security guards at KABC-TV when a Hispanic man dressed in a Dodgers uniform with number thirty-four on it drove up to the main gate and said, "I'm Fernando Valenzuela. And I have an appointment at Eyewitness News."

The mere fact that this man spoke perfect English should have tipped off the guards that there was something wrong here. But they were so delirious at seeing "Fernando" that they merely waved him in. It was only after the guards called the newsroom to share the happy news that Fernando Valenzuela was on his way up were they informed that they had just been victimized by a hoax. By this time, the Fernando impostor was nowhere to be seen. The poor security guards were placed on high alert throughout the TV station. And one of the most infamous chapters of Eyewitness News starring Dr. George was about to unfold on live television.

While security guards searched every square inch of the twenty-three-acre ABC Television Center, the fake Fernando had found his way to the actual studio where Channel 7's newscast was being broadcast live and "yours truly" was doing the weather. Thirty seconds later, and the impostor would have been captured by the security guards who were closing in on him. But your friendly, neighborhood weatherman—namely me—looked up and saw "Fernando" in our studio. And I got so excited, I pulled him onto my weather set so I could share Fernando Valenzuela with our viewers.

Oh my goodness. As I've been told—everyone in the studio knew that it wasn't Fernando. My irate news director, who was watching all this happen on TV in his office, knew it wasn't Fernando. All of our stunned newsroom staff knew it wasn't Fernando. And worst of all, our viewers at home knew it wasn't Fernando. The only person who was convinced that this really was Fernando Valenzuela of the Dodgers was me. And I held KABC-TV hostage on live television for ten minutes as I had "Fernando" teach me how to throw his famous screwball pitch. I didn't learn the truth until after we had finally gone to a commercial. To this day, I never found out what our security guards did with "Fernando." I admit, like many batters who faced the real Fernando—I struck out. But it did make for a very interesting newscast.

And now that I've told the truth on me, let me tell you some interesting things about my famous mates at work that perhaps you didn't know.

Jerry Dunphy: Let's start with this. Did you know Jerry almost didn't come to Los Angeles in the first place? In his book *News Is People: The Rise of Local TV News and the Fall of News from New York*, author Craig M. Allen writes that in 1960 Dunphy was offered the job of hosting NBC's *Today* show. Jerry even went to New York City where he auditioned for the network. Allen, who's a professor with the Walter Cronkite School of Journalism and Mass Communication at Arizona State University, says Dunphy instead chose to anchor *The Big News* at KNXT-TV in Los Angeles because at $65,000, it paid more.

Jerry Dunphy loved doing the news. But let me tell you something that Jerry loved just as much—music. He was a regular at some of Beverly Hills' most popular establishments that featured piano bars. When Jerry passed away in 2002, an article in *Los Angeles Magazine* said Jerry liked to frequent such nightspots as the Four Seasons and the Polo Lounge after his newscasts, and enjoyed dancing to classics by Cole Porter and Rodgers and Hart. Of course, music played a big part in the Dunphy family. Well-known record executive and producer Mike Curb—you remember The Mike Curb Congregation—married Jerry's daughter, Linda. Mike Curb also served as California's lieutenant governor. Mike's famous father-in-law wrote two hundred songs. Among the songs written by Jerry Dunphy and Mike Curb were "Somebody Special," which was recorded by Bobby Vinton "Cowboy's Christmas," recorded by Wayne Newton; and what could well have been the soundtrack to Jerry's storied career, "From the Desert to the Sea," which was recorded by popular country music singer T. G. Sheppard.

Christine Lund: She started out wanting to be an English teacher. But two years after graduating college, Christine was named news director at a small UHF station in Aurora, Illinois—WLXT-TV Channel 60—which was on the air only evenings and weekends. It went out of business a year later. But where some people may see problems, Christine sees possibilities.

And when she was teamed with Jerry Dunphy at KABC-TV, Christine helped turn Eyewitness News into a ratings powerhouse during the 1970s and 80s. Take it from Dr. George, my friends. Channel 7 wouldn't have been number one without Christine Lund. My goodness, you talk about resonating with an audience!

To say Christine Lund is an animal lover is perhaps the greatest understatement of all. Christine adores animals and had a ranch in the San Fernando Valley where she raised horses. One year, Christine rode one of her horses with an equestrian unit along Pasadena's Colorado Boulevard in the famed Rose Parade. My wife, Sue, and I were in attendance when Christine got married on her ranch in a ceremony that was held in a horse stable. Her husband was a doctor who had deeply touched Christine by the way he cared for her ailing father.

Christine Lund was a delight to work with. But on one newscast, Christine's bright sense of humor got her in trouble. Because my former teammate is such a class act, I don't think she'll mind if we have a little fun with this. Channel 7 Eyewitness News was live on the air. And either Johnny Mountain or I was doing the weather using camera #4 on the far right side of the news set. Even though Christine was not seen on camera during the weather segment, the other three studio camera shots were shown on monitors in the control room in case the director and the producer wanted to switch to those shots. Christine decided to have a little fun off-camera (or so she thought) by putting a white piece of tape on her nose as she leaned into the shot on camera #3 and waved to the folks in the control booth. There was just one problem. As Christine was waving with the tape on her nose, her eyes glanced downward to the on-the-air monitor. And she noticed that this was all being broadcast live throughout Southern California. An immediate look of horror swept across Christine's face, and she quickly darted off-camera in embarrassment. It broke everyone up. And it was one of my favorite moments with one of my all-time favorite colleagues.

Paul Moyer: He loves golf. If you're ever looking for Paul, you might start at one of the greatest golf courses in the world—the Riviera Country Club in Pacific Palisades, California. To see Paul spending his day playing at Riviera is, shall we say, just "par" for the course. Mr. Moyer is quite an athlete. He was a pretty good baseball player, having played for both Torrance High School and the University of Arizona. Paul even had the major league Pittsburgh Pirates interested at one point. But my friend was far more successful in making his best "pitch" on local

TV news. On the home front, Paul was so popular, he was even named honorary mayor of Brentwood.

But I truly think Paul would have given up all of the above to live life in the fast lane as a race car driver. And on April 16, 1988, his dream came true. It happened on the only weekend of the year when speeding is actually legal on the streets of Long Beach. It's all part of the annual Toyota Grand Prix of Long Beach. And our own Paul Moyer took the checkered flag to capture the Pro/Celebrity Race. Now if Paul is honest, he will admit that his effort was greatly aided by Jay Leno, who I'm told apparently slowed down Moyer's competition in a mishap on one of the turns. (Nobody gets hurt in these celebrity races.) But Paul really did win the race, defeating such legendary auto racing champions as Dan Gurney and Parnelli Jones, as he covered the ten laps in his Toyota Celica GTS averaging more than fifty-seven miles an hour. Talent must run in the Moyer family. Paul's nephew, Micah Ohlman, now anchors the news on KTLA-TV Channel 5 in Los Angeles.

Ann Martin: One of the most exceptional anchors that has ever been in our business. And I can tell you firsthand that Ann is as down-to-earth as anyone I had the pleasure of working with on the roster of Eyewitness News. Dignity, style, and sincerity are words you hear from colleagues who remember Ann Martin with fondness. She came to Channel 7 in 1976 from Seattle, where Ann had originally responded to a newspaper ad for the job of "weather girl" at KIRO-TV. But it wasn't long before Ann had fought her way into doing news reporting. In the words of author Beth Fantaskey: "Why did I sign up for this? Because we grow by challenging ourselves."

And while we're on the subject of challenges, Ann Martin will never forget her first day on the job at Channel 7 Eyewitness News. She had just arrived in Los Angeles from Seattle. And her first assignment was to rush to downtown L.A. and do a breaking news live remote on the settlement of a major strike. It was such a big story, Channel 7 broke into its afternoon entertainment programming for Ann's remote. She did an impeccable job. Ann had all of the details—interviews with both labor and management officials—in a reporting job that was nothing less than superb. The entire newsroom watched our new teammate in action. There was just one problem. In signing off the remote, Ann reverted back to an old habit from her previous job. "For Channel 7

Eyewitness News, this is Ann Martin reporting live from downtown—Seattle." Ann probably died a thousand deaths when she realized what she had done. Yes—we laughed. But we were not laughing at Ann. We were laughing with her. Everyone knew what an excellent job Ann had done in her very first remote under pressure. And we all realized that day what a great addition our brand new reporter was going to be. This journalist that one Southland television executive described to the *Los Angeles Times* as "arguably the preeminent female anchor in the marketplace" would enjoy an eighteen-year career at Channel 7 Eyewitness News and another fourteen years at crosstown Channel 2 News. I'm just happy that Ann Martin decided to move from doing the weather to anchoring the news. Because if she had stayed in the weather department, I don't think Dr. George's career forecast at Channel 7 would have been all that bright!

Harold Greene: When I initially reported for work at Eyewitness News in Los Angeles in the early 1970s, Harold Greene was my 6 p.m. newscast producer. But he was just getting started. Harold performed every job in the newsroom and learned how to put together a newscast from the bottom up. He's been a cameraman. He was a newswriter. And these invaluable experiences helped lay a foundation of success in an extraordinary career that spanned the greater part of four decades. My goodness, it's hard to remember a time when Harold Greene wasn't doing the news in Southern California during that span—and being an integral part of each news operation where he served. Yes, Harold was my friend. But I had selfish motives. I was always hoping that his incomparable skills as a journalist and a broadcaster would rub off on me. After all, I was just an old schoolteacher moonlighting in the weather department. But Harold could do anything.

As an anchorman, he garnered the highest ratings his hometown of San Diego has ever seen. As a reporter at KABC-TV, Harold won a Golden Mike Award for his live coverage of the Cerritos air disaster in 1986. As an investigative journalist, Harold went behind enemy lines to give viewers a firsthand look at L.A.'s most dangerous gangs. Harold lived on Skid Row, moving in with the homeless for an unprecedented report on the hopelessness of those trapped in a life of misery and despair. I remember one night at the Emmys when two of Harold's documentaries competed against each other in the same category.

You have to be good if you can afford to root against yourself at television's most prestigious awards ceremony. This talented man was so versatile, he even won a Golden Mike in 1984 for his work on Eyewitness News—doing the sports. His résumé includes three Edward R. Murrow Awards and twelve more from the Los Angeles Press Club, not to mention his own star on the Hollywood Walk of Fame. Harold brought a unique blend of professionalism and credibility to the table. He didn't just read the news but presented it from his vast array of experience honed by years on the street. There wasn't anything he hadn't seen. Harold Greene put the "eyewitness" in Eyewitness News.

Laura Diaz: When this journalist first reported for work at KABC-TV in Los Angeles in 1983, she was so capable and extremely prepared to go out in the field and report on news. And there was a very good reason for that. Few reporters in a major market like L.A. have ever gone through a baptism of fire in learning how to be a reporter like Laura Diaz. She came to Eyewitness News after having worked for TV stations in far smaller markets like San Luis Obispo and Fresno. It was a journey in which Laura not only reported the news, but on many stories she also had to shoot her own footage with a camera, edit the videotape on her own, and write her own scripts. Laura did everything. Her first assignment at Channel 7 Eyewitness News was to work out of its Orange County Bureau alongside two veteran (and shall we say, kind of hard-nosed) reporters, Barney Morris and Ed Arnold. And Laura Diaz more than held her own. Did she ever. Ed says he was impressed right off the bat. This "rookie" knew all the elements of reporting. She was a consummate professional—a hard worker who wanted to be judged on her ability as a reporter and not on her looks. That work ethic led to one of the most remarkable careers in Los Angeles broadcast news history.

Laura Diaz not only reported the news, she became one of the most successful anchors the City of Angels has ever seen. Along the way, Laura broke through barriers to become the first Hispanic woman to anchor a weekday TV newscast at an English-speaking station in Southern California. Laura was a member of the Channel 7 Eyewitness News team for nineteen years before she moved to KCBS-TV, where she anchored the Channel 2 newscast for another nine years. But she never forgot her roots as a reporter—having earned fourteen Emmys for excellence.

Most importantly, Laura is a dear friend who I absolutely enjoyed being able to call my teammate.

Stu Nahan: Probably the most colorful and engaging person I ever met. When you walked into Channel 7's sports department, Stu would be smoking a cigar at his desk and talking to one of his many famous friends. It could be Lakers owner Jack Kent Cooke or hockey Hall of Famer Gordie Howe. There wasn't anyone Stu didn't know. And he was one of the best-liked people in the world of sports. His office was always a beehive of activity. Stu loved to play poker. And many nights, he'd have a card game going in the sports department right up until airtime at eleven. There were days when Stu would fly to Las Vegas to play cards, always making sure he was back in time to do the newscast. If anyone called, they were told Stu was "on assignment." Over the years, Stu was a strong supporter of the Southern California Sports Broadcasters organization, serving twice as its president. He even moonlighted in the movies, appearing in *Brian's Song*. And it wasn't fight night for Rocky Balboa unless Stu Nahan was at the ringside microphone for all six *Rocky* movies. Stu never considered himself a "star." But he's got one . . . on the Hollywood Walk of Fame.

Stu had the most interesting résumé of any of my colleagues. He had a dismal career in minor league hockey (and admittedly so), playing for the old Los Angeles Monarchs. Stu tried his hand in television as a children's host. He was "Skipper Stu" in Sacramento and "Captain Philadelphia" in the City of Brotherly Love. But Stu loved to tell his adventures as the number two play-by-play announcer for a minor league baseball team. The radio station Stu and his partner worked for couldn't afford to send them on the road for the team's away games. So they would recreate the ball games in the studio, getting the pitch-by-pitch information over the teletype and using sound effects to make it sound real on air. Stu would spend most of the game in an adjacent studio preparing the teletype info for his partner, and then step in and do the play-by-play for an inning or two in the middle of the game while his partner took a break. As Stu tells it, his partner liked to relax on his break by having a drink (or two).

One day, that habit had an unexpected effect on the broadcast. The baseball team was playing a doubleheader out of town in Portland. Back at the studio, Stu's partner had a drink during his break in the middle of the first game . . . another in between games . . . and even more in the middle of the second game. By the eighth inning, the lead announcer was on the air and desperately needed to go to the bathroom. But Stu was nowhere to be seen. (He was in another studio checking the teletype for updates.) Stu was listening to the broadcast when at one point, it sounded like rain was falling. His partner told listeners, "A sudden storm has just broken out here in Portland." Stu says he ran to the other studio and found his partner, shall we say, putting a trash can to good use. Sure enough, in sixty seconds the deed was done, with Stu's partner telling the audience that the skies had just cleared.

Stu Nahan lost his battle with lymphoma the day after Christmas in 2007 after gracing our world for eighty-one years. Stu loved the movies. And Larry Stewart of the *Los Angeles Times* wrote a marvelous article on a memorial service that would have tickled the irreverent Stu. It was held at a movie theater in the Sherman Oaks Galleria where popcorn, sodas, and Raisinets were served. Speaking to an audience that was a Who's Who of the L.A. sports world, Kings Hall of Fame announcer Bob Miller took aim at Stu's lack of skills as a goalie in minor league hockey. After giving up eight goals in a single game, Miller (with tongue in cheek) said a despondent Stu Nahan tried to commit suicide by standing in front of a moving bus. "But it went through his legs."

Bob Banfield: He is one of the most beloved people that has worked at Channel 7. For decades, Bob was such a treasured asset to our newscast. He is among the most respected reporters who ever appeared on Los Angeles television. And he's an even better person and teammate. In the Inland Empire, where Bob served as Eyewitness News Bureau Chief from 1980 until his retirement in 2010, our station couldn't have wished for a better ambassador. When Bob came to work each day to report news in Riverside and San Bernardino Counties, he never knew what challenging story he would be called on to cover. Whether it be an out of control brush fire threatening homes, snow in the mountains closing main arteries to traffic, or winds strong enough to topple big rigs like toys, Bob and his crew were resilient, flexible, and highly dedicated to meeting each test—no matter what. Bob Banfield wore many "hats," literally.

Bob's road to Eyewitness News included some very interesting stops along the way. Banfield and famed football coach Lou Holtz share the same small hometown, East Liverpool, Ohio (which has been dubbed the Pottery Capital of the World). In 1948, a car dealer came to see his daughter in a high school play and noticed Bob on stage as well. The car dealer offered eighteen-year-old Bob Banfield a job as a junior announcer at a local radio station. And that prompted young Bob to change his plans to go work at a steel mill. As Bob got more broadcast experience, he moved on to a bigger town—Zanesville, Ohio (population 25,486), where he became a "whiz" on WHIZ radio and TV. Whatever there was to do, Bob did it. He hosted a children's show as Ditto the Clown. And he was the star of musical variety programs like *Breakfast Party* and *Bob Banfield's Open House*. I've actually seen tape of Bob on TV with an organ player singing the Johnny Mercer song "My Sugar Is So Refined." Oh my goodness!

But every once in a while, Bob got to go do some news, using a small camera to take some pictures of a breaking story. In 1967, Bob Banfield was hired by Channel 7 Eyewitness News in Los Angeles to be a reporter. He was paid twenty dollars a story—if it made air. Bob never had to look for a job ever again. It was one of the most remarkable runs in broadcast history—forty-three years. And what was the steel mill's loss is journalism's gain.

On June 28, 2012, our dear friend Bob Banfield lost his battle with cancer at the age of eighty-two. There was such a public outpouring of deep affection from the many lives he touched over the years. One Southland newspaper ran this headline about Bob's distinguished career in broadcast journalism and his legacy: "If he was there, the story mattered." At the funeral service, Eyewitness News cameraman Dave Busse spoke for all of us about our teammate who was so loved: "Bob Banfield taught us all that honesty, integrity, humility, and just being a nice guy never goes out of style." My friends, it's one thing to say that Bob is irreplaceable. But then again, how can you replace something in our hearts that will never be removed?

Gene Gleeson: When it comes to longevity, he is a mere rookie compared to Bob Banfield. Gene "only" lasted thirty years at Channel 7 Eyewitness News. He was a pivotal player in the success of KABC-TV. When you talk about someone with trust and believability, Gene Gleeson was second to none. And when he retired in 2010, Gene was still at the top of his profession—just as he had been for decades.

In television news, Gene was the complete package. As a reporter, he was among the finest storytellers I ever saw. His commitment, dedication, and experience made a difference each and every day. This was a journalist you wanted on the scene as history unfolded. When the Berlin Wall fell in 1989, Gene Gleeson was there for Eyewitness News. As a private pilot, Gene used his vast knowledge in his live reporting on the space shuttle . . . from its initial mission on April 12, 1981 to the *Challenger* and *Columbia* disasters. He was the very first reporter that was allowed to pilot the B-1 bomber in a flight that actually went supersonic. For years, Gene anchored the morning and midday editions of Eyewitness News. In all my years that I worked at Channel 7, I don't know if we had a teammate that was better liked and respected than Gene Gleeson.

But did you know Gene Gleeson got his baptism in broadcasting as a rock and roll disc jockey? Gene was a mere twenty years of age when he worked for his father's radio station in the Inland Empire of Southern California—KFXM "Tiger Radio." And even though he was the boss's son, Gene still had to work the graveyard shift at one point—midnight to 6 a.m. The listening audience was so small in the middle of the night, Gene says he used to call a good friend of his at a competing radio station and they would win each other's contests on the air. But on August 23, 1964, Gene Gleeson was one of the disc jockeys on stage when the Beatles performed at the Hollywood Bowl. Once the concert was over, the Fab Four ran offstage to jump into a limousine. And in the mad dash, Ringo Starr tripped over Gene's foot onstage. The following year, the Beatles had a hit single called "Day Tripper." You have to wonder if Gene Gleeson was the inspiration! In retirement, Gene has become a tourist, as he and his beloved wife, Traute, travel the world with the same enthusiasm with which he covered it.

Ed Arnold: Don't tell him I said this. But there isn't a nicer person in the business. Ed served on the Eyewitness News team from 1975 to 1986, where he was a fixture on our sportscasts and later as an insightful news reporter as a member of our Orange County Bureau. Over the years, Ed was a "Rock of Gibraltar" on the local sports scene, covering the "games people play" for both Channel 7 and Channel 5 News, in addition to being an influential force within the Southern California Sports Broadcasters organization. Since 2000, Ed has been anchor and managing editor of the Southland's only newscast that takes a daily in-depth look at the important stories and issues of the day, *Real Orange* on KOCE-TV.

Now you would think that a highly respected journalist like Ed Arnold might be the product of some of the finest news people harvested from what Edward R. Murrow described as "this vineyard that produces words and pictures." Yes—Ed does have an impressive résumé. But his journey actually began in the world of rock and roll radio, deep in the heart of Texarkana, Arkansas. That's where fourteen-year-old Ed Arnold started out by playing records on a rhythm and blues station that also featured such homespun disc jockeys as "Country Cousin Jim" and "Uncle Dudley". Ed remembers a young Elvis Presley in 1954 performing in their radio studio with just a guitarist and a bass player to promote his local concert. Ed later graced the airwaves of Los Angeles on radio stations that featured jazz and easy listening, in addition to being the voice of public television KCET and a mainstay of its fundraising efforts for more than a decade.

My friend Ed Arnold is also the most courageous person I've ever seen in broadcasting. I've worked with so many over the years. But it takes guts, courage, and unwavering faith to be able to stand up in public like Ed and say, "I believe in God." Ed has answered a unique calling in his life. Oh, Ed never signed off his sportscasts with a sermon. He doesn't believe in forcing his faith on others. But there are windows of opportunity. And when the ministry at the Crystal Cathedral in Garden Grove, California, asked Ed to be its announcer for its nationally seen *Hour of Power* television program each week, he saw it as an inspirational way to serve the Lord. That was back in 1970. More than forty years later, Ed is still serving. And he has never accepted one dime for this work at his church. There aren't enough pages in this book to document all the charities to which Ed Arnold has reached out and made a monumental difference. Ed will never talk about it, but he has always donated from his heart. And that, my friends, speaks volumes.

Elmer Dills: There are lots of folks who have worked as restaurant critics in the Southland media over the years. But nobody has ever had the impact of Elmer Dills. For nearly three decades, Elmer dished out his reviews on Channel 7 Eyewitness News with honesty and integrity so that the viewers he served would have the best information on where to spend their hard-earned dining dollars. But have you ever wondered where Elmer developed this appetite for knowledge on the subject of food? "Diplomatically" speaking, Elmer Dills served this country for more than twenty years as an officer with the Central Intelligence Agency. Among his many duties, Elmer was assigned to arrange dinners with VIPs and heads of state in the many countries to which he traveled for the CIA. It's no longer a "top secret" that before becoming a famous chef, Julia Child also worked for a U.S. spy agency during World War II. I find it fascinating that these two renowned food experts, Elmer and Julia, also had a hunger for espionage at one point in their careers. I guess there's nothing like having a recipe for drama to spice up one's life!

Elmer Dills's interest in the art of cuisine actually began long before he signed up with the CIA. When Elmer was going to college, he was manager of the student cafeteria on campus. After serving Uncle Sam overseas all those years, Elmer came back to the states hoping to parlay his expertise in dining into a real career meal ticket. He started out in print at the *Los Angeles Herald Examiner* writing restaurant reviews at fifty dollars an article—with Elmer paying the food tab out of his own pocket. In 1976, Dills expanded his menu with a show as the "Dining Doctor" on KABC TalkRadio. Two years later, Elmer's restaurant reports became a staple on Channel 7 Eyewitness News for decades.

And now I'm going to take you behind the scenes to give you the real lowdown on how Elmer Dills put together his report card on the restaurants he graded throughout Southern California. Elmer imposed nothing less than the highest of standards on himself to eliminate any possible suspicions about his credibility. He couldn't be bought. He accepted no favors. And Elmer always paid his own bill. His work ethic was impeccable. When Elmer Dills first visited a restaurant, he took no TV cameras. They had no idea he was coming. The reservation was made under another name. Elmer would dine unassuming with a group of up to eight people, which at times included my wife and me. Dills would insist we all order something different so that he could sample as much of the menu as possible. He thoroughly checked out the bathrooms for cleanliness. Nothing escaped Elmer's attention—the service, the wine list, the ambiance—each and every detail. Elmer Dills knew that his review could very well mean success or failure for that particular restaurant. He wanted to be fair. Over the years, the viewers of Channel 7 Eyewitness News placed their unwavering trust in Elmer Dills. And KABC-TV mailed out millions of Elmer's $10-or-under restaurant guide, *Dine Like a Prince . . . Pay Like a Pauper.*

Elmer's dedication to excellence continued in his travel reports for our newscast, most notably the popular "Fred and Elmer" series with Channel 7 News reporter Fred Anderson. Elmer had a love for windsurfing. And when he married his beloved Lynne at Universal Studios, the local Gladstones turned its restaurant into a virtual beach for the wedding (at which I was honored to serve as an usher). Mrs. Fischbeck and I had a delightful relationship with Elmer and his wife. We even took several vacations with the Dills, including one unforgettable trip to Tahiti. As you can imagine, with Elmer planning everything, it was nothing less than paradise. On September 15, 2008, we lost our dear colleague. Elmer Dills was eighty. The news director who had first hired Elmer at Channel 7 Eyewitness News—Fox's president of station operations, Dennis Swanson—flew to Los Angeles to deliver the eulogy at the funeral of his longtime friend. It was indeed a celebration of life. Mark Twain once said, "Twenty years from now, you will be more disappointed by the things that you didn't do than by the ones you did do. So throw off the bowlines. Sail away from the safe harbor. Catch the trade winds in your sails. Explore. Dream. Discover."

Bruce Herschensohn: The highly respected political "think tank" who served on the Channel 7 Eyewitness News ticket for thirteen years (1978–1991) with his incisive commentaries and debates. Bruce brought a résumé that was unparalleled. He was one of the most influential advisors in the Richard Nixon White House as Special Assistant to the President. But did you know that Bruce is the only person who ever worked for Eyewitness News who made invaluable contributions to a team that actually won an Academy Award? It's a journey that began in 1950 when eighteen-year-old Bruce Herschensohn went to work as a studio messenger for RKO Pictures shortly after graduating from high school. After serving in the Air Force, Bruce began his own movie company—Herschensohn Motion Picture Productions. And he was later named by President Johnson to be director of motion pictures and television for the United States Information Agency. It was during Bruce's tenure at the USIA that the agency received four Oscar nominations for its acclaimed documentaries, including *Czechoslovakia 1968*, which won the Academy Award for Best Documentary Film. Over the course of this extraordinary work, Bruce was involved with such film legends as Charlton Heston, Paul Newman, Gregory Peck, James Cagney, and director John Ford. Bruce Herschensohn wore many hats for these projects—including producer, director, writer, and cinematographer. Bruce did the editing, and he even composed the music.

Now I've got to be honest with you. I didn't know about my friend Bruce's brush with Oscar until recently. And I worked with him at Channel 7 Eyewitness News for more than a decade. Bruce never talked about it—ever! This is one of the most humble, warm, and friendly gentlemen that I've ever known. Is he also bright and brilliant? Well, of course. My goodness. Bruce worked at the White House.

I was awestruck by how genuinely nice he is. When you pass Bruce in the newsroom, and he asks, "How are you doing?," he really wants to know! Remember his sharp debate confrontations with former U.S. Senator John Tunney on Eyewitness News? It was a political war of words that became a real "can't miss" on Los Angeles television: Bruce on the right and John on the left. Off air, these two guys were marvelous friends despite their ideological differences. They still are. Don't you wish we could bottle the goodwill generated by these two giants of intellect and inspire our nation to be less divided and vindictive toward those we don't agree with?

It was Bruce Herschensohn who arranged for Eyewitness News anchor Jerry Dunphy to be the first journalist to interview Richard Nixon following his resignation as President of the United States. This KABC-TV exclusive was broadcast in Southern California after the network's *Monday Night Football*. What was supposed to be a forty-five minute interview ended up being extended to an hour and a half. It was quite an event. And security at our TV station was oh-so-tight with the Secret Service in charge. Bruce rode with former President Nixon as they were flown in by helicopter to the Channel 7 studios in East Hollywood. Now since I was not scheduled to be a part of the Nixon program, I decided to drive home after the 6 p.m. newscast and have a quick dinner with my family before returning for the 11 p.m. news. When Mr. Nixon walked onto the set and shook hands with Jerry Dunphy, I am told the former president asked, "Where is our weatherman, George?" And that led to a mad scramble to find me— a manhunt that ended in the KABC parking lot where I was getting into my car for the drive home. When I heard that the former president had summoned me—well, my family was just going to have to wait. After all, Mr. Nixon had "executive privilege." And you know something, he couldn't have been more kind and gracious.

Bruce Herschensohn has dedicated much of his life to promoting the sharing of ideas . . . in which his participation helped raise the level of discourse and the quality of that exchange. He ran for the U.S. Senate twice, coming within just a few percentage points of getting elected in 1992. But it is in the landscape of education where Bruce has made—and continues to make—invaluable contributions to these forums of higher learning. Bruce has taught at both the University of Maryland and Whittier College. He has been a distinguished fellow at the Claremont Institute as well as the John F. Kennedy School of Government at Harvard. For the past fifteen years, Bruce has been teaching classes on U.S. foreign policy at Pepperdine University's School of Public Policy, where he has also served on the university's board (and at times as chairman) since 1990. And somehow, my friend has also found the time to write no fewer than twelve books on a wide range of subjects. I can't even begin to tell you how many times I've talked with Bruce at our workplace concerning the important issues of the day. As a teacher myself, I deeply admire Bruce's strength in speaking out and his willingness to engage, to listen, to enlighten, and to grow. Malcolm S. Forbes once said, "Education's purpose is to replace an empty mind with an open one." And as long as Bruce Herschensohn is on the job assisting discovery in his classroom, the pursuit of knowledge will always be a commitment taken to the highest "degree."

John Schubeck: One of the brightest and most talented news anchors that I ever had the delight of working with in broadcast journalism. But John's story is also one of the saddest. He was my friend and my teammate. I only wish more could have been done to help John in his desperate time of need.

Very few people have ever been blessed with the highly successful career that John Schubeck enjoyed. He anchored local TV newscasts in the major markets of New York City, Chicago, Philadelphia, and Los Angeles. When I first joined Channel 7 Eyewitness News in 1972, we couldn't have had a better anchor team than Joseph Benti and John Schubeck. They were simply the best. In 1974, John signed on with KNBC-TV to anchor the Channel 4 News. Nine years later, Schubeck moved to crosstown rival KNXT-TV (now KCBS) where he assumed anchor duties on the Channel 2 News. For seventeen years, John was one of the most recognizable TV news figures in Southern California. And he was so intelligent, having earned his law degree during the day while he anchored newscasts at night.

John also led a very carefree life. I remember Schubeck flying to Europe at a moment's notice to spend the weekend playing golf, visit relatives, or drive cross-country before returning to work on Monday. But John also had a problem—a serious battle with the bottle that I didn't know about until it was almost too late. During our time together at Eyewitness News, John and I enjoyed a wonderful relationship. I knew that my friend drank socially from time to time. But I never saw John drink at work. And Schubeck didn't let alcohol affect our newscasts in any way—not even for one moment. Like I said, if John had a problem with alcohol . . . he didn't do anything that would have tipped me off.

Years later, I got a call. Someone who deeply cared about John Schubeck told me that our friend was in way over his head with drinking. And I was asked to take part in an intervention with several others in a last-ditch effort to save John. The intervention took place in Thousand Oaks, where John had no idea what was about to happen until he arrived. A group of us pleaded with him to put the bottle down and enter a residential rehabilitation center immediately. I will never know if John had the capability at that point to understand the urgency of this personal crisis in which he was drowning. We even had his bags packed for this most important trip. John accepted and said he would enter rehab. But after we left, John Schubeck backed out. And he never went. I'm told John's son was very upset and distraught—telling the father he loved that he was killing himself. But it was a plea that went unheeded.

John Schubeck passed away on September 26, 1997. The cause of death was listed as kidney and liver failure. In its obituary, the *New York Times* described John as one of the most distinguished newscasters in the country. In his final years, the only television job John could find was at a small station in the Southern California desert. The acclaimed news anchor who once commanded a salary of $1 million a year reportedly died penniless. One of John's former colleagues at KNBC is said to have paid for his funeral and burial out of a deep love and respect that we shared. John Schubeck was just sixty-one.

Barney Morris: A most revered anchor and reporter who delivered the news for most of three decades in Detroit, Philadelphia, San Diego, and Los Angeles. As a journalist, Barney was the epitome of professionalism—integrity, trust, intelligence, and news judgment. He was fair. He was well-liked and highly respected by his colleagues and the people he covered. And out in the field, Barney was just the finest.

Case in point: Election Night 1984. The biggest story of the evening was by far Ira Reiner being elected in the hard-fought race for Los Angeles County District Attorney. Every TV station in Southern California was on hand inside a local hotel ballroom, primed for live coverage of Reiner's victory statement. As Reiner's supporters and a large army of news media waited for the candidate to come out, Barney Morris situated himself on the far right hand side of the stage. Even Barney's Eyewitness News remote producer at the scene had no idea what his reporter was doing. But Barney did. And this impeccable newsman was about to teach a lesson on how a seasoned reporter gets a scoop. When Reiner finally emerged and came to the podium . . . Barney Morris walked across the stage with a Channel 7 microphone in hand and began a live interview of the victorious candidate. Barney Morris had outmaneuvered every station in town. And his "exclusive" interview with the man of the night was broadcast live on each of their newscasts. Barney had simply given them no other choice.

My friend Barney is also the most inspirational person I have ever been blessed to know. You see, Barney Morris had an illness. It's called alcoholism. But instead of going down in defeat, Barney became a guiding light to his fellow alcoholics as he reached out to those trapped in a downward spiral of drinking, loneliness, and despair. Barney's incredible personal story became a light at the end of a dark tunnel for the lost and forgotten who were desperately seeking some semblance of hope.

Barney's drinking cost him his first marriage. The bottle became too much for his wife to handle, and she divorced him. But Barney's wife had serious issues with her own health. And the court gave him custody of the couple's six children. Barney could have gone off the deep end at that point. And he did fall off the wagon a number of times. The last time Barney got drunk . . . he almost killed a man in a bar fight. That forced Barney to seek help by walking through the door of Alcoholics Anonymous. It was a relationship that remained intact for more than three decades. At first, Barney's grip on sobriety was fragile at best. He initially resisted going to A.A. meetings, having a sense of not belonging. But over time, Barney's feelings of inadequacy ended up shining a light on his need for the fellowship and the encouragement that these gatherings provided. And weeks and months of recovery led to years of staying sober.

Barney Morris later remarried, and his family in time grew to include eight children in all. He became a cornerstone of A.A.'s Tuesday night meetings in Santa Monica, California, called "The Pacific Group." Barney said he found in Alcoholics Anonymous what he had been looking for unsuccessfully in the bottle. And with his gift of communication, Barney took his life-saving message of sobriety across America at speaking engagements for A.A. If you had a need—Barney Morris had the time. He was always on call. There wasn't anything Barney wouldn't do for a recovering alcoholic. He cared that much. Barney was indispensable.

On March 14, 2003, Barney Morris died from heart failure at the age of sixty-six. But he continues to make a difference. Barney's recorded messages that have guided so many drinkers to sobriety through his unique blend of humor, passion, and urgency are available on the Internet. The late Sam Shoemaker is a beloved Episcopal priest who was so instrumental in the founding of Alcoholics Anonymous. Reverend Shoemaker wrote a poem about the mission that Barney Morris cherished—to lend a helping hand and save victims from the ravages of drink, pain, and agony. The poem is called "I Stand By The Door."

I stand by the door.
I neither go too far in . . . nor stay too far out.
The door is the most important door in the world.

It is the door through which men walk when they find God.
There is no use my going way inside and staying there,
When so many are still outside.
And they, as much as I, crave to know where the door is.

And all that so many ever find
Is only the wall where a door ought to be.
They creep along the wall like blind men,
With outstretched, groping hands,
Feeling for a door . . . knowing there must be a door.
Yet they never find it.
So I stand by the door.

As a journalist, Barney Morris helped the world be better informed. As a human being, he made it a better world.

Heroes Who Give Hope

When a man becomes a fireman his greatest act of bravery has been
accomplished. What he does after that is all in the line of work.

~ CHIEF EDWARD F. CROKER ~

FDNY, 1899–1911

Someone once wrote some thoughtful words that can be applied to every humble and courageous firefighter I have ever met. "What you call a hero . . . I call just doing my job." It is a calling like no other. When they respond to duty, they have a willingness to endure the ordeal of whatever it takes to help those in need. Firefighters conquer the seemingly insurmountable barriers of danger and fear with strength of heart. In the face of tragedy, they offer comfort and compassion. And they serve unselfishly so that when the alarm rings again, they can answer with bravery that knows no limits.

In this chapter, I want you to meet a most exclusive club of caring firefighters from two organizations who I've had the distinct honor and pleasure of knowing for more than a quarter of a century. They reach far beyond the fire lines with a mission that is symbolic of man's humanity to man. And these heroes bring a message of healing and hope to burn survivors who have been forced on a journey of pain, loss, trauma, and in some cases ridicule and anguish.

The Alisa Ann Ruch Burn Foundation

Let me begin with what is a living memorial to a little girl who died in a tragic fire at the age of eight. The story of this loving angel with blonde hair and big blue eyes has made all the difference in a world she didn't live to see. In May 1970, the Ruch family with their three small children decided to hold a backyard barbeque at their Van Nuys home to celebrate the coming of summer.

At one point, fire raced out of control up the lighter fluid can the father was holding. It exploded. And little Alisa Ann Ruch was engulfed in flames. In a moment of panic, Alisa Ann ran around the house toward the garage and then back to the patio door—where her aunt, who was a nurse, grabbed a sheet or a tablecloth, wrapped it around her niece, and rolled her on the ground to put the fire out. Alisa Ann suffered severe burns on 97 percent of her body. Her five-year-old brother David was burned badly on his face and hands. David was rescued by his father, who suffered burns on his arm.

Alisa Ann Ruch

The children were rushed to Sherman Oaks Community Hospital, where Alisa Ann was given only a 1 percent chance of surviving. David, who had burns across nearly one-fourth of his body, would pull through. For the next five weeks, Dr. A. Richard Grossman and his dedicated team of specialists fought to save Alisa Ann. Only one year before, it was Dr. Grossman who convinced Sherman Oaks Community Hospital to devote two beds that would be used exclusively for burn patients. Talk about this doctor's vision . . . those two beds would lead to what is now regarded as one of the finest and most comprehensive burn facilities in the entire world—the Grossman Burn Centers.

On June 28, 1970, eight-year-old Alisa Ann Ruch lost her fight for life. The Ruch family believed that with sufficient burn prevention education, little Alisa Ann might not have died in that fire. And in the midst of their loss and grief, her parents reached out to Los Angeles County firefighters to create a foundation in their daughter's name to promote the message of fire safety. Alisa Ann's family had been deeply touched by two county firemen who had been severely burned during an emergency call . . . and by the heartfelt response by concerned colleagues to provide support for their physical, emotional, and psychological recovery.

In 1971, the Alisa Ann Ruch Burn Foundation was born. The Sherman Oaks Community Hospital donated a storage closet for the unpaid volunteers and firefighters to use as their first base of operations. This tiny "office" was home to some very big hearts, who embarked on an even bigger mission. Barbara Horn, who served as foundation president and has given so unselfishly in dedication for decades, had these words about those first volunteers: "Their ability to dream remains an integral part of our burn foundation character. Their vision, sacrifices, and contributions are the key to shaping our future . . . and the future of those we serve."

In its inception, the foundation targeted two crucial needs: establishing programs in public schools to educate children about fire safety, burn prevention, and treatment; and giving assistance to burn survivors. Fires and burn injuries take such a catastrophic toll—nearly 2.5 million people suffer burns each year. Between eight and twelve thousand of those patients will die, while another 1 million will face the burden of permanent or substantial disabilities. These horrifying experiences can happen in the blink of an eye. But many of the survivors will be severely scarred physically for the rest of their lives. And they will be scarred emotionally and mentally as well.

The financial cost is another steep mountain burn survivors and their families must face. The initial hospitalization of a patient who has been burned across 30 percent of their body can run as much as $200,000. That's just the beginning. Continued long-term treatment for reconstruction, rehabilitation, psychological counseling, and physical therapy will cost a fortune—and beyond. For some four decades now, the Alisa Ann Ruch Burn Foundation has accepted the challenge of providing invaluable support and hope for burn survivors who are in need. A relief fund was set up to give financial assistance to those affected by disaster and facing life-threatening emergencies. This includes money to help pay for hospital bills, medical supplies, therapy, housing, food, and transportation.

This foundation is driven by its desire to succeed and a refusal to compromise its commitment and integrity. Defeat is not an option. But in the beginning, fund-raising was indeed limited. It started with small donations that were sent to the Ruch family in letters and cards as word spread that they wanted to help others in Alisa Ann's memory. One by one, fire departments across Southern California signed on to be a part of this growing foundation of love that now has such a rich history of accomplishment.

If I may say so, firefighters are a most competitive bunch. And there isn't anything they wouldn't do to outperform their colleagues from a neighboring fire department in raising funds for burn survivors. In fact, they are nothing less than ingenious in finding ways to do so. They held pancake breakfasts, dinners, dances, golf tourneys, bike rides, rodeos, wine and cheese tastings, and bowl-a-thons. In 1972, the Torrance Fire Department decided to hold a fund-raising spaghetti dinner for the public—all you can eat. I'm told that the fire chief donated his cooking talents for the cause. And the community "ate it up." It has been an annual tradition for the Alisa Ann Ruch Burn Foundation for some forty years now. There's a recipe for success! Some, shall we say, "hunky" L.A. firefighters posed for a calendar to heat up some female passions and raise money for this worthy cause. It became a best-seller. Another innovative fire department held a Firefighter Bachelor Auction for single ladies. Talk about girls' night out! Sound the alarms! The sexiest men in uniform strutted their stuff on the runway. Even a high-tech calculator couldn't keep up with all the bids that came pouring in. In case you're wondering, Mrs. Fischbeck refused to let me go on the auction block. Even charity has its limits, I guess. But then again, this is one weatherman who doesn't need any personal "storm clouds" in his life!

In 1985, some firefighters and friends of the foundation came up with a unique way to try to connect all the dots to these individual fund-raising efforts throughout the year . . . and by doing so, create an even bigger event. In the words of Frank Sinatra—"Start spreading the news"—which is how Dr. George was asked to come on board. Foundation officials decided to hold a relay in which my firefighter friends and I would climb onto a couple of fire trucks and drive to different cities across the Southland to pick up the money raised during the past year for the Alisa Ann Ruch Burn Foundation. I was designated as the official relay "baton." Whenever our little caravan would arrive at one fire station, I would accept the check for the foundation, then board another fire truck and head to the next city.

That first year of the relay, we visited fifteen different fire stations from our starting point in Monrovia in a one-day humanitarian journey. And what a heartwarming event it was to be a part of. Our caravan included a real-life hero who became my friend for life—Rick Pfeiffer, a captain who served thirty-six years with the Inglewood and Los Angeles County Fire Departments. I think Rick had more fun than anyone else during the relay because he got to drive a classic restored 1952 American LaFrance fire truck. You should have seen us at each relay point as we arrived with red lights and sirens along with a police escort. Because I was involved, Channel 7 Eyewitness News covered the relay. And each community turned out in droves to take part. You couldn't help but be deeply touched by the inspirational burn survivors who accompanied us on the fire trucks. No one could miss their big smiles. During that first relay, we were able to collect checks totaling $30,000 for the Alisa Ann Ruch Burn Foundation and its mission to enhance the quality of life for burn survivors.

Now I don't want anyone to think that I took part in this relay with any kind of selfish personal agenda to put the public spotlight on me. Oh my goodness. First of all, I was asked by the foundation to participate. They wanted someone who was fairly well-known to help increase awareness of the relay, the foundation, and its dreams. Yes— images of me receiving the checks at each fire station were shown on the news. But I saw this as a unique opportunity to focus the public's attention on the dedicated firefighters and volunteers who had worked hard all year to make the relay a success. You know, in years past when you watched the Jerry Lewis MDA Telethon (when he was a part of it), you saw the donations pour in from across America on Labor Day. But Jerry did his absolute best to make sure viewers knew what happened the other 364 days of the year within his "Love Network" that made this possible. I saw that as my job as well. I figured that if Dr. George can get your attention on our newscast, then I could share a most important message about some wonderful folks who sacrificed around the year to make a big difference in the lives of so many through the burn foundation. It's been said that no one is more cherished in this world than someone who lightens the burden of another.

Burns do not recognize boundaries. And neither do the services provided by the Alisa Ann Ruch Burn Foundation. It's been estimated that 50 percent of all burn injuries are preventable. And the goal of this foundation is to make those injuries obsolete through its burn prevention education programs. Knowledge is the enemy of ignorance. It's like a book that famed author and storyteller Garrison Keillor says "is a gift that you can open again and again." The money donated to the foundation goes to educate over twenty-five thousand elementary school students each year with its program called Firefighters in Safety Education. This educational project is run in coordination with fire departments across the state to teach schoolchildren vital information that includes the "Stop, Drop, and Roll" technique (*stop* if your clothes catch on fire, *drop* to the ground, and *roll* on the ground to extinguish the flames).

The largest percentage of burn injuries among babies and toddlers are caused by scalds. Hot liquids can burn just like fire. The Alisa Ann Ruch Burn Foundation initiated the Baby Blues Program, which provides scald and burn prevention kits to new parents throughout California. Many children who struggle to recover from severe burns also face another steep obstacle—the fear of returning to school. Through the foundation's Back to School Program, the survivors' insecurities and anxieties over how classmates may react to their scars and appearance are addressed. And the program works with both student peers and teachers to form a supportive school environment to meet a need that is so critical. The Alisa Ann Ruch Foundation sponsors burn survivors support groups to create a forum of interaction and emotional support for survivors and their families. If distance or transportation are a problem, then teleconferences are arranged. But feelings of loneliness and isolation will be confronted—no matter what.

As the foundation's services expanded, so did the organization. Regional offices opened in San Francisco and Fresno in addition to its Southern California base. Foundation efforts to reach out to burn survivors were extended statewide. And even though eight full-time staff members of the foundation were hired to carry out the day-to-day operations, the cornerstone of this organization are the volunteers—five hundred in all—who have always been the lifeline of a mission to positively affect each and every burn survivor and their loving, devoted families.

Each year after the annual fund-raising relay was over, I was always worried about whether I would be asked back. I was sure they could find a big celebrity who was a lot "cuter" to replace this old schoolteacher. But my friend, Fire Captain Rick Pfeiffer, made sure my invitation was always in the mail. You see, Rick had some pull within the foundation, having served four years as its president. And it wasn't long before the relay became three relays across Southern, Central, and Northern California each year. And they pulled out all the stops to make sure I was the "baton" at all three. Another foundation president, Barbara Horn, always accompanied me on these trips. Corporate donors provided whatever transportation was needed to get us there, including airplanes, helicopters, and motorhomes. I even remember the thrill of transferring from one fireboat to another in the middle of the breakwater in a "daring" move that I think must have scared my fellow boatmate Barbara half to death!

There's a saying from a wise person named Nancy Coey that I think truly epitomizes the wonderful people who make up the roster of the Alisa Ann Ruch Burn Foundation: "When work, commitment, and pleasure all become one and you reach that deep well where passion lives, nothing is impossible." They have allowed me to serve as their "baton" for more than two and a half decades of relays. The caravans have grown to include at least thirty vehicles, with the California Highway Patrol leading the way. You don't know what true excitement is until you have gone "Code 3" with the CHP on the burn relay. Fifty fire departments across the state are now proud participants in this massive effort, with firefighters volunteering their personal time year-round to ensure that the next relay is even more successful. But the backbone of this success are the donors who give from their hearts with endless generosity. The burn foundation is now raising up to $250,000 from its annual relays.

While we're on the subject, let me tell you the story of Ellwood "Woody" Reed, who served as a captain in the Los Angeles County Fire Department for over three decades. Woody and his wife, Louise, loved the Alisa Ann Ruch Burn Foundation. For years, Woody was an eyewitness to the heroism of the firefighter brotherhood and to the devastating impact on someone who suffers a severe burn injury. So Woody and Louise opened a family trust in which they spent twenty-two years saving up for a gift as partners with an enduring drive to help others. In April of 2011, Woody passed away to be with his beloved wife who had died in 2002. But this hero had one more job to accomplish before he left us. Woody bequeathed his family trust of $500,000 to the Alisa Ann Ruch Burn Foundation to benefit the lives of burn survivors for years to come. This gift is now funding the Ellwood and Louise Reed Bridge to Life Scholarship, which provides financial assistance to burn survivors in their pursuit of higher education. What a legacy of love.

I don't know if you've ever felt the pain of seeing severely burned children fight for life in a hospital after brave firefighters rescued them from a devastating inferno. I have. It is a heartwrenching sight that I will never forget. And so often, many of these kids, if they survive, will be forced to have dozens of skin graft surgeries. It is a road to recovery that can cause emotional trauma that may never go away.

That's why I want to tell you about one of the happiest places on earth, where tears and heartbreak are simply not allowed. For nearly three decades, the Alisa Ann Ruch Burn Foundation has operated a free summer camp for burn survivors ages five to sixteen. It's called Champ Camp. It began back in 1984 at the Cottontail Ranch in Malibu. But the week-long camp is now held at the Wonder Valley Ranch east of Fresno. Each summer, nearly 150 young burn survivors are flown or driven to the camp with volunteer chaperones and counselors to enjoy a wonderful opportunity to build their self-esteem and develop lasting friendships with children their own age. The Alisa Ann Ruch Foundation also operates a camp for adult burn survivors called the Getaway. And just like Champ Camp . . . the foundation pays for everything.

Children in the real world can be cruel. Some will make fun of a child with burn scars—relentlessly teasing them and asking invasive questions. But at Champ Camp, burn survivors feel more comfortable with other children who are facing the same challenges. This is where they can come to be kids again. My friends, I've been to Champ Camp. And let me give you a firsthand report on how they put the *wonder* in Wonder Valley. There's horseback riding, swimming, a water park, archery, and minibikes. It's a fun-filled summer vacation that offers social, physical, and emotional growth for children in surroundings that emphasize their inner beauty. Here's what burn survivor Maria Melendrez, who started going to Champ Camp at the age of five, told the Fire Department Network News: "It's like a whole different world. It's where a burn survivor can get to be who they really are. We don't have to hide from anyone. We don't have to be ashamed of what they say. It's a wonderful feeling." And you know what, Maria now wants to become a firefighter so that she can reach out with love and help change the lives of many . . . like the Alisa Ann Ruch Burn Foundation has changed hers.

So the next time you see the burn relay on the road or you have a chance to attend an Alisa Ann Ruch Foundation fund-raiser—reach into your wallet or your purse. And give from deep in your heart. By doing so, you will help these caring firefighters put an arm around burn survivors, wipe away their tears, and let them know they will never be alone ever again. Their motto is "We make a life by what we give."

A Lifeline of Compassion—and a "Quest" to Restore

Firefighters never die. They just burn forever in the hearts of the people whose lives they saved. ~ SUSAN DIANE MURPHREE

The date was October 22, 1996 . . . when firefighters from the cities of Los Angeles and Glendale risked their lives to protect homes from a fast-moving Calabasas-Malibu wildfire that forced thousands of residents to flee. The brave men and women who were on the fire line that fateful day answered the call not knowing if it would be their last. For some, it nearly was. Firefighters get scared too. Ambrose Redmoon once wrote, "Courage is not the absence of fear, but rather the judgment that something else is more important than fear."

Suddenly, the winds shifted. Without warning, the direction of the fire changed dramatically. And flames overran the positions of Bill Jensen and Scott French of Glendale Fire Station 24 and two L.A. City firefighters on a narrow side street off Corral Canyon Road. All four were seriously burned. But Jensen, who was just one year away from retirement, was fighting for his life. This twenty-nine year veteran of the Glendale Fire Department was in grave condition, having suffered third-degree burns over 73 percent of his body.

Doctors at Grossman Burn Center gave Jensen just a 5 percent chance of surviving. Ironically, Jensen wasn't even supposed to be on duty that day—he was sent to the Calabasas-Malibu fire only after he agreed to swap shifts with a friend. Bill Jensen eventually pulled through, but only after enduring forty operations and 3,500 skin grafts. Jensen's longtime colleague, Scott French, was burned on 30 percent of his body and underwent surgery on his face, ears, and elbow. The dedicated staff at Grossman Burn Center was deeply indebted to this hero. Firefighter French had been heavily involved in fund-raising for the facility. Bill Jensen and Scott French were two of only twelve firefighters who were assigned to Glendale Fire Station 24. And this is a close-knit team that was hit hard by the devastating news about their injured comrades.

Their teammates, family, and friends kept an around-the-clock vigil at the burn center. They started a prayer chain with someone offering a prayer every fifteen minutes as these survivors desperately fought back with flame-tortured skin and the agony of their burns. An army of firefighters from throughout Southern California also showed up to express their heartfelt support and made themselves available in case blood donors were needed.

The Glendale Fire Department received an avalanche of cards and donations from the public wanting to help in some way. As the days passed and the three other firefighters were allowed to go home, Bill Jensen's brave battle continued. At one point, his kidneys stopped working, and doctors feared that his body might be shutting down. But they never gave up. And Jensen never gave in, buoyed by the love and support of this bedside vigil.

Tom Propst of Glendale Fire Station 27, who looked up to Jensen as his mentor, was emotionally touched. But Propst noticed something else that was about to change his life—something that would ignite a cause affecting the lives of burn survivors for years to come. In the hospital room next to Jensen, Propst saw a man who was fighting for his life after being severely burned in an industrial accident. He lay in bed wrapped in gauze from head to toe. But unlike Bill Jensen, this man had no one in his room. He had no family . . . not a single person to offer a prayer or reach out with even a semblance of hope. It was a lonely picture of despair that hit Tom Propst hard in the deepest roots of his heart. How could this possibly be? It ignited a fire of a different kind, compelling Propst and his fellow firefighters to make sure this never happened to another burn survivor again—by creating a lifeline of support, help, and compassion.

Dr. Albert Schweitzer, a missionary who believed that helping others through service and kindness was both a responsibility and a joy, once said, "Wherever a man turns he can find someone who needs him." Through the tireless efforts of Glendale firefighters Tom Propst, Stuart Stefani, Craig Hammond, and dispatcher Lori Fitch, Firefighters Quest for Burn Survivors was born to meet that need—with a motto, "Together we will make a difference." That's what I like about these people. They don't say *we can* make a difference; they vow *we will*. That's the focus you can always expect from these firefighters who see physical and emotional pain that burn survivors suffer on a regular basis. The majority of burn injuries take a lifetime to heal. And it can create a mountain of debt that can take ten lifetimes to pay off. So if you want to help—it takes money, organization, public awareness, volunteers, dedication, boundless enthusiasm, and firefighters with endless amounts of heart. How's that for a "quest"? It certainly sounds like a team that Dr. George would love to be a part of.

In June of 1997, Firefighters Quest for Burn Survivors held its first rally to raise money for those in need. Quest's executive director Propst asked me to be the "human baton" for the caravans of vehicles from participating fire departments, collecting checks as we made stops at fire stations across Southern California. Quest raised $16,000 during its first rally. But it was just getting started.

And what an honor it was to be able to ride in this caravan of heroes along with a mountain of a man who brought a message of inspiration to this event—firefighter Bill Jensen. He was burned so severely in the 1996 Calabasas-Malibu fire that Bill was never able to return to work at the Glendale Fire Department where he served the community for nearly three decades. But at the first rally as he rode in the Quest caravan, Bill Jensen courageously reached out to his fellow burn survivors to let them know "You are not alone. We are one. Together we will make a difference." I have so many reasons to feel so blessed about my involvement with the folks at Quest. It has allowed my wife and me to forge an everlasting friendship with Bill and Sue Jensen. For sixteen years and counting, Bill has continued to serve Firefighters Quest for Burn Survivors, touching us all with his monumental will to live and his extraordinary grace and courage. Scott French, who was also seriously burned in the Calabasas-Malibu fire, has had an immeasurable impact on Quest over the years with his unselfish dedication and support. Take Dr. George's word for it. These are two servants whose acts of bravery and charity are truly heroic.

Since its inception, the Quest Rally for burn survivors has grown in size and donations each year. In 1998, the caravan raised $70,000. In recent years, Quest has received as much as $280,000 in checks during a single rally. That's a lot of "lifting" for an aging weatherman and "baton" like me. But Channel 7 Eyewitness News anchors Gene Gleeson, Phillip Palmer, and Kathy Vara (now with KNBC-TV) also generously volunteered to help the Quest Rally with their immense depth of spirit. The annual caravan for Firefighters Quest for Burn Survivors now covers 1,200 miles with 110 stops in six Southland counties over five days, led by an elite motorcade from the California Highway Patrol.

The volunteers who serve Quest spend a busy year collecting donations from agencies, organizations, corporations, and caring individuals. Firefighters from Southern and Central California have joined this network to demonstrate their commitment. The year-round journey to the Quest Rally includes such fund-raising events as golf and fishing tournaments, a steak fry, a car show, a raffle (with a donated trip to Paris), a health fair in Catalina, a spaghetti dinner in South Pasadena,

"Ski Day" at Mountain High, and a beach festival. I have been to a number of these important events for Quest. And over the years, it has been so heartwarming to reconnect with old friends within the Quest family with hopes of making new friends as well.

I've told you how Quest was formed. I've told you who is involved and how they raise money. And now I'm going to tell you what they do with it. And what a wonderful story it is. Quite simply, Quest values life. George Bernard Shaw once said: "You see things; and you say 'why?' But I dream things that never were; and I say 'why not?'" Every cent that Firefighters Quest for Burn Survivors has ever accepted in a donation has been given to its intended target. Every cent has either been given to burn survivors and their families or to programs of support. That's 100 percent over sixteen years. Now how can that be done, you may ask. Every person that serves Quest is an unpaid volunteer. That's the way it always has been. Executive director Tom Propst is an unpaid volunteer. He makes a living as a battalion chief for the Glendale Fire Department. Tom has been there for thirty years. But since 1997, he has also run Firefighters Quest for Burn Survivors. I know Tom. And I can't imagine how he does both of these important jobs within one life. On any given day, Tom is part of a dedicated group of people who makes sure that Quest is running in a highly efficient manner, focused on the mission of helping burn survivors make it through devastating situations. Let me repeat this: Every one of them is an unpaid volunteer. The late author and professor Leo Buscaglia has said, "Too often we underestimate the power of a touch, a smile, a kind word, a listening ear, an honest compliment, or the smallest act of caring, all of which has the potential to turn a life around."

Yes, Quest has organizational expenses. But it also has corporate supporters and civilian sponsors that take care of those costs so that the firefighters and volunteers can apply each and every dollar raised at the annual rally to having a positive impact on the lives of every burn survivor they can reach. And it is a crucial job. Firefighters Quest for Burn Survivors helps pay hospital bills for patients who cannot afford to do so. This includes therapy, medications, specialized bandages, pressure garments, form-fitting facial masks, and counseling. Quest is ready to provide family assistance while their loved one is hospitalized, including housing, food, and transportation. I've seen

Quest donations enable children in the hospital to have strollers and wagons, as well as toys and books to make their stay a little easier.

Quest helps support a group called L.A. Troupe Theater in Education, which annually teaches thousands of kindergarten through second-grade students the vital basics of fire safety and burn prevention with entertaining live performances at public schools. If you donate to Quest, you help pay for young burn survivors to go to summer camps, where they can enjoy such activities as horse riding, river rafting, and crafts. And the Quest Grant Program offers scholarships to paramedics to attend advanced life support classes that teach the enhanced care of the burn injured patient.

I've saved perhaps the best for last . . . because I believe what I am going to share with you is the most important mission of Firefighters Quest for Burn Survivors.

I can tell you this firsthand because I have been an eyewitness to this success story for the cause of helping others. In the early 1950s, there were only ten burn centers operating throughout the entire country. Now there are two hundred. And thanks to its compassionate donors, Firefighters Quest is able to provide substantial and vital support for major burn centers across Southern and Central California.

Very few bodily injuries are as traumatic as burns. I've seen critically burned patients fight to live after flames seared through their flesh and muscle, destroying blood vessels and nerves. Their immune system is so weakened that the body is overwhelmed by infection for which it has no defense. As one doctor put it: they are among the sickest patients you'll ever see in your lifetime. The firefighters of Quest are a blueprint for the commitment and the conviction of dealing with the injustice that burn survivors must face. Firefighters know that fires cripple. Fires disfigure. And fires kill. Quest has a relentless devotion to financially helping burn centers that do far more than just aid its patients in enduring survival. They restore lives.

There is an inspiring profile of courage involving one of the burn centers that donations from Firefighters Quest for Burn Survivors have helped support for years. The UC Irvine Regional Burn Center has an impeccable roster of skilled hands and a long résumé of miracles. I want to tell you how they rescued one burn survivor from the depths of a torturous hell. And it had nothing to do with a fire.

Fifteen-year-old high school honors student Cheryl Bess was kidnapped by a maintenance worker at the public housing project where she lived with her mother. Cheryl's assailant unsuccessfully tried to rape her in his van. He then threw a quart of sulfuric acid on his terrified victim—an attack that severely burned, blinded, and disfigured her—before he left the teenage girl for dead, wandering helplessly in the desert for five hours before she got help. The monster who did this was eventually caught and put on trial. He had previously spent sixteen years in prison for the attempted rape of a three-year-old girl. For the horror he caused this time, the man described by the judge as "cruel, vicious, and callous" was put away for thirty-four years. He died behind bars. Cheryl Bess may have had her face and her sight stolen in this unspeakable attack. But she never lost her dignity. Cheryl was guided through the slow and agonizing healing process and the arduous years of skin graft surgeries by Dr. Bruce Achauer and his team at the UC Irvine Regional Burn Center—a team that I will describe as God's angels on Earth.

As one newspaper headline put it, Cheryl "hasn't just survived . . . she's thrived." Her unwavering bravery and determination to recover against all odds led to an invitation to the White House and the Oval Office, where Cheryl and her mother, Norma, were honored by President Bill Clinton. There was an outpouring from admirers around the world who sent cards, letters, and donations to a special trust fund that was set up for Cheryl. And this courageous young woman graduated with honors from Saddleback College in Mission Viejo, where Cheryl pursued her love of music by working as a disc jockey on the campus jazz radio station.

But Cheryl also had a passion to give back to what she called "humankind" by reaching out to other burn survivors to heal their emotional scars. She participated in the burn recovery group sponsored by the Orange County Burn Association, where Cheryl offered support and encouragement. I mean, here was a woman who had been blinded and disfigured in a horrible crime . . . and she's telling other burn survivors "Everything's gonna be OK" (a motto from a popular morning radio show that Cheryl was a fan of).

On June 8, 1998, there wasn't a dry eye as the caravan for Firefighters Quest for Burn Survivors pulled into eleven fire stations across Orange County with red lights and sirens. We had some special guests riding with us aboard the bright red fire engines on this day of inspiration.

The tears of triumph flowed as firefighter Bill Jensen teamed up with Cheryl Bess to offer hope and love to their fellow burn survivors. Oh yes—that made the news. And did Quest ever collect a whole bunch of new people to join its cause that day! Bill Jensen and Cheryl Bess are two of the brightest lights to serve this noblest of endeavors. And the message they shared will hopefully prevent other burn survivors from becoming prisoners of themselves and carrying deep scars within over their lifetimes. As one burn survivor told the *Los Angeles Times*, "If we have someone who's been there before who thrives . . . it's not so frightening."

My friends, I want to thank you for taking time to read one of the most important chapters of my entire life. Firefighters Quest for Burn Survivors and the Alisa Ann Ruch Burn Foundation is a subject no one will ever accuse me of being "objective" about. The dictionary defines hero as "A legendary figure endowed with great strength or ability . . . admired and emulated for achievements and qualities." The firefighters I have described in this chapter will be the first to tell you they are no heroes. I beg to disagree. Then again, it is this humility that makes them so special. And I am deeply honored to know them. Admiral William F. "Bull" Halsey Jr. said, "There are no great men, only great challenges that ordinary men are forced by circumstances to meet."

It has been said it is the duty of firefighters to regularly hold others' futures in their hands, often at great peril to themselves. They are quiet heroes, fiercely dedicated to the belief that their best work is work done for others. There is a poem that I would like to share with you in part. The author chose to remain anonymous. We may not know who wrote it, but it has a message we must never forget.

He is the guy next door.
He is a guy like you and me
with . . . worries and unfulfilled dreams.
Yet he stands taller than most of us.
He is a fireman.

He is a man who saves lives because he has seen too much death.
He is responsive to a child's laughter . . . because his arms have
held too many small bodies that will never laugh again.
He doesn't preach the brotherhood of man.
He lives it.

The Rest of My Life—
I'm Just Getting Started

Reports of my demise are greatly exaggerated.

~ SAMUEL CLEMENS ~

The Rolling Stones have been lying to us. Time is not on our side. In 1992, I turned seventy. And there isn't any amount of preparation you can do to get ready for it. You can't study for it like an exam. It just slaps you in the face like a cold washcloth. John Glenn, who at seventy-seven was the oldest astronaut to fly in space, said it best: "There is still no cure for the common birthday." As a veteran weatherman, I will say this: Once you turn seventy, those five-day forecasts do take on a whole new perspective.

My assignments at Eyewitness News were slowly but gradually reduced. It's not as if I had to wear a name tag those times when I appeared on Channel 7 News again. The security guards at the KABC-TV main gate still recognized me. But I was beginning to spend more and more time at home. No official retirement day was ever really set. It didn't look like the finish line at the Boston Marathon with lots of loud horns, cheers, and celebration. It just kind of sputtered to the curb like a Model T and shut off. But my friends, I've got nothing to complain about—not after the career I enjoyed at one of the most successful news operations our industry has ever seen. You know, very few people in television news have been as blessed as I have, given the wonderful opportunity I had of serving the audience of Eyewitness News for twenty years.

Before I left, I had the absolute delight of working with a new teammate in the weather department. I've already told you what a joy it was to be with such people as Dallas Raines and Johnny Mountain. And Rick De Reyes couldn't have been a better fit on our team, what with his eagerness to learn and a deep desire to inform our viewers. Being the new "kid on the block", Rick had to work some tough shifts like weekends and early mornings. But nothing could possibly dampen Rick's enthusiasm in being a member of Channel 7 Eyewitness News. This is a young man who is so bright and intelligent, a hard worker who gives such dedication and commitment, a friend who is a pleasure to be with and to work with. Rick has also been of immense help to me in putting this book together. And I would like to share with you some thoughtful words Rick De Reyes has written about the time he and I spent together.

> *Dr. George graciously trained me when I was hired as a weatherman at KABC-TV. He could've ignored me. After all, he was still one of the biggest names in Los Angeles TV news. Instead, he spent countless hours explaining the idiosyncrasies of Southern California weather. I could never repay him for the kindness he showed me. And he did it with such passion and humility. I was just starting there. But he treated me like family. My life is so much richer having met him.*
>
> *—Rick De Reyes*

Rick was a valued member of the Eyewitness News team for eight years. Boy, do he and I share a lot in common. Rick's remarkable journey in life has included doing the weather for a place that I hold near and dear to my heart—KOB-TV in Albuquerque. Rick De Reyes is a friend I truly treasure. And I am so grateful to be remembered in such a special way by someone who I will always cherish as my teammate.

In 1992, as I looked forward to whatever challenges the future might present, I also glanced back with fondness at the wonderful memories I have of my time at Channel 7—thanks to the loyal viewers who invited us into their homes each and every day. You never knew what was going to happen in our newsroom on a day-to-day basis, especially on the phone. If our viewers had a question, and they asked for the weather department, the operators put them through directly. We had people call to ask for the forecast, saying they were planning a wedding, a picnic, a birthday party—you name it. Not that we could actually change the weather to help them out. But we were always happy to share the latest information. There were also days when we were surprised by someone in our viewing audience who would call us seeking a little help.

One day, the phone rang. I picked it up and said, "Weather Department . . . Dr. George." And the caller said: "George, this is Marlon Brando." I was absolutely speechless. I mean, this is one of the most acclaimed actors in motion picture history on the phone. "I'm calling from a movie set in Canada. We're filming a scene outside, and I need to know at what temperature would my breath freeze?" (I think he really meant to ask how cold does it have to be to for your breath to be seen.) I solved his problem. Marlon Brando seemed satisfied. The entire phone call lasted no more than sixty seconds. Just another day in the newsroom. We really didn't get that many celebrity phone calls. But I did pick up the phone one time and it was a viewer with some weather questions—Zsa Zsa Gabor. In her unmistakable accent, she asked, "Are you my 'kooky' weatherman?"

Another one of my favorite stories occurred during one of my many visits to the National Weather Service office at the Federal Building in Westwood. On one such visit, I got onto the elevator to go to the eleventh floor. And as I chatted with a friend of mine, a man who was standing in front of me wearing sunglasses turned around and said, "You're Dr. George. I watch you every night!" Of course, Ray Charles didn't know what I looked like. But he recognized my voice. And I found him to be so delightful.

Being the weatherman on Channel 7 Eyewitness News did lead to some interesting offers coming my way. On November 10, 1977, I appeared on TV's *Mickey Mouse Club*. The program guide says that in a special weather segment, I taught the Mouseketeers how to simulate tornadoes and clouds in your house. To be honest, I don't remember that. But I do hope I also told our young viewers, "Don't do this at home." And in 1974, I actually got to make a TV movie. It was a murder mystery called *The Girl on the Late, Late Show*. It didn't make a "killing" in the ratings. But it did feature such well-known performers as Van Johnson, Walter Pidgeon, Yvonne De Carlo, Mary Ann Mobley, and Burt Convy. I portrayed a cat psychiatrist. My role was so unimportant that I didn't even get mentioned in the on-screen credits. I also didn't receive any more film offers after that. But I did have a "Close Encounter of the Third Kind" with a real movie star.

One afternoon in the mid-1970s, I was in a Westwood parking lot on my way back to the car when I heard a woman calling out, "Hey, Dr. George!" I looked around. And here was movie legend Mae West walking over to me—along with two of the biggest bodyguards mankind has ever seen. I had never met this screen icon before. But Mae wanted to tell me that she had known my uncle, motion picture cinematographer Harry Fischbeck, who had worked on a number of classic films in Hollywood's silent era. At one point, Uncle Harry was the personal cameraman for movie idol Rudolph Valentino. One more thing—and I swear I'm telling the truth. Mae West gave me this invitation: "Why don't you come up and see me sometime?"

Now here was a woman who was already in her eighties. And yes, even then Mae West was still one of the sharpest people I had ever met. She loved to talk about the Golden Age of Hollywood with a vast array of knowledge that made her a virtual human time capsule. And with the encouragement of "My Little Chickadee"—Mrs. Fischbeck—I embarked on a visit with one of the most fascinating people in the annals of entertainment.

The place where Mae West lived, the famed Ravenswood Apartments at 570 North Rossmore Avenue, is a Hollywood star itself with a jazzy neon sign on the roof. It once housed such famous tenants as Clark Gable and Ava Gardner. In fact, the Ravenswood has been declared an official Historic-Cultural Monument . . . Number 768 by the City of Los Angeles. As I entered the apartment building, security was tight. I had to be cleared by the front doorman, the elevator operator, and two huge bodyguards on the sixth floor who walked me to apartment 611, saying, "Miss West is expecting you." I entered alone, sat on the sofa, and couldn't help but notice that everything was white. That included the carpet, the furniture, the walls—even a piano that featured a thirty-two-inch white nude statue of its famous resident. The penthouse apartment featured a spacious view that stretched from Beverly Hills to Los Feliz. And in walked Mae West dressed in, what else, all white.

For the next hour, she was the most gracious of hosts, verbally taking me on a history lesson of the film capital of the world. Did you know that Mae West only made twelve motion pictures in a career that didn't begin until she was thirty-nine—a little late to be starting out as a sex symbol? Yet she is ranked by the American Film Institute as the fifteenth actress on its list of greatest film legends. Mae said Paramount signed her to a two-week contract in 1932 and allowed her to stay at the Ravenswood it owned because it was close to the movie studio over on Melrose Avenue. Mae West ended up liking the two-bedroom apartment so much that she bought it. And it remained her home for forty-eight years. Mae told me that she invented her on-screen sexy "persona" at a time in the 1930s when nudity and even swearing were strictly off-limits. But behind the scenes, Mae West cannily created her image that became larger than life by writing most of the movies and Broadway plays she starred in. Mae was an original—actress, screenwriter, and playwright. Every woman who has ever worked in a movie, either on camera or in production, owes a debt of gratitude to Mae West and her influence within the industry over the years. And you know something—I found her to be so delightful. It is an experience I will never forget. On November 22, 1980, Mae West passed away in her beloved apartment in the Ravenswood. She was eighty-seven. There is one more thing I learned during my visit. She may have been a movie star, but Mae West was so secure in herself as a real human being that she always kept her name, address, and telephone number published in the phone book—until the day she died.

Opportunity Comes Knocking—Again

Life is a gift. And it offers us the privilege, opportunity, and responsibility to give something back by becoming more. ~ Anthony Robbins

By the fall of 1994, I had not worked for two years. But even though I hadn't "officially" retired, the thought of seeking another job had never crossed my mind. And then I received a phone call at home. Bill Applegate, the general manager of KCBS-TV in Los Angeles, wanted to know if I would be interested in doing anything for Channel 2. I answered that I may be an old racehorse . . . but if there was another race coming, I was eager to go. Applegate had a long résumé with ABC local TV stations. My old boss, Dennis Swanson, hired Bill to be news director at Channel 7 WLS-TV in Chicago. And Applegate later ran the news operation at WABC-TV in New York City for General Manager Bill Fyffe, who had been my first news director in Los Angeles.

As you can see, Bill Applegate and I had a few things in common. And we came to a quick agreement about my new duties at Channel 2 News. Money certainly wasn't an issue. Don't tell Applegate, but I would have taken anything they offered. After all, I was just a simple teacher in search of a new classroom.

Applegate didn't want me to do the weather. Instead, I was hired to be a special correspondent to do mini-documentaries on a variety of subjects with what the station's press release called "a mixture of cheer and old-fashioned common sense." I was assigned my own producer to put these documentaries together. But I was also asked to give my input on the subjects that we explored in our mini-docs—including science, technology, and the people and places that define the City of Angels. I have nothing but praise and deep appreciation for the way I was treated by the management and fellow staffers at my new home at famed CBS Columbia Square on Sunset Boulevard in Hollywood.

Now there are some folks in town who may think that by moving down the television dial to Channel 2 News, I was showing disloyalty and a lack of respect to my previous employer at KABC-TV. In the words of legendary UCLA basketball coach John Wooden, "Goodness gracious sakes alive!" How could anyone possibly think I would ever do that? I am writing this book as a personal valentine to my many years at Channel 7 Eyewitness News. I only accepted Channel 2's offer after I had been away from work for two years. I certainly wasn't pounding the pavement looking for a job. But the offer was made. It sounded interesting. And to be honest, I really wasn't ready to retire yet. So I said, yes.

And I'm not the only person who has ever gone from Channel 7 to working at Channel 2. There was one news director at Channel 7 Eyewitness News who later did the same job at KCBS-TV. And no fewer than two general managers at KABC-TV have gone on to become the GM at Channel 2 as well—including John Severino. During my tenure at KCBS-TV, I was reunited with some special folks who had also been my teammates at Channel 7, including my friend and anchor Ann Martin, an extraordinary reporter named Mark Coogan, Eyewitness News veterans Larry Carroll and Paul Dandridge, and sportscaster Jim Hill. And in 1995, seventy-three-year-old Jerry Dunphy signed on to anchor Channel 2 News after a twenty-year absence from the station. Because Jerry was 387 days older than me, I figured Channel 2 was keeping me on to attract a "younger" audience. What an enjoyable journey. But when my contract ran out in late 1997, I wanted to try something new at the age of seventy-five.

The Gift of Volunteering—and Giving Yourself

Volunteers are the only human beings on the face of the Earth who reflect this nation's compassion, unselfish caring, patience, and just plain love for one another. ~ ERMA BOMBECK

When I finally walked away from television news, I still wasn't ready for a life of playing shuffleboard and bingo. I've had the guiding light of passionate role models throughout my life who taught me how volunteering for a worthy cause can indeed have a lasting impact on others. The question is: How do I get involved? And where? I got my answer one night at a Neighborhood Watch meeting on my street in Woodland Hills. A Los Angeles police officer told our group the department was looking for civilian recruits to serve on the LAPD's Volunteer Surveillance Team. One of my neighbors, retired firefighter Don Sampson, suggested that he and I ought to sign up. And so we down to the West Valley police station and joined.

Now please don't think that after I reported for duty the LAPD just handed me a gun and a badge and then unleashed "J. Edgar Fischbeck" on the streets to take a bite out of crime. That's not how this program works. These unpaid, unarmed volunteers are given extensive training in surveillance, safety, and radio procedures. The team members work in tandem in unmarked cars, helping uniformed officers in patrol cars several blocks away. If the volunteers spot any suspicious activity, they immediately radio the police dispatcher, and officers quickly respond. I can tell you firsthand that members of the Volunteer Surveillance Team are never put in unsafe situations. No team member has ever been injured. And I served with this proud team for more than a decade.

The LAPD's Volunteer Surveillance Team has assisted in thousands upon thousands of arrests, including those of rapists, drug dealers, car thieves, and graffiti taggers. We even track down students who are truant from school. Most volunteers usually work once a week on a three- to four-hour shift. But I've been on stakeouts that have lasted until two or three in the morning. My wife, Sue, thinks I'm getting a little too old for that. But she was oh-so-proud when her "old man" actually saw a thief snatch a purse from an unsuspecting woman—and I called it in. The bad guy was captured within minutes. And the victim got everything back. No volunteer has ever overstepped their boundaries and tried to make an arrest themselves. I am so grateful and in awe of the men and woman of the LAPD who are willing to risk their lives "to protect and to serve" the good people of Los Angeles.

Now some folks may think that at times widespread crime has turned our city into a real zoo. And it wasn't long after volunteering to patrol the streets of L.A. with police that I decided to see if I could also try to make a difference at the ultimate "animal house." That's when I called the Los Angeles Zoo to see if I could lend a helping hand there as well. Let me first apologize for making such a "stretch" of a comparison in building a literary bridge between these two subjects. But I hope it worked!

Zoo officials were looking for volunteers to work as docents. Now you may wonder (as I did) what a docent is. They are the folks who are trained to help further the public's understanding of the zoo. That sounded like a good job for someone like me. And because I didn't want any money, it seemed like a good fit for the zoo. After training each Saturday for months and passing the official examination, I became a docent at the Los Angeles Zoo. And was I ready to get to work!

My job was relatively simple. Once a week, I would give tours of the zoo. Now these tours could be given to the public at large. They could be entire classes from various schools. Or they could be groups of tourists from anywhere in the world. For Dr. George the Docent, it was equal opportunity for all. Everybody got the same treatment and the absolute best tour I could give. And did I ever have to do my homework! Just like forecasting the weather, I had to know everything about the zoo. Because if I didn't, the visitors would be sure to ask questions about it. As a docent, preparation on my part was essential.

The Los Angeles Zoo is home to some eleven hundred animals, representing more than 250 species, 29 of which are considered to be endangered. The zoo entertains 1.5 million visitors each year. And when Dr. George was on duty, I made sure I greeted our guests, helped unload the buses, pointed out which gates they should head to, and even watched and entertained their children while Mom and Dad bought tickets. Giving tours of the zoo is one of the most wonderful jobs I have ever had. And it also gave me the chance to meet animal lovers like actress Betty White, who has served as chairwoman on the Board of Trustees of the Greater Los Angeles Zoo Association. (I think that means she was a lot more powerful than a docent like me. Betty is also funnier than I will ever be!)

I served the zoo as a volunteer for twelve years. And when my poor aching legs wouldn't let me give tours anymore, I signed up for another program taking some of the zoo's animals to visit rest homes and nursing facilities across the Southland to bring smiles to their patients and residents. Of course, we could only take little animals that were warm and fuzzy. I don't think we would have been allowed to tie a rhinoceros outside a nursing home and then go tell the residents: "What is big—has a horn on its nose—lives in a river—and likes to eat people? Take a look out the window!" No, I don't think that would have worked.

My friends, when you decide to become a volunteer, you are making an investment in someone else with a gift of hope and inspiration. A caring person named DeAnn Hollis has said, "The heart of a volunteer is not measured in size, but by the depth of the commitment to make a difference in the lives of others." We need to be available—willing to be involved—and not so focused on our own needs that we are blinded from seeing the needs of our fellow man. We may not have much to offer.

But if we can just reach out and do our small part—together we can do a lot with a little.

Over the years, I'd go wherever I was asked. "Anyone who'll have me" was my motto. I've always believed that no one should ever decline an invitation to opportunity. One night in 1991, I was honored with the Media Excellence Award by the good folks who run the Lincoln Training Center in South El Monte. And I fell in love. They have a mission at Lincoln: "Turning disabilities into possibilities." For forty-nine years, this compassionate team has been training men and women with disabilities to learn job skills, gain confidence, and achieve success in the workplace. The Lincoln Training Center now works its magic at three facilities across California including Fresno and Roseville. Each year, Lincoln celebrates nearly six hundred success stories in which trainees are matched with a meaningful job to earn a paycheck and self-esteem.

And when I was asked to come on board and help, I can't begin to tell you what a privilege it was to participate. They had a number of jobs for Dr. George to do. I narrated a promotional video for the center. One year, anchor Ann Martin and I cohosted the annual "Affair of the Heart" fund-raising event. And there were the numerous open houses. But my favorite "job" was getting to go down to the South El Monte center and visit the special people who were being trained. I'd have to hide behind the desks because they would hug me to death! There's no shortage of love and pride at the Lincoln Training Center. And they have built a successful partnership with more than fifty job sites throughout the entire state where Lincoln continues to make a profound difference in the life of a person with a disability.

The word *courage* has been defined as the state of mind that enables one to face hardship or a struggle with confidence and resolution. There are a number of courageous people that must climb a steep mountain each day, trying their best to cope with the lack of physical abilities that most of us take for granted. For example, how would your life be affected if you suddenly lost your eyesight? It's estimated that more than 25 million Americans suffer from blindness or significant vision loss. That includes 21 percent of those who are age sixty-five and older.

The Braille Institute in Southern California is a godsend. It operates five regional centers across the Southland and offers 140 community outreach programs. Just because you have lost your sight doesn't mean you have lost all hope of a fulfilling life. Nearly one-third of all Americans who are legally blind are now employed. And the dedicated staff of the Braille Institute is able to offer support services and training free of charge. Volunteers are crucial to this mission. And I was honored and humbled when the Braille Institute asked me to take part in a wonderful project aimed at opening the door to the world of literature to those without sight.

In a commitment that I cherished, I would report for duty at the Braille Institute's Los Angeles Sight Center on Vermont Avenue. And I would go into a recording studio where I would read entire books aloud so they could be taped and transformed into audio books for the blind and visually impaired to listen to. Now I'll be the first to admit that I'm no professional announcer. But the folks at the Braille Institute assured me that "Dr. George" audio books would indeed help fill a great need in the center's library and book club. I recorded all kinds of reading material including novels, technical books, and literature on my favorite subject of science. The library's audio collection has now grown to one hundred thousand titles and 1.2 million volumes, including magazines and periodicals. And if one of the Braille Institute's patrons brought in their favorite book, I was always available to help put it on tape just for them.

The Braille Institute is a marvelous team to be a part of. And it has quite a roster of volunteers. For example, have you ever heard of Wes Parker? He's one of the greatest fielding first basemen in the history of baseball, having won six consecutive Gold Glove Awards and helped lead the Los Angeles Dodgers to a World Series title in 1965. Wes Parker is now hitting home runs for the Braille Institute. It's a commitment that began years ago when a newspaper reporter who had lost his sight asked Wes to come to the Institute's L.A. Sight Center and read to a group of blind men and women. It became a love affair. For more than a decade, Wes has taught a weekly class on sports at the Braille Institute, in addition to having served on its Board of Directors. He's not only brought popular sports figures like Tommy Lasorda and former Dodger great Ron Cey to speak to his class, Wes has even treated his students to an annual Dodgers game. At the Braille Institute, Wes Parker is indeed an MVP—as in "Most Valuable Person." It's a donation of self that pays dividends. As a human blessing named Shanterra McBride once said: "I am a recipient of unconditional love. I am a volunteer."

There is one other place I would like to tell you about. It's where a "Help Wanted" sign is always posted for those who are loving and caring. Whenever I would receive a request to visit someone in the hospital, I always felt that it was a calling from God Himself. How could I say no to that? And during my hospital visits, there were no frowns or tears allowed in the room of my intended patient. My job was to provide a smile, a prayer, and lots of hope. That's my prescription for healing!

I remember the time when one of our newswriters at Channel 7 who was working the overnight shift asked me if I could call his mother, who was in the hospital after having undergone a mastectomy. As you can imagine, she wasn't feeling all that well physically and emotionally. He asked me if I could make a phone call, thinking Torrance Memorial Medical Center was too far for me to drive from my home in Woodland Hills. Little did he know. The next morning, my newswriter friend had worked hard all night. And he virtually crawled to Torrance to visit his mother. And lo and behold, there was Fischbeck in bed with Mom, giving out "Dr. George" buttons to the entire nursing staff at the happiest hospital on earth. And you want to know what? I received a whole lot more from that visit than I could have possibly given. That's the way God planned it.

Veterans' hospitals have been the scene of some of my most emotional visits. You want to talk about heroes. In every bed, in every room, and on every floor there were brave men and women who had valiantly served their country. But now some of them were struggling to recover from severe wounds or illnesses, the loss of a limb, or crippling mental health issues, while others had been given just days or even hours to live. Soldiers who have been eyewitnesses to the horrors of war have a saying: "All gave some. Some gave all." Each time I reached out to shake their hands as a heartfelt thank-you note, I wanted to remind these veterans that their service to our country has not been forgotten. The visits I made to visit our hospitalized veterans over the years were a stark reminder to me as to just how fragile life really is. Perhaps the poet laureate of baseball, Vin Scully, said it best during a Dodgers broadcast when he talked about one injured player's condition. "Andre Dawson has a bruised knee . . . and is listed as day-to-day." And then Scully paused before saying: "Aren't we all?"

Adversity is anything but a rare commodity. Facing storms and shipwrecks in our lives isn't a matter of *if* but *when*. Author George Iles once wrote, "Hope is faith holding out its hand in the dark." There were a number of times when I was asked to reach out to someone who was waging an uphill battle against a killer called cancer. There isn't a family in America who hasn't felt the landscape of pain and suffering caused by this dreaded disease. I vividly remember visiting a man in the hospital who was in the final days of his courageous fight. There is nothing you can ever do that will prepare you for these moments. I tried to comfort my new friend by rubbing his feet while trying to share tender words of kindness and understanding with his loved ones. His son later wrote me a thank-you letter that so touched my heart.

> *Dear Dr. George,*
>
> *When my father was ill with cancer, he told me how much he enjoyed you on the news. I called you and asked you to visit him in the hospital. You not only took the time to see him . . . but visited the entire floor. He passed away shortly after that. He enjoyed your visit so much. And I will always be grateful to you. Thank you again!*
>
> *Joseph*

This is why I could never decline these kinds of requests. My friends, "no" is the worst word in the entire English language. There is one more hospital visit that I want to share with you. And it is one of the most heart-breaking. On May 6, 2008, I was asked by a friend of mine at Channel 7 Eyewitness News to accompany him to the City of Hope in Duarte so that we could visit a veteran Los Angeles police officer who was dying of leukemia. Several months earlier, my friend had written a story about the officer's fellow cops who had shaved their heads in support of their colleague after he had lost all his hair through radiation treatment.

At the City of Hope, the officer's hospital room was virtually sealed to prevent infection. I cannot with mere words describe the emotions that overwhelmed me as I embraced this stricken officer's wife with a hug. Going in, I knew this was a Christian family. And the Bible instructs us to "encourage one another and build each other up."

Doctors would only allow one person in the room at a time. So I put on the required surgical gown and mask—and entered. This was a touching moment like no other. And I was deeply humbled as I greeted this hero. For twenty-seven years, this policeman went to work every day willing to put his life on the line protecting people he didn't know so that the city he served could be safe. A loving husband and father of two children, he was a treasured community asset as one of the founders of the annual "Cops 4 Tots Car and Motorcycle Show" that raised money for the bone marrow unit at Children's Hospital.

This was a man who loved his job. But he also loved God. And as we talked in those brief moments, I shared with him the message from 1 Thessalonians 4:17–18, "And so shall we ever be with the Lord. Wherefore comfort one another with these words." Five days later, God brought this police officer home to Heaven at the age of forty-eight. There was such an outpouring of love for this man at his funeral. The church was filled with officers who had served alongside him for years on the mean streets of Los Angeles. On this day, they were there to honor their fallen teammate and to humbly worship God who loves and protects them in one of the toughest jobs of all. As a hymn was sung, a veteran LAPD sergeant sitting in the front row raised his hand in faith, asking for the Lord's strength as these officers serve with bravery and commitment.

An Ordinary Man—An Extraordinary Honor

His style of weather reporting was groundbreaking. He combined his thorough knowledge of forecasting with his friendly and understandable presentation, to become an icon to his millions of viewers. I enthusiastically recommend Dr. George Fischbeck for the Governors Award. ~ STAN CHAMBERS, KTLA-TV NEWS

My friends, I am so humbled by the gracious words of this legendary journalist who has enjoyed the greatest career in broadcasting in the history of Los Angeles television. The year was 1972 when KABC-TV took a huge gamble and hired a small town schoolteacher to forecast the weather on Eyewitness News. Here I was all by myself on the biggest stage of my life, basically starting a new career at the tender age of fifty. I was so worried that this might not work out; I kept my family back in Albuquerque in case I had to return home in defeat. Little did I know that I was about to embark on an unbelievable journey at Channel 7 that would span two decades. But in all honesty, I really didn't think anyone would notice. After all these years, I was still just a teacher in my heart.

But someone did notice. In 2003, the Academy of Television Arts & Sciences announced that I would be given the prestigious Governors Award for what the Academy called a lifetime of broadcasting achievement. Oh my goodness! This is something that a former science instructor at Monroe Junior High School doesn't even have a right to dream about. Now I could easily say that I was named to receive the Governors Award because the Academy didn't have anyone else to consider that year. But that was certainly not the case. In fact, the other finalist was far more deserving. Bob Eubanks is nothing short of a legend in television and radio, having hosted *The Newlywed Game.* He's a New Year's Day tradition broadcasting the Rose Parade for some thirty-eight years now. And as a highly popular rock and roll disc jockey on KRLA, Bob mortgaged his house in 1964 to financially back and promote one of the most famous concerts of all time—the Beatles at the Hollywood Bowl. Not bad for a guy who got his start as a doorman at the Egyptian Theatre in Hollywood. When the TV Academy's Board of Governors heard the presentations for its Governors Award nominees in 2003, Bob Eubanks was represented by the beautiful and talented Leeza Gibbons of *Entertainment Tonight* and *Extra* fame. Goodness gracious, even on my best of days, I'm certainly no Leeza Gibbons!

The nominees themselves do not appear before the Academy's Board. But a number of my former teammates at Channel 7 and colleagues in Los Angeles television did write letters to the Board on behalf of Dr. George—including Stan Chambers, Paul Moyer, Laura Diaz, Ann Martin, Ed Arnold, and Bruce Herschensohn. I will always be grateful to the Board for having selected the "old weather guy" to be the recipient. But champions are not forgotten here. Two years later, the excellence of Bob Eubanks was honored with the TV Academy's Governors

Award, in a rich tradition that allowed this broadcast immortal to take his deserved place in history.

On September 6, 2003, the 55th Annual Emmy Awards were held at the Academy's Leonard H. Goldenson Theatre—named after the man who had founded the ABC Television Network. When that moment came for me to accept the Governors Award, I was joined onstage by a number of talented weather forecasters from across the Los Angeles dial, including Mark Kriski of KTLA-TV and Mark Thompson of KTTV-TV. Let me put it this way: there aren't enough "millibars" in the universe to measure how much that meant to me. And as if that were not enough, look at these special folks who actually paid for ads in the official Emmy Program to say "Congratulations!"

Dr. George,
  You are an inspiration to all of us.

Stan Chambers

Thank you for teaching us to reach for the stars! Your dedication, your enthusiasm, and love of life have and continue to be an inspiration.

With love,
Laura Diaz

You are a true original who taught us all, both on and off the air. No one deserves this honor more than you, my friend.

Your buddy,
Paul Moyer

And in a heartfelt act of kindness and class, the management at KABC-TV—it will always be my home—graciously placed a full-page ad in the Emmy Program with pictures of my teammates, Dallas Raines and Johnny Mountain, saying: "Congratulations Dr. George!" They didn't have to do that. But on January 24, 2009, the folks at ABC7 did it again. On the night that I received the Lifetime Achievement Award at the 59th Annual Golden Mike Awards, here's a full-page ad that appeared in that official program—from KABC-TV.

"A consummate professional, a caring member of the community, and our good friend. ABC7 congratulates Dr. George Fischbeck."

That deeply touched my family and me in such a special way, on a very special night. There was one more ad in the Golden Mike Awards program I would like to share with you . . . a heartwarming note from two most valuable people.

> *Dr. George,*
>
> *Your telling the weather story while interjecting your vast knowledge and your kind humor laid a road map for the rest of us. We all felt your enthusiasm—even when that darn cut-off low created a weatherman's woe! You are an icon . . . and our hero.*
>
> *Dannie and Dallas Raines*

I'll say it again—I have been so blessed. If I may, I'd like to close this chapter with an expression of appreciation and affection. "Thanks for being my friend. Thanks for thinking of me. Thanks for caring about me. Thanks for everything you did for me. You shouldn't have. But I'm so glad you did."

Life's Greatest Blessing— The Love of Family

It's been said that no man on his deathbed has ever looked into the eyes of his loving family and said, "I wish I'd spent more time at the office." In the words of Winston Churchill: "There is no doubt that it is around the family and the home that all the greatest virtues, the most dominating virtues of human society, are created, strengthened, and maintained." My friends, in all the twenty years that I was invited into the homes of our loyal viewers of Channel 7 Eyewitness News in Los Angeles, it was time that my wonderful family unselfishly and graciously allowed me to be with all of you. And in return, I tried to make up for that lost family time by being the best husband and father to the wife and children that God Himself blessed me with.

But it all started with my partner in life . . . my "co-anchor" and my best friend. On April 17, 2013, the former Susanne June Reif and I celebrated our sixty-fourth wedding anniversary. I think by now you could safely say "and they lived happily ever after." I admit that I may not have been the handsomest guy available at the time. And I was far from the most successful. But Sue must have been in love with me because she certainly didn't marry me for my meager $2,600-a-year salary as a schoolteacher. And she has stood by my side—for better or for worse— through thick and thin—no matter what.

Unfortunately, we live in a world where commitment doesn't mean as much as it used to. I would like to share a few thoughts on this from a man of inspiration, Greg Laurie, who's the senior pastor of the Harvest Christian Fellowship in Riverside, California. The good reverend says our society is becoming more and more disposable. We've become conditioned to throwing things away when we're done with them. They make disposable cameras for short-term convenience. You can even buy clothes that are made from paper. You wear it once then toss it in the trash. It's simple. No muss. No fuss. You use it, throw it away, and go on to something new.

But Laurie points out that marriages have also become disposable as our divorce rate soars past 50 percent. Once a relationship starts to have growing pains and the challenges of commitment begin to set in, hearts that used to be overflowing with love become cold and empty. And for one spouse, it's time to bail out. For many, "till death do us part" has now become "till one of us doesn't want it anymore." What's called irreconcilable differences have cut a path of destruction through so many lives and left little children emotionally scarred for life. No one seems to understand that what may be grounds for divorce could also be grounds for forgiveness. In the words of Pastor Greg, building a marriage that will stand the test of time is not just finding the right person. It means being the right person as well.

If anyone asks me what my formula for happiness is, I answer with "faith and family." I don't know what I would have done over these many years without my devoted Sue. Speaking as a husband, I certainly don't deserve her. But for some reason in His love and grace, the Lord thinks I can do the job. And each day, I fully commit myself to doing my absolute best to prove Him right. But while we're on the subject, my friends—let's seek a "second opinion."

> *Dear Friends,*
>
> *In my life I have been blessed to find a man who is warm, gentle, and caring to me and our family that we have created . . . as well as his viewers and students whom George considers his friends. We've shared my husband throughout the years with what seems to be millions of people. And he has always had time for all of us.*

We missed him when he had to travel or speak to various groups. But his kindness, compassion, and true love for all people is what really has held us together over all of the years. Despite all of the hours he dedicated to his work and helping various organizations, he always seemed to have quality time for our family.

I found a man who can be proud of who he is . . . and who is loved and respected far more than he realizes. Sixty-four years ago when I decided to marry this man, I knew it was going to be an adventure. But I had no idea what an incredible life we would have together.

George has given me the beautiful gift of love . . . and another incredible gift, our family! My dear husband: I've loved you for sixty-four years so far. Let's try for another fifty.

Love,

Sue Fischbeck

If I were to ask you to write a list of things that you couldn't possibly live without, I would hope that at the top of your list would be *family.* That's the way it has been since the very beginning when God saw Adam's loneliness. "It is not good that man should be alone." And Eve was created. As Matthew Henry wrote in the seventeenth century: ". . . under [Adam's] arm to be protected, and near his heart to be loved." The late writer and journalist Jane Howard said, "Call it a clan. Call it a network. Call it a tribe. Call it a family. Whatever you call it, whoever you are, you need one."

The Fischbeck Family Tree Blooms . . . and Bears Fruit

While we try to teach our children all about life, our children teach us what life is all about. ~ Angela Schwindt

On August 4, 1955, our little "Fisch" tank was filled. Nancy Ellen at 4 pounds, 7 ½ ounces—and fifteen minutes later, George Frederick at 4 pounds, 11 ounces. To paraphrase the sayings: it's double the giggles and double the grins, twice as much to love, if you're blessed with twins. During all the years I was a teacher in Albuquerque, both Sue and I had to work to meet the financial challenges of our family's population explosion. But what we received in return—these two gifts from above with hearts entwined—multiplied our blessings in a loving way that is immeasurable. Mr. and Mrs. Fischbeck may have had twins, but our family was one of a kind.

In many ways, this book that I am writing is like putting together a "family album"—recounting memories of our children that we will cherish forever. I've already told you about the time Sue came home only to be horrified in discovering that her science teacher husband had placed a gopher snake in the crib for infants Nancy and George Junior to play with! Then there was the time curiosity got the best of little Fritz (my son's nickname) when he looked into a box I had brought home from school . . . only to scream when he pulled out a tarantula, toss the eight-legged creature up in the air, and have it land on sister Nancy. If science is about discovery—life at home was an outright adventure!

George Junior and Nancy, 1973

But then there was the joy of our two children so proud to watch Dad on public education television with their classmates in school, as this marvelous technology allowed this humble instructor to expand the horizons of teaching. Of course, doing the weather for top-rated KOB-TV News in Albuquerque presented a different challenge for the Fischbecks. Whenever we'd have a family outing, I was starting to be recognized in public and at times was asked to sign something or pose for a picture. It was important for

Sue and me to teach our kids to have humility and always be gracious toward others. Television news was merely another classroom for their father to teach in. There is no more important job that a parent can have than to teach their children kindness, love, respect, appreciation, friendship, praise, the gift of encouragement, and the blessing of sharing.

In 1972, our family was separated for months when George Junior and I moved to Southern California so that I could begin my new job at KABC-TV. Even though Fritz attended his senior year of high school in our new home, he and I flew back to Albuquerque so that George and Nancy could graduate together. That was so important to our children. They loved each other. And in a matter of days, our family was reunited in Los Angeles once again. We were one. We always will be.

Once the family had moved into our new house in Woodland Hills, both George Junior and Nancy enrolled at nearby Pierce College to continue their education. At one point, Fritz decided he would take some time off from school to get a job. My son was quite skilled as a carpenter. And he was able to put his talents to good use at the ABC Television Center, where George was hired to build sets for the programs that were in production there. Forgive me if I sound like a father that is bragging. But young George Junior excelled at everything he did at ABC. He worked on some very elaborate sets for the TV shows and met a lot of stars. Best of all, I was able to see my son a great deal because KABC-TV was on the same lot.

Sue and I were so proud of our children. Trying to raise a family in a world of temptations and distractions is a steep mountain for loving and caring parents to try to scale each day. It's been said that you give your children life, but you cannot live it for them. You can do your best to teach them right from wrong, but you cannot always decide for them. Life is made up of choices. At times, there is a thin line that divides making the right choice or heading the wrong way. But the positive and productive lives that Nancy and George Junior chose for themselves were the best "thank-you note" that their mother and father could have possibly ever asked for. My friends, that is why the next chapter of my beloved family's journey in life is the hardest story that I will ever have to tell.

The date was December 10, 1977, when I received an emergency call at our home from Pacoima Memorial Hospital . . . notifying me that my beloved son had lost his life in a tragic accident. George Junior was just twenty-two years of age. It was a sudden feeling of loss in my heart that I hope no other parent or family will ever have to experience in their lifetime. To lose our boy at such a young age in an unexpected tragedy like this overwhelmed my wife and me with stunned disbelief. While our family was paralyzed by the deepest depths of sorrow, I think it hurt our daughter most of all. Nancy dearly loved her twin brother with all of her might. She and George Junior came into this world together, just fifteen minutes apart. And they will never, ever be separated. It's been said that while death leaves a heartache no one can heal, love leaves a memory that no one can steal.

In lieu of flowers, our family asked our friends and the public to make contributions to the hospital where our son had died. And in 1981, Pacoima Memorial Hospital announced that the George Fischbeck Junior Memorial Shock and Trauma Center was being established to save lives in those most desperate of situations. As the years have passed, there hasn't been a day that Sue, Nancy, and I don't think of Fritz. We are still trying to get over what happened three and a half decades ago. But then again, my family wouldn't be hurting if we had not first been touched. A very thoughtful teacher and author named Hillary Stanton Zunin said, "The risk of love is loss, and the price of loss is grief. But the pain of grief is only a shadow when compared with the pain of never risking love."

As this book is being written, it brings joy to my heart to tell you that my loving family has only grown closer. Our faith has given us strength, comfort, and hope. You know, I've seen a lot of news from across the nation and around the world during my long career in television. And you couldn't help but see what you get when you put your faith in mankind: war, crime, poverty, homelessness, hatred, discrimination, and greed. Those are man-made problems. I remember the great Vin Scully looking back at September 11th, 2001, and calling it "a day in which God must have wept, wept over man's inhumanity to man."

My friends, the storms of life are going to affect all of us from time to time. Even Dr. George has shed tears of sorrow and sadness. But my loving family has always been there for me with an everlasting commitment of love and encouragement. Even on my best days as a weatherman,

I could only give my viewers a five-day forecast. But you know, if those of us in this angry world of ours can stop looking around and pointing fingers—and instead look up in faith—I promise you a bright and sunny future that will last today, tomorrow, and forever.

We Are Family . . . My Celebration of Life

What greater thing is there for human souls than to feel that they are joined for life—to be with each other in silent unspeakable memories. ~ GEORGE ELIOT

You may have noticed that whenever I did the weather at Eyewitness News, I always had a smile that would never go away. I know you haven't seen me on television in . . . oh my goodness, has it been sixteen years now? But that smile is still there. I've got a lot to be happy about. Her name is Nancy. She's still my "little girl."

Nancy's second home as a child was KNME-TV in New Mexico, where she got her first taste of the live television experience. Her excitement on regular visits to the station and enjoyment of people and their stories led to a blossoming career that ranged from a stint as an intern at KETC-TV in St. Louis to being an ABC network page at KABC-TV in Los Angeles. Nancy has always been a "people person." She gets that from me.

If Sue has been my right-hand partner, Nancy has been my left-hand partner—steady and reliable with a ready smile and joy for life that affects all who meet her. Whether she's cheering the Channel 7 Eyewitness News "basketball team" versus the Harlem Globetrotters in a game at the Forum—or handing out "Dr. George" buttons at one of the myriad of events she worked with me, my daughter has always been wholehearted. I am so proud of Nancy's sense of adventure and genuine interest in the world's different cultures that have taken her many places. She shares both my curiosity and love of life.

My Dad is the kind of man who can smile and put an understanding face on the worst weather—or problem.

Despite the fact he introduces himself as "kindly, lovable, humble, ole man Fischbeck"... the innovative path he cuts through life is as large as the heavens on which he reports.

From a darkened Griffith Park Observatory Planetarium, Dad would take audiences on a "Mission to Mars!" He made every day like that—a fast-paced adventure to beyond where the simplest question could blossom into an experiment he culled from some mysterious crate in his garage—suitable for a class of expectant young scientists.

Whether Dad woke my brother and me in the middle of the night for a trip to the roof to observe a meteor shower, or trotted us down the red carpet of a posh awards show... we knew we were loved. And every day we spent with him was, and still is, a gift of the cosmos.

Wherever my father goes, he greets strangers with a "Good Friend" or "Hello" in more languages than I can count. How can I express my feelings for someone I love as much as I love him? Only by loving unreservedly and without limits... and, like him, by meeting each day and experience with energy, enthusiasm, and laughter.

Nancy is not only my daughter, she's a mother as well. And that has made Dr. George an oh-so-proud grandfather. I like that job! I have spent so much of this book reflecting on what has happened in years past. But my granddaughter, twenty-three-year-old Leilani Spring Fischbeck, gives our family boundless enthusiasm about life that is still to come. *Leilani* means "heavenly flower" in Hawaiian. And my friends, this is one flower that is indeed blooming.

Spring (as I like to call her) is about to graduate from college having earned a bachelor's degree in health sciences with a major in health administration. And she has aspirations of earning a master's degree and becoming a certified physician assistant (PA). This is a highly trained health care professional who can actually practice medicine under the limited supervision of doctors and surgeons. A physician assistant can do just about everything that a doctor does, including perform minor surgeries. Spring is already licensed as an emergency medical technician. And she's gaining invaluable experience serving as a volunteer at a major trauma center in Southern California.

My granddaughter is about the same age as my son, George Junior, was when he died in an emergency room as dedicated doctors and nurses valiantly tried to save his life. Did what happened that fateful day influence Spring's choice to enter the medical profession? Absolutely. In fact, Leilani is hoping to parlay her years of training and sacrifice into becoming a physician assistant in the emergency room, where she can be a beacon of hope in a time of someone's greatest need.

> *From the beginning, you were always my "Opa" (the German translation of grandfather). Opa, I remember spending afternoons at your house playing intriguing games of chess, while listening to classical music and dancing around in the living room. You have encouraged me to try my hardest when it comes to anything I set my mind to. And that is why I have come this far!*
>
> *I love that things are still the same whenever I come over, for twenty-three years now. And every time that I sit down at the piano bench to play, you lie down on the carpet next to the piano until I complete my set. You are so supportive of everything I choose to do. And you have taught me a skill so useful when it comes to public speaking, interviews, or performances ... that I love speaking in public. You have given me a confidence and happiness that I will carry my entire life.*
>
> *I have been inspired by you and the family to help people in emergency situations ... understanding how suddenly tragedy can strike after losing Uncle George in the traumatic accident. Thank you for being so supportive of my medical career. You have inspired me to grow and strive through difficult situations ... and "never give up."*

Opa is the type of grandfather who wants to make sure everyone is happy, and values his family's love every time we get together. Whether we are spending an afternoon playing spades as a family, or if he is helping me quiz for a premed exam . . . he is always letting us know how much he loves all of us.

His love goes a long way . . . for his family, his dear friends, his fans. His love radiates to us all.

Leilani Spring Fischbeck

My granddaughter epitomizes what the late writer Alex Haley once said: "The family is our refuge and our springboard; nourished on it, we can advance to new horizons. In every conceivable manner, the family is link to our past, bridge to our future."

My friends, in closing, may I share with you the hope that all of us will wake up each day and look upon it as a precious gift. When you look at a person's tombstone, it marks the day they were born . . . and the day they passed into eternity. They probably had nothing to do with either. But they had a remarkable chance to make a difference in between. We all do. Life is an invitation to opportunity. As I celebrate my ninetieth year in this journey of mine, I am so blessed to have a deep appreciation for the gift of life. My goodness, it is such a privilege to even be here at this point. On August 22, 2002, I underwent open heart surgery at UCLA Medical Center where Dr. Hillel Laks and his marvelous team replaced a valve. The operation must have been a success because I'm still here . . . and as grateful as ever.

Please don't waste this day. Go out and give of yourself. Hug someone. Put a smile on their face. Make an investment in someone else . . . even if it's just for a moment. We can make a difference. But you just have to care. One day, I was driving on a Southland freeway. And as I passed a California Highway Patrol officer, I honked and waved. I never really thought about that again—until I received this letter in my mailbox at Eyewitness News.

Dear Dr. Fischbeck,

For about the next half hour, I couldn't stop smiling . . . thinking I had received some type of recognition for the job I was performing. I have been waved at by many people in the course of my employment. And it always gives me a good feeling like I have accomplished something.

But the enthusiasm you showed just happened to make that particular day special. I just wanted to say "thank you" for the simple thumbs-up gesture. It made my day more enjoyable.

Sincerely,
"David"
California Highway Patrol

Light a candle of friendship in your window . . . so that another will want to share. Margaret Mead once said, "Never believe that a few caring people can't change the world. For, indeed, that's all who ever have." You can take it from a teacher named Dr. George—the message of encouragement that you write on the blackboard of life will never be erased.